NOT THE MOORS MURDERS

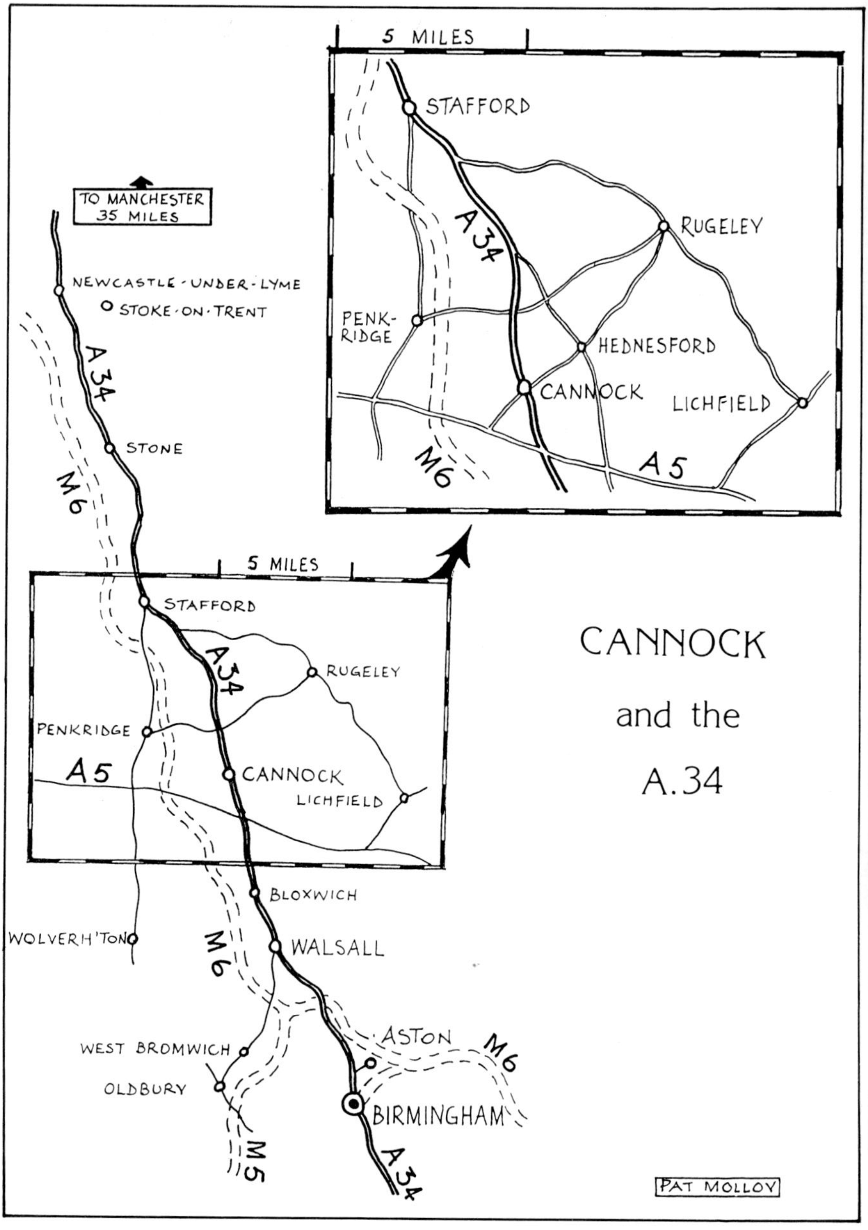
5 MILES
STAFFORD
RUGELEY
PENK-
RIDGE
HEDNESFORD
CANNOCK
LICHFIELD
A34
M6
A5
TO MANCHESTER
35 MILES
NEWCASTLE-UNDER-LYME
STOKE-ON-TRENT
STONE
5 MILES
PENKRIDGE
BLOXWICH
WOLVERH'TON
WALSALL
ASTON
WEST BROMWICH
OLDBURY
BIRMINGHAM
M5
CANNOCK
and the
A.34
PAT MOLLOY

Not the Moors Murders

A Detective's Story
of the biggest child-killer hunt
in History

Pat Molloy

To Barry, with all my best wishes.

Pat Molloy

'Ship Inn', Fishguard
9th June/90

GOMER

First Impression - 1988

ISBN 0 86383 473 6

© Pat Molloy

All rights reserved. No part of this publication may be reproduced or transmitted in any form or by any means, including photocopying and recording, without the written permission of the copyright holder, application for which should be addressed to the publisher. Such written permission must also be obtained before any part of this publication is stored in a retrieval system of any nature.

Printed in Wales at Gomer Press, Llandysul, Dyfed

Dedicated to the Memory of
Harry Bailey,
the man who bore the brunt

CONTENTS

	Acknowledgements	9
	Introduction	12
1	Without Trace	17
2	Dominoes and Door-knockers	42
3	A Job and a Half	66
4	Life's Like That	90
5	The N.F.A. Factor	120
6	Trouble Down Below	141
7	Rock Bottom	152
8	Caught in the Rush Hour	168
9	Mister Whitehouse, I Presume	187
10	All in the Game	209
11	The Loneliest Place	231
12	Nemesis	248
	Postscript—A Costly Lesson	261

ACKNOWLEDGEMENTS

The Author is deeply indebted to a number of people for the photographs which illustrate this book. He thanks the Chief Constable of Staffordshire, Mr. C. H. Kelly, c.st.j., c.b.e., q.p.m., d.l., ll.b., and Detective Chief Superintendent Malcolm Bevington, the Head of Staffordshire CID, for allowing him access to the photographs contained in the Cannock Chase murder files and so readily agreeing to supply all he asked for; the Editors of the *Daily Express*, the *Birmingham Post and Mail* and the *Wolverhampton Express and Star,* three newspapers which also gave invaluable help to the Midlands police forces involved in the investigations; Frances Cartwright, of the *Express and Star* Picture Library, whose courtesy and help in guiding the author through the picture files thrown open to him by her Editor made this part of his research such a pleasure and provided the bulk of the photographs he has used; the late Lewis Williams, Staff Artist of the *Birmingham Post and Mail*, who gave the author a number of his original sketches when they met during the Christine Darby murder investigation.

NAMES

For various reasons, a number of names have been changed or omitted from this story. They have been changed where they occur in accounts of enquiries carried out by the author and other officers of the outside enquiry teams, and they have been omitted where they relate to victims who survived their ordeals. Real names are used in relation to the murder victims and those engaged in the efforts to detect those murders.

He who is shipwrecked the second time
cannot lay the blame on Neptune

(Old English Proverb)

INTRODUCTION

I knew what was coming as soon as he spoke: "Let's see, Pat," he said, "*you* were on the Moors Murders, weren't you?"

"No, I wasn't."

"Oh, I always thought you were. Didn't they say in the papers when you retired that you were on the Moors Murders?"

"Not the Moors Murders. The Cannock Chase Murders."

"Ah, yes. I remember. Myra Hindley, wasn't it. And that chap . . . Ian . . . what's his name?"

I took another swallow from my pint, placed it on the bar counter and gathered up my patience as I had done so many times before, in countless other bars, over nearly twenty years. "No," I said. "Myra Hindley and Ian Brady committed the *Moors* Murders. They abducted young children, sexually assaulted and tortured them, killed them and hid their bodies up on the moors between Lancashire and Yorkshire . . . on Saddleworth Moor, not far from Oldham. That's why they were known as the Moors Murders. The murders themselves were committed in Manchester."

"I always thought that's what *you* were involved in."

"No, not the Moors Murders, the Cannock Chase Murders, an entirely different case. The Moors Murders happened around the same time and people always seem to get them mixed up."

"So what *were* the Cannock Chase Murders? Why should I think that was Hindley and Brady?"

"I suppose it's because they involved young children too: little girls, seven or eight years old, abducted and then taken up to Cannock Chase, sexually assaulted and murdered."

My questioner gathered his thoughts for another try. A sip from his glass seemed to help the process, and gave others in the bar the chance to turn their ears in our direction. "Let me get it right," he said. "Where exactly is Cannock Chase?"

I smiled as I remembered: "That's a good question. When the first of them happened, twenty-odd years ago, I didn't know the place myself, even though I was stationed within twenty miles of it. But I know now. Cannock Chase and those murders became so much a part of my life, and every other detective's in the Midlands, that I could never forget the place."

I took a pen from my pocket, made a sketch on a beer mat, and explained: "Cannock Chase is a great open space of around eighty-five square miles, about twenty miles north of Birmingham, with Cannock to the south of it and Stafford to the north. It's a beauty spot, a popular picnic area and a favourite place for courting couples. Much of it is forestry and the rest a great spread of heath and moorland. Looking for bodies there was like looking for needles in a haystack, I can tell you."

"So they were a lot like the Moors Murders, then? No wonder I get them mixed up."

"Not to us they weren't."

He seemed surprised.

"No, they weren't. Mind you, when Hindley and Brady were arrested—in October, 1965—the police investigating the disappearance of a young girl in Birmingham were in very close touch with the men in charge of the Moors Murders team . . . Arthur Benfield and Joe Mounsey."

"So there were a lot of similarities?"

"Yes, but not where it mattered. I dealt with a lot of murders in my time, as you know, but give me the one where you have the killers in custody from the beginning; where you've caught them red-handed with a corpse in their house and an eye-witness to the murder. Then you only have to find the bodies of the others they've killed. *That* was the difference between the Moors Murders and the Cannock Chase Murders. They had them in the cells from the start. What we had was bodies, no damn suspect and nobody to tell us anything; just the seven hundred square miles and four million population of the West Midlands for starters, and not a clue which door to knock on first. It's hard work whichever way round you get it, but give me a Moors Murder every time. You're half way home before you start." I laughed. "In the trade we used to call murders like that ready-made!"

*   *   *

I tried to explain the widespread confusion about these two cases. "Hindley and Brady have over-shadowed just about everything in the child-sex-murder business over the past twenty years," I said. "It's hardly surprising, is it? The psychiatrists had a field day with them, and the news media and writers like Emlyn Williams turned them into cult-figures, what you might call the personification of evil. Then there was that tape-recording of little Leslie Ann Downey screaming for her mother while the two of them had her tied to the bed, raping, torturing and then killing her. I've heard it. It's no wonder people in court burst into tears when it was played. Then Lord Longford takes Myra Hindley under his wing, calls her a 'thoroughly nice person' and tries to get her paroled. And to cap it all, after twenty years in gaol, they are brought by helicopter back to Saddleworth Moor on the promise that they'll help the police to find other bodies buried there, and they even find one. No wonder Hindley and Brady come automatically to mind when people think of child-murder. That kind of publicity would make anybody immortal, even though child-murder isn't such a rarity any more."

"Oh, I never looked at it that way."

"Well, that's it," I said. "The Moors Murders have become famous, not because they were difficult to detect, but because Myra Hindley and Ian Brady made such fascinating subjects. That's why you automatically think of them when you start talking about child-murder. That's how they've come to epitomise the child-murderer."

There was a lull in the conversation. Talk of murder drifted into an argument over the abolition of the death-penalty and the politics of it. A referendum in that bar at that moment would have brought it back overwhelmingly. We gradually began to break away into our separate discussion-groups, turning to other earth-shaking topics, bent as ever on solving as many of the world's problems as could be tackled before closing time.

But by now I was far away . . . a hundred and forty miles away, for my thoughts remained on Cannock Chase. I could not help reflecting, as so often over the past twenty-odd years, on how the Moors Murders had so completely overshadowed the series of child-murders that had cast such a massive pall of fear over the Midlands in the 1960s. And how, for all their infamy, the Moors Murder investigations pale into insignificance compared with those into the Cannock Chase Murders. As I had reminded that questioner in my local pub, they remain the most extensive child-murder investigations in history.

Furthermore, had the lessons we learned at Cannock been acted upon, the fiascos of the later investigations into the "Black Panther" kidnapping and murder (of Leslie Whittle) and the "Yorkshire Ripper" murders might never have arisen to stain the professionalism of the British Police Service. They should and could have been learned, but they were not. In Shropshire, Staffordshire and Yorkshire a few years later, the same mistakes wreaked havoc, created a crisis of public confidence and forced Parliamentary debates when they were revealed so dramatically (in Yorkshire at least) in the form of further needless murders.

I had tried my best to pass those lessons on, but it seems no one was listening. When I remember that, I cannnot help but remember the old proverb: *He who is shipwrecked the second time cannot lay the blame on Neptune.*

*   *   *

My reverie was broken by a voice from a far corner of the bar. "What about doing it?"

Brought back to earth, I looked across and asked, "Doing what?"

I should have known without asking, because the next words were also familiar.

"Writing about the Cannock Chase Murders. You can write . . . you write books . . . when are you going to write about Cannock Chase?"

Another question I had answered a hundred times before. "One day," I called. "I've thought about it. One day I'll get around to it." I laughed and tapped the side of my head with the tip of my forefinger. "It's all in here. I'll get it out one day."

CHAPTER ONE

WITHOUT TRACE

In January, 1965, the big topic among detectives the length and breadth of England and Wales was the formation of Regional Crime Squads, an idea stemming directly from the concern felt by the Home Office about the chaos that had marred the opening stages of the investigation into the Great Train Robbery of August, 1963. Never again, it was being said, would small police forces have to cope with sudden and overwhelming major crime investigations without rapid reinforcement from a strong team of highly mobile and experienced detectives.

Those of us already seconded from our forces to such small, experimental joint ventures as the North and South Staffordshire Crime Squads had our hearts set on becoming part of the new organisation. The big day, it seemed, was to be next month; the National Co-ordinator had already been appointed. It was rumoured that the Regional Crime Squad in the Midlands would have its headquarters in Birmingham and branches in Wolverhampton, Coventry, Leicester, Northampton and Stoke-on-Trent. That was where my sights were set: Stoke-on-Trent, the city in whose police force I had served for nearly fifteen years, and where I had been a detective for seven.

I had joined the force in May, 1950, and had been put into the CID after seven and a half years walking the city beats. With thirteen years' service, I had been promoted sergeant, and, in line with force policy, transferred in that rank into the uniformed branch. And then I was lucky. After only five months in uniform I was put back into the CID as a Detective Sergeant in the central division. I had then been given the task of setting up one of those new-fangled "Criminal Intelligence Sections", of which there were five in the country, modelled on that in New Scotland Yard. That in itself was an historic innovation which would eventually spread nationwide to form the very heart-beat of the investigation of "high-class" crime and criminals. But it was quite new then, and it was a job that gave me a unique knowledge of crime and criminals in the North Midlands. It made me, I suppose, a natural choice for the joint-force experiment in mobile crime squads, begun in the Spring of 1963 by the Staffordshire County Police and the small city and borough forces contained in the county.

It was very much an experiment, a scratch force of small groups of Detective Sergeants (four of us in North Staffordshire) provided with cars and dual-channel radio sets. By comparison with what was to follow it was an unsophisticated start, but it represented the very first departure from the "boundary mentality" inevitable when you have one hundred and eighty separate police forces in the country (to-day, a quarter of a century later, there are forty-three).

Small in number we might have been, but we had already made our mark, and, working an average of ninety hours a week (CID officers were not paid for overtime in those days), had been called in to help on many major crime investigations, including many difficult murders.

* * *

It was on such a murder investigation (in Burton-on-Trent, at the beginning of January, 1965) that I first heard of the abduction, rape and attempted murder of a nine-year-old girl in Walsall. My three fellow Detective Sergeants and I had been on the Burton investigation for a week or more. George Reade and Ron Hammond, our opposite numbers on the South Staffordshire Crime Squad, had not been able to join us because they had been called in to help on the Walsall case. But now they had joined us, and we were having our evening meal in a tiny pub across the bridge from Burton, on the Ashby side of the River Trent.

It was a typical Crime Squad meal break: the dominoes were out, the cold pork pies had been cut into quarters and were thick with mustard. We drank our pints of Bass bitter, fed our incipient ulcers with those leaden pork pies, and, while the rest of the boys got down to serious dominoes, Detective Sergeant George Reade and I talked about the five-week enquiry that had kept him away from the Burton murder.

"What was in that rape job then, George? Did you have any luck with it?"

He leaned back in his chair, the hunch of his shoulders pressing his chin into his chest, the long ash of his cigarette dropping onto his tie. He spoke in a rather strangled voice and with a Hampshire accent on which his eighteen years' service in Walsall had left its mark: "That kid will never be the same again, Pat. Nearly dead she was. Another twenty minutes in that ditch and she would have been."

"Any clues? Anything similar happened in the area?"

"Very little," said George, puffing clouds of smoke while his lungs protested with a rasping cough. He brushed away the cigarette ash and stilled the cough with a draught of beer that emptied his glass, which he put down with a bang to draw his partner's attention to the fact that it was his turn to pay. He hunched himself even more, the permanent crease in his forehead deepened, and he coughed again. "But he's *got* to be local, Pat. That poor kid shouldn't really be alive and it's amazing she can give us anything at all, but she can. Whether or not it's reliable after all she's been through is another matter, but there are a couple of things she does seem to remember. First, she was able to take us from the street where she was picked up to the spot where she was found, and second, she said that when they got there she asked him where they were and he said 'Bentley.' It's out on the west of Walsall, a big, derelict scab of a place."

"Did he say anything else? Any name? Anything about himself at all?"

A shrewd and very able Walsall Borough detective of the old school was George Reade. He and I would eventually become founder-members of the Midlands Regional Crime Squad, and then neighbouring Divisional Detective Chief Inspectors, while he would go on to achieve fame as the Detective Superintendent who led the CID team that brought about the conviction of the IRA's Birmingham pub bombers on twenty-one counts of murder. And even more fame when, eleven years after his retirement, he came back to fight his way successfully through the longest ever hearing in the Court of Appeal, to keep them in prison and defeat a long, fiercely orchestrated and vociferous campaign to free six guilty men and to discredit him, his colleagues and British justice.

George never uttered a word that hadn't been thoroughly digested and he had this habit of sinking back into his shoulders and puffing away reflectively before answering questions. "Only a name, and it's probably not genuine anyway," he said, after a long silence. His cloud of cigarette smoke swirled around us and he coughed again. "Called himself 'Uncle Len' and told the girl her mother had sent him to fetch her to her aunt to collect Christmas presents. The description she gave us could fit anybody. And then there's a car. A Vauxhall. You know, one of the big ones, with the fins at the back. The 'Cresta' model."

"*She* told you that?"

"No. The car's from a witness. The kid can only say it was a big car. The witness saw it there at the time she must have been either in the car or in the ditch. He says it was a Cresta, with a hand spotlamp fixed to the front door pillar, at the end of the windscreen on the driver's side."

"Should be easy enough to find," I ventured.

"I'd have thought so, but we haven't found it yet. Jim Collins [the head of Walsall CID] has put every man we've got onto the job, but we've got nothing so far."

"And what about the kid? He raped her?"

"Yes, the bastard. He picked her up at nine at night and she was found half-dead at nine-fifty. It's amazing after what she went through, but the route she took us from where he picked her up in Bloxwich across to Bentley must have been right. The time fits in perfectly. They arrive on this wide, open road across the Bentley slag heaps and he rapes her . . . in the car I'd say. It was pitch-black there. Tore the poor kid apart. She remembers screaming with the pain, and the last thing she remembers is him putting his hands around her neck and squeezing. He must have just thrown her out of the car and she rolled into the ditch. Left her for dead. How the hell she was found that night God only knows. It was so bloody dark down there, and it was chucking it down with rain. It was a miracle this fellow came by on his bike and heard her moaning."

"Jesus," I said. "And what's the state of her now?"

"The doc. says she would have been a gonner in another twenty minutes at the most. She was torn around the vagina and badly bruised around the neck, but otherwise physically not too bad. It's her mind they're worried about. Looks as though it's turned her brain, so you can judge what her evidence is worth. Poor bugger. She'll never be the same again, Pat.''

"Attempted murder?"

George laughed and picked up his pint. "Not bloody likely. Our chief isn't going to have an undetected attempted murder on the books. Rape it is. For now anyway. We'll see what else we make of it if we ever catch the swine."

And then his partner interrupted us: "Shall we deal you in?"

George and I turned towards his table, moved our pints over, and drew a hand from the spread of dominoes, while I asked one last question: "And nothing else like it in the area?"

"Nothing," said George. "Nothing involving a kid that age anyway."

That didn't surprise me. That kind of a thing was a rarity then, even though we are talking of only twenty-odd years ago. But times were changing, and though we couldn't know it, what George and I had just been talking about was the first incident in what were to become known as *The Cannock Chase Murders*.

*   *   *

Our Burton-on-Trent killer having been arrested and charged, my colleagues and I returned to our Crime Squad base in Hanley, Stoke-on-Trent. I had operated from there for about a year as one of the team of four Detective Sergeants (two from the City and two from the County), with both an investigative role (cultivating informants and targetting criminals who operated across the force boundaries) and a support role (giving local officers the benefit of two pairs of experienced detectives to help with their investigations of serious crimes and their dealings with travelling criminals). Our work naturally brought us into contact with detectives across a wide area of the Midlands and the North-west, and with other local crime squads, so the four of us regarded ourselves as front runners in the Regional Crime Squad stakes.

On 8th February, 1965, the Stoke-on-Trent Branch of No. 4 Regional Crime Squad came into existence, the very first in the country, and we Detective Sergeants became the nucleus around which it was formed. We were joined by four Detective Constables who were paired off with us, DS and DC, each pair being allocated a car fitted with specially-developed multi-channel radio sets. We were to be on twenty-four hour call, the car was to be kept at the home of the Detective Sergeants to facilitate immediate call-out and (the greatest innovation of all to detectives who had spent much of their lives submerged in the stuff) *we were to be freed of paper-work* so that we could concentrate on catching criminals whose expertise, organisation and scale of operation had hitherto put them beyond the reach of the conventional detective. All in all it was a very exciting prospect.

"You are concerned with the criminal, not the crime," we were told at our first briefing by the Detective Chief Inspector and Detective Inspector who were to be in charge of the branch. "Our terms of reference are clearly set out in Home Office Circular No. 249 of 1964. What they tell us is that we don't take the scene of a crime as our starting-point, like we did back on divisional CID; what we do is to start with the criminal, the guy who commits the big stuff, the guy who has probably never been convicted or even arrested. We all know some of them, don't we? Well, our job is to identify the best of them and to set our sights on getting them. Call them our "targets" if you like. We shall watch them day and night, see where they go and who they mix with, identify all their associates, put informants on to them or try to make informants of some of their associates. We'll have the time . . . all the time we need. No more paper work, no more preparing files of evidence and going to court. That's for the divisional men. We're being given the kind of chances we've dreamed of—to go out and get the bastards we've all been dying to get at."

Regional Crime Squads are more than twenty years old now, and so much a part of the scenery that it is hard for to-day's detective to appreciate what this meant at the time, to understand what an historic departure it represented from all that had gone before in criminal investigation. We weren't simply doing a job, we were embarking on an exciting way of life that would keep us away from our families for ninety and ninety-five hours a week, twenty-seven days a month, 353 out of the 365 days of the first year of our branch's existence, as we put everything we had into establishing ourselves.

"And another thing," said the DCI. "We are one branch of several, in one of nine Regional Crime Squads covering the whole country, which means we are part of a large organisation that can be concentrated anywhere from the Scottish border to Land's End to help on major crime investigations. In our region alone, there are sixty of you, in teams of two, with thirty cars, all fitted with multi-channel radios that can be tuned in to whatever frequency is used where we happen to be operating. And our region can be teamed up with other regions, and so on and so on, so that we can concentrate as big a team of experienced detectives as anybody can ever need."

And that was exactly how it turned out. We spread our wings over police boundaries which had hitherto seriously inhibited the fight against the professional criminal. We were rushed to major investigations all over the Midlands, while, in the times between, we got our teeth into, and put away, professional criminals engaged in such heavy crime as armed robbery, safe-blowing, burglary and receiving stolen property, who had hitherto laughed in our faces.

It is impossible to exaggerate the thrill of it all; of that life of early morning raids, door-kicking, car-chasing, intensive surveillance and difficult murder investigations. It remains for me, as I know it remains for all of my colleagues who lived through those days, one of the most rewarding experiences of the most rewarding career I could have wished for.

*   *   *

It was an exciting year, which ended for me in my first encounter with a spate of what were believed to be child abductions in the Birmingham and Walsall areas.

It was a brief encounter, and for a while no different from many another call for assistance we had had during that first hectic year. It came on Saturday the 1st of January, 1966, as we were nursing our New Year hangovers: *"Report to Bloxwich Police Station in Walsall Borough at 7 a.m. tomorrow, Sunday the 2nd. The Stoke, Wolverhampton and Birmingham squads are being put in to help Walsall in the search for five*

"Disappeared without trace": Diane Tift as she was last seen (a composite photograph).

Express & Star

and a half year old Diane Joy Tift, who has been missing from home since last Thursday afternoon."

My partner, Detective Constable Roy Ashley, and I were there dead on time, and the briefing room in the old police station was packed. A large wall map displayed the Borough of Walsall and its environs, and there was a blackboard on which were pinned sheets of typed foolscap showing officers' names and the territories allocated to them. The briefing officer, the head of Walsall Borough CID, took the stage and we were called to order.

"Gentlemen," he said, raising a hand holding a large photograph of a smiling little girl with cheeky eyes and fringed light-brown hair, "this is Diane Joy Tift, five-and-a-half years of age, born on the 28th of March, 1960. She lives at 2, Hollemeadow Avenue, on the Blakenall Estate at Bloxwich."

He pointed a billiard cue at a spot on the map in the built-up area to the north of Walsall town centre. "Diane Tift was reported missing from home last Thursday evening at seven o'clock. In fact she was last seen at around half past one to two o'clock when she left her grandmother's home in Chapel Street." The point of his billiard cue moved to a spot on the map which he told us was half a mile from the child's home. "There is one sighting, though, which might be reliable. We don't quite know yet. When Diane's mother was in the launderette near the grandmother's home at around three o'clock, she was told by another daughter, Susan, that Diane had just walked by the launderette window. There's some doubt about this sighting because Susan hadn't got her glasses on, though she's adamant about it. If she's right, it's possible that Diane had gone from her grandmother's home to the shopping-precinct to play. At all events, she has just disappeared without trace."

He motioned to one of the detectives on the stage and was handed some notes. "We've done a thorough house-to-house there," he said, "but we haven't yet picked up a single other sighting; nor is there any sign of her being accosted by anybody or of what might have happened to her when she went around the corner out of Susan's sight, if indeed Susan actually saw her. She just disappeared into thin air."

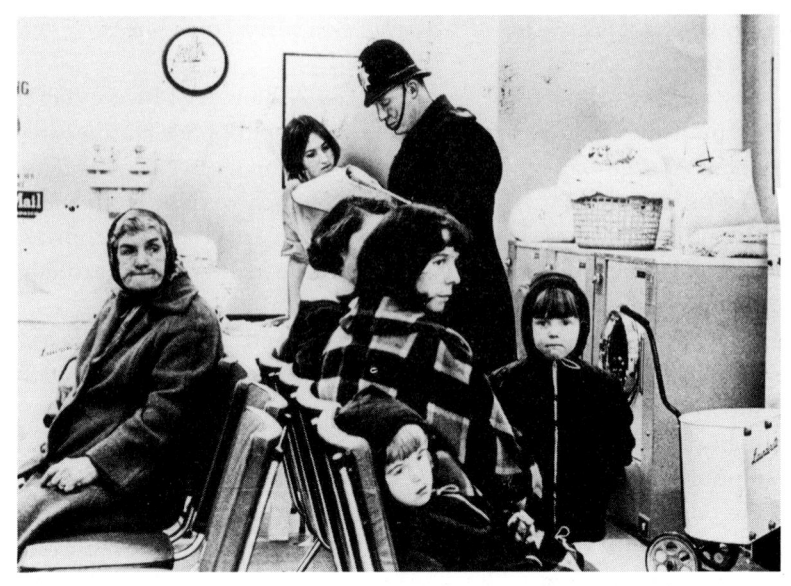

The Bloxwich launderette, scene of the last supposed sighting of Diane Tift.
Express & Star

He consulted his notes again, and described circles on the map with his billiard cue. "We have already done a lot of searching: dogs and line searches across here, here and here . . . allotments, open ground, derelict buildings and so on . . . and" . . . (the point of his billiard cue moved on) . . . "we've dragged stretches of water in these areas. What we have brought you all here for to-day is to do a systematic search of every house and outbuilding in this area here." He described a wide sweep around the huge Hollemeadow Council Estate. "And I mean a thorough search. I want you to look under every bed, in every cupboard, in every chest of drawers, under every staircase, in every loft and in every shed and rabbit hutch of the houses allocated to you. You will work in groups, each group containing local officers. The groups will be broken down into pairs . . . crime squads keeping to their crews of two . . . and each pair will be given a map and allocated a list of properties. You will go to the estate in your groups and start off from what will be your rendezvous points for the whole exercise. I suggest that those of you who are strangers to the area do a recce first to find your bearings. Any questions so far?"

One of the Crime Squad men from the Birmingham Branch raised his hand: "Any connection with Margaret Reynolds of Aston do you think, sir?"

"I was coming to that," said the briefing officer. He consulted his notes again: "For the benefit of those of you who are not familiar with the case, I want to mention a possible connection with another missing child, in Birmingham. It was nearly four months ago, on the 8th of September, a Wednesday. Margaret Reynolds, not quite seven years of age, born on the 16th of October, 1958, also disappeared into thin air. She went missing at Aston after leaving home in Clifton Road to go back to school after lunch. She and her sister parted to go to different schools and that was the last seen of young Margaret. In fact, she didn't go back to school, she just disappeared. There's been no sign of her since, and the police at Birmingham have not found a single clue as to what might have happened to her. We have a poster here with her picture on it." He held it up for us all to see.

Clifton Road, Aston, Birmingham, where Margaret Reynolds "just disappeared".
Express & Star

Margaret Reynolds as she was last seen, on her way to school (a composite photograph). *Express & Star*

What he could have added was that, in the thick of the early enquiries into Margaret Reynolds's disappearance, the arrests of Ian Brady and Myra Hindley (in October, 1965) had sparked off a flurry of activity between the Incident Rooms in Birmingham, and Manchester where they were being held. Betrayed to the police by Hindley's brother-in-law, whom they had tried to bring into their sadistic killing-for-kicks campaign of random murder, they had been arrested for axing to death a young man they had lured into Brady's home. Now they were suspected of abducting and killing children of about Margaret's age and of disposing of their bodies, and no one could guess how far afield they might have operated.

Hindley and Brady were saying nothing about anything, and the joint investigation being conducted by Cheshire's head of CID, Detective Chief Superintendent Arthur Benfield, and his Lancashire counterpart, Detective Chief Superintendent Joe Mounsey, was having to make its way forward without any help from them.

The poster of Margaret Reynolds showed her wearing the clothes she had had on when last seen in Aston, and carrying a child's green umbrella identical to the one she had been carrying when she disappeared. The face in the picture belonged to the missing child, but it had been superimposed on the body of a girl who had modelled for it. "Remember that umbrella," said the briefing officer. "And by the way, remember this." He held up a pink-coloured plastic handbag with a white handle and diamond-shaped pieces of white plastic across the breadth of the flap. "Diane Tift had a handbag identical to this as a Christmas present, and she was carrying it when she went missing last Thursday. And one last thing: whatever you happen to turn up in the way of stolen property on this operation, forget it. You'll be depending entirely on the co-operation and goodwill of the householders because you have no power to demand entry. You'll need all the tact you can muster for some of them, I can tell you. Any more questions?"

There were none, so the crowded room broke into a hubbub as names were called out by group leaders and men pushed their way through the throng to join them. Then, warmed by mugs of coffee, and me wearing my battered sheep-skin coat and a muffler, we swarmed out into the cold, grey, drizzle of the morning to our cars, to join the convoys for Blakenall and Bloxwich. By eight o'clock we were poised at the starting ends of our blocks of houses, and the long haul began.

*　　　　*　　　　*

We walked the roads, closes and crescents of Blakenall, in freezing rain, until darkness stopped us, and we were back on the job at the same time next morning and the one after it, in equally appalling weather conditions. After three days we had done it. *Six thousand* houses were searched from top to bottom and not a stick or stone left unturned, or drawer or wardrobe not turned out, or chicken coop not dug under, or dust-clogged attic not clambered over.

Our unannounced arrivals at eight o'clock that Sunday morning found virtually everyone in bed and threw every household into disarray. The amusing experiences we related to each other on our regroupings for meals and debriefings were legion. In one of the first houses my partner and I searched, for example, I went to open the door of the cupboard under the stairs, only to be stopped by the man of the house. "Er . . ." he began uncomfortably. "Er . . . look . . . there's something I'll have to explain to you."

There was. The cupboard was full of builders' and decorators' equipment and materials, as was his attic and the shed in the garden outside.

"What the hell's all this?" I asked.

"Er . . . it's from work, you see . . ."

"Work? What work?"

He was a lorry driver for a builders' merchant in Walsall and he had obviously been robbing his employer blind for a very long time. He had the look of a man facing the gallows as we uncovered his Aladdin's Cave. But he had allowed us into his house without a murmur of protest and we had not left a stone unturned in our searching of it, so we had a bargain to keep. "Look," I said. "You'd better get rid of this bloody stuff sharpish, and I'll be back again tomorrow to check that you have. You can thank your lucky stars you've been so co-operative with us. You'll never be this lucky again, old son."

Just about everyone on that massive search had similar stories to tell. Had we not been bound—and quite properly so—by the *quid pro quo* we had set ourselves, we could have filled the cells in Walsall and Bloxwich, and we could have handed a bonanza to the Walsall Borough CID. The co-operation we had from the people of that town over those three days was phenomenal. And almost total. There was one objection; one solitary instance where the householder told the officers he knew his rights and they could only enter with a Magistrates' Search Warrant. Strangely enough, that gentleman, a Walsall Borough Councillor, was a leading member of the Watch Committee, the body responsible for the administration of its police force, and a pillar of Walsall's local government!

As for the object of the exercise, the finding of some clue to the whereabouts of little Diane Tift, we came away empty-handed. If there were a connection between her disappearance and that of Margaret Reynolds, eight miles away in Birmingham, we had found nothing to support that either. One thing was certain: if Myra Hindley and Ian Brady had abducted and killed Margaret Reynolds, they could not have taken Diane Tift. When she disappeared, they had been in custody for three months.

In any case, the two Midlands disappearances were beginning to come together in the minds of the senior detective officers in charge of what had now become full-scale murder investigations. Both girls had disappeared without trace, in daylight, on days when the shops in the districts closed for the half-day. They were roughly the same age. But above all—though it might be a coincidence—*there was the proximity to both scenes of the A.34 Southampton to Manchester Trunk Road.*

Detective work, particularly in the investigation of major crimes, is not guess-work. Theorising on the grand scale is for Sherlock Holmes, and Agatha Christie's fictional sleuths. Real detectives confine themselves to keeping an open mind and drawing reasonable conclusions from known facts, remembering always that "reasonable" conclusions are those which do not overstretch credibility or extend into flights of fancy. When they have done this, the rest is largely down to routine and automatic procedure, with a leavening of experience and professional instinct, all very tightly controlled by a discipline and organisation which admits of no freelancing or wandering off at ill-judged tangents. No room in this approach for the antics of fictional detectives which have become so familiar in American TV cops and robbers series and their British imitations.

So what did the senior investigating officers have in Birmingham and Walsall? Open-mindedness dictated that all non-criminal explanations had to be explored: had the girls wandered off and fallen into pools of water, or entered buildings and become locked in, or fallen down wells or colliery shafts, or otherwise incapacitated themselves and died in hidden places? Thus the searches: the houses and outbuildings of six thousand residences in Bloxwich alone; twenty-five square miles of open land in Birmingham and Walsall; countless pools, streams, old shafts, flooded quarries and sewers dived and dragged by frogmen; any number of derelict ironworks and factories searched on the wastelands bequeathed by the Industrial Revolution; around fifty thousand people interviewed, and many thousands of posters and leaflets distributed;

Briefing the volunteers in the search for Diane Tift. *Express & Star*

"Countless pools, streams, old shafts, flooded quarries and sewers were dived and dragged" in the search for Diane Tift. *Express & Star*

"Anniversary Checks" (networks of check-points set up to monitor the presence and movements of people and vehicles in given areas on the same days of other weeks); countless hours of foot-slogging, door-knocking, searching and questioning notched up by hundreds of uniformed and plain-clothed police officers.

So much for the possibility of a non-criminal explanation, but the possibility that the girls had been kidnapped dictated an overlapping criminal investigation. Men convicted of, or known to have committed, indecent acts on children, or to have a penchant for hanging around school railings at play-time; commercial travellers, lorry drivers and delivery-men, absentees from shops and factories, certain classes of mental patient, servicemen on leave, men convicted of indecency with children and now on the loose after being released from prison—all to be found and questioned, and their whereabouts at the material times to be ascertained and verified.

The whole nation became involved in these investigations, with circulations to all police forces and news items and appeals in local, regional and national newspapers and on every television and radio network in the country.

And the result of it after four whole months? Nothing. A massive public response and a mountain of paper-work. But at the end of it all, nothing. Not a single sighting of either the missing girls or whoever might have abducted them. All that remained when my partner and I left Walsall to go to the assistance of another force in another investigation on the 5th of January, 1966, was the A.34 connection.

That trunk road, an important one in those early days of Motorway construction, running north-westwards from Southampton for two hundred miles, through Hampshire, Berkshire, Oxfordshire, Warwickshire, Birmingham, Walsall, Cannock and Stafford and thence, through Cheshire, to Manchester, was a thread that not only ran through the riddle of what had happened to Margaret Reynolds and Diane Tift, but also attached itself to several encounters between car drivers and young children in the Walsall area, over several months... encounters which might have been innocent requests for directions, or intended kidnappings.

Above all, it was a thread that attached itself to the raping and attempted killing by "Uncle Len" of that poor, nerve-torn little nine-year-old in Bloxwich, in December, 1964. *She, too, had been picked up from a spot within yards of the A.34!*

*   *   *

We were sitting in the Squad Office at around four o'clock in the afternoon of Wednesday 12th January—a week after we had returned from Cannock—when the DI burst in. "They've found Diane Tift. It's murder!"

"Where?" we chorused.

"On Cannock Chase. Near a place called Pottal Pool."

"Where's that?"

Detective Sergeant Alan Everall, a Staffs. County man, got up and walked over to our large wall-map. He took out his ball pen and placed it on a cross-roads south of Stafford. "Here," he said. "On the A.34, nearer Cannock than Stafford, where the Penkridge to Rugeley road crosses it."

We crowded around him and looked at the great spread of scrubland and forest called Cannock Chase.

I looked at my watch. "Do they want us?"

"Cannock Police Station, eight o'clock tomorrow morning," said the DI. "All of you. Be prepared for a long stay. They've called in the Yard and it's going to be a big one. They want every available man, so they're calling in the Birmingham, Wolverhampton, Coventry and Stoke Branches, and CID men from Wolverhampton, Walsall, Brum and Coventry. Eight o'clock. OK?"

*   *   *

We had learned more than new police techniques during our first year as a Regional Crime Squad. The domestic problems associated with seeing precious little of our families were, perhaps, the most potent of our new experiences, along with having to drive fifty or a hundred miles home at the end of a day's work, as often as not with a few pints inside us. Pre-breathalyser days they might have been, but the penalties of coming to grief in a Crime Squad car miles from home were real enough, as some of my comrades were unlucky enough to discover, and yet in the nature of our job—long, gruelling hours, and the need to frequent pubs and clubs to meet the villains and our existing or potential underworld informers—the risk was not easy to avoid. I did, though, for a whole month, when my doctor diagnosed a suspected ulcer. Although I carried on working, I was ordered off the beer (even though I still frequented the pubs and clubs), and the carton of milk and packet of arrowroot biscuits on the back seat of my car became a standing joke in the Squad.

But there was something else about our Crime Squad experience . . . something which caused every car on No. 4 Regional Crime Squad to carry a box of dominoes, a pack of cards and a pegging board on the back seat. Whenever one arrived at a police station as part of a concentration of manpower to begin a major investigation, there was a delay before deployment, a period of initial chaos before the manpower so hastily assembled could be sorted into cohesive teams, given orders, and put out onto the streets.

That period of hanging about, which we on the Regional Crime Squad had christened "Doms [Dominoes] Time", would never be less than an hour and had even been known to extend to half a day or more. So our first action on arriving at a strange police station was to find the canteen or some other cosy corner of the building, lay on some tea and set up a dominoes and cribbage school, to which all—regardless of whether they belonged to the Squad—were invited, while we waited for orders.

Many's the pound that changed hands during those sessions, while rumour abounded and fact or firm instructions were impossible to come by. For these were the days when many Provincial police forces still followed the tradition of a century-and-a-half by "Calling in The Yard", with its mystical "System" (the administrative set-up), to investigate difficult murders, and few had yet mastered the art of preparing for such large-scale contingencies, training staff to set up the organisation without undue delay, and being ready to put the show on the road at extremely short notice.

It was really a period of transition, a time when the very existence of Regional Crime Squads was beginning to dispel the mystique of "The System", to spread the art of major investigation and to make Provincial police forces self-sufficient. It would not be stretching things to say that the series of investigations on which we were now setting out would, in the Midlands at least, be the catalyst that above all others would hasten that process. It was an experience for which I would have cause to be profoundly grateful when I reached the higher levels of CID command, for it was there that I identified and analysed the strengths and weaknesses of our approach to a murder investigation, and formulated my own ideas on how to prepare oneself and one's subordinates. In short, I was embarking on one of the most rewarding experiences of my thirty-four year police career.

*   *   *

So, at Cannock's old police station on that bitterly cold Thursday morning in January, the well-honed team of hardened detectives forming the Midlands Regional Crime Squad had come together, the dominoes were out, and the Band of Brothers, as we felt ourselves to be, was binding itself together in good-natured banter while waiting to be sent into action. That took the whole morning, for it was noon, after several false starts, before we received our first orders: "Go out in batches of four cars to Mansty Gulley on Cannock Chase, and rendezvous at the scenes-of-crime tent for a briefing by Detective Superintendent [Harry] Bailey [Deputy Head of Staffordshire CID], then come back here for a full briefing by Detective Superintendent [Cyril] Gold [of New Scotland Yard's Murder Squad] . . . two o'clock should do it."

Back into the box went the dominoes and out we swarmed.

Even now, at noon, with a sick-looking sun squinting from behind the mist that shaded into thick hoar frost covering the fields on the southern edge of Cannock Chase, it was cold . . . bitterly cold, with a temperature still below freezing; the kind of weather that puts an iciness on the tip of your nose. We stood huddled, hands in pockets, inside the large white tent alongside the hedge and astride the water-ditch, just inside the field gate from the

Detective Chief Superintendent Harry Bailey (Head of Staffs. CID) sets up his incident post at Mansty Gulley. *Express & Star*

narrow road which runs parallel to, and about half a mile west of, the A.34 trunk road that was to dominate this investigation.

"Here," said Harry Bailey, pointing down into the muddy water of the ditch, "is where they were found."

There was a murmur of surprise at the word "They", so he quickly pointed out that he believed both Diane Tift *and* Margaret Reynolds to have been found there. "The man who found the bodies first saw a bundle of clothing and immediately realised it was the decomposed body of a child, but then a police officer walking along the ditch saw what he at first thought was a stone and then found was a skull. It now looks as though that was Margaret Reynolds, and there is very little of her left. Diane Tift was probably dumped right on top of her. We've had a preliminary post-mortem and it seems that Diane Tift was probably suffocated by her pixie-hood and sexually assaulted. I'd be surprised myself if we ever find what killed Margaret Reynolds, she's so badly decomposed."

I had met Harry Bailey before and had been very impressed by him. He was not my boss, in the sense that we served in different police forces—he in the Staffordshire County force and I in the Stoke-on-Trent City force—but I already knew him well enough to like and respect him. We had first come into contact through my service on the old North Staffordshire Crime Squad in circumstances which had given me the ideal opportunity to judge him as a man and as a leader of men. I had been highly impressed not only by his shrewdness, but also by his easy manner with subordinates, which yet did not diminish their respect for his rank. In my own City force, where discipline was still of the rigid, military variety, such relationships were unknown above the level of Sergeant.

He was a large, taciturn man, with the rounded face of a farmer, and somewhat flabby lips that tended to splash the words they uttered; absolutely unflappable, clear in his orders, firm in his support for his men and easy company in a bar.

Harry Bailey was standing on the stage with the Yard man for the afternoon briefing. As at Bloxwich only ten days before, the room

Harry Bailey (right) meets the men sent from Scotland Yard to help him: Detective Superintendent Cyril Gold (centre) and Detective Sergeant Eric Bailey. *Express & Star*

was packed to the doors, and there was the usual array of maps, plans, posters and photographs. Piles of "Action" forms, questionnaires and statement forms filled tables at one side of the briefing room.

None present had ever heard of Cyril Gold of the Scotland Yard Murder Squad, but, as we were to discover, he was an old hand at murder investigation. Rather small, nattily dressed and topped off with a pert, tweed trilby, he had a pointed nose and angular features, all of which marked him more as a race-track punter than a Detective Superintendent, but I remember him above all as a thoroughly knowledgeable and shrewd detective, and as a gentleman. He spoke quietly: "Gentlemen," I remember him saying, "we have a stinker here." Then he went through the facts of the disappearance of the two girls, of the harrowing experience of the little girl at Bentley, near Bloxwich, and of the several other incidents which might, or might not, be connected with them.

His theme was the A.34 . . . at Aston in Birmingham, several times at Bloxwich, and now where the road crossed Cannock Chase on its way north.

Harry Bailey (right) and Cyril Gold (centre) at Mansty Gulley.
Express & Star

Arthur Rees, Chief Constable of Staffordshire (second from left) visits Mansty Gulley with Cyril Gold (centre) and other senior officers.

Express & Star

"So far we have nothing at all to go on," he said. "No sightings of any consequence, no pick-ups, no vehicles, no suspects. The PM [Post Mortem Examination] results and the Lab. might give us something, I don't know. But for the moment, it's down to you. It will be house-to-house, "Actions" and turning over likely offenders, and we shall hammer it gentlemen until we get there."

Then he called on his Sergeant, Eric Bailey, also of the Yard, whose job it was to set up and run the famed "System". "For those of you who are not familiar with the system," said Gold, "Eric Bailey here will hold a separate briefing. He'll explain it all to you and how you will play your part in it. Listen to him carefully. Without the System, we'll soon get ourselves into a hell of a mess. There's going to be a mountain of paper work and if we don't start as we intend to go on, the whole thing will collapse around us."

There were forty men who did not need to go to Eric Bailey's lecture on "The System". By now it had become our bread and butter. We on No.4 Regional Crime Squad had worked under enough Scotland Yard Murder Squad men to know the score and to know "The System" pretty well inside out.

CHAPTER TWO

DOMINOES AND DOOR-KNOCKERS

I could never have dreamed, as we listened to our briefing at Cannock Police Station and prepared to set about "door-knocking" for the Cannock Chase Murder Investigation that, ten years later, I would be a visiting lecturer at the National Police Staff College (at Bramshill in Hampshire), and my subject would be *"The Investigation of Major Crime, including Murders"*.

My opening to the lecture was always the same: "Ladies and gentlemen," I would say, "my subject to-day is the investigation of major crime, and I would like to begin by suggesting that every major crime—indeed, every major incident—brings chaos in its early stages. Those who organise their chaos will emerge from it more quickly than those who don't. So I like to sub-title this talk 'Organising your Chaos'."

There would be a ripple of laughter, and I knew that among my audience were detectives who understood exacly what I was talking about; detectives who had had their own version of "Dominoes Time" when called to help in major investigations and waiting for orders. They would nod understandingly when I talked of the chaos which marked the first days of the investigation into The Great Train Robbery, and when I described how, in a series of murder investigations in the East Midlands, the enquiries were stopped in their tracks for several days while a huge back-log of telephone messages, statements and questionnaires was cleared by a belatedly reinforced Incident Room staff. Presumably those who should have been foot-slogging outside were biding their time playing dominoes while the confusion was sorted out!

My audience murmured with the pangs of experience when I said that a manual index and filing system can grow so large as to become unmanageable; no longer pointing the way to possible solutions, but demanding neat conclusions to irrelevant lines of enquiry and swallowing them up for ever inside its hundreds of drawers . . . a clear indication that the officer in charge had lost control of it.

They smiled in disbelief when I told them that Home Office boffins were working on a computer system to overcome it all and that I had seen and tried the prototype. It was indeed on the way, though it would be ten more years coming, even from 1976! It would not supersede "The System" even then, but it would certainly make it infinitely more manageable.

I explained to them how the basis of an efficient Incident Room (which embodies the famed "System") is a discipline within which nothing is conceived, initiated, acted or reported upon without reference to the system. Nothing is done which is not put on paper as a permanent record. Every message, every incoming enquiry, every idea for a line of enquiry, every query, every further action, every witness-statement and questionnaire, is recorded and fed into the central index for comparison and evaluation. At any given time, the officer in charge of the investigation should know from that system the current state of the investigation and the progress of any particular line of enquiry.

"The System," I would say, "is the 'Nerve Centre' of the investigation. What it all boils down to is progress-chasing, cross-referencing, analysing and evaluating . . . each line of enquiry being tracked through to its conclusion and being sent out again and again until it has reached it, while everything is cross-referenced in the index so as to avoid duplication of effort and to bring together enquiries with a common link."

At the root of the system, I told them, is what is known as the "Action" form, on which every line of enquiry is initiated. It may be of a specific nature or a general one. Specific, for example, in asking for the interview of a named person who resembles a "Photofit" picture; general, for example, in setting in motion a separate line of enquiry like the interviewing of all the owners of a particular make of motor car.

It is a search for common factors—especially when two or more investigations are linked—for, in the end, it is the common factor that will point the finger at the culprit. In the Incident Room, which is the power-house of the investigation, the common factor is the product; method and management are the motive power, and discipline the engine oil.

Unfortunately, all this was in the future. We were still in 1966, and those in charge of the Cannock Incident Room were not quite ready for us. So the dominoes came out again and we played until we could decently go out to the nearest pub for a pint.

It was not until ten o'clock the next day, *twenty-six hours after our arrival in Cannock,* that we picked up our first "Action" forms and set out into the icy fog to find the Cannock Chase Murderer.

*   *   *

At our level we were not, and did not expect to be, privy to the workings of the "Inner Cabinet" of Detective Superintendents and Chief Inspectors who headed the investigation. Nor, of course, were we present to see the examinations of bodies and scene, or the Home Office Pathologist's post mortem examination, or the taking of material for scientific examination. For we were at the sharp end of the investigation . . . the door-knockers, any of whom could come face to face with the murderer at any door we knocked on. We depended on our morning briefings for an indication of how we were doing and whether or not we were required to change direction.

We learned from our first morning briefing that Harry Bailey had been right when he told us at the murder scene that we were unlikely ever to know what had happened to Margaret Reynolds in her last moments in the hands of her killer. All that was left of her were her skeleton and a shoe. We heard from the Yard man, Cyril Gold, that Diane Tift had died of a mixture of strangulation and suffocation, when the pixie hood she was wearing had been pulled over her face and its neck-band pulled tight around her neck. Traces of semen found in her anal passage were thought by the Pathologist to have drained from her vaginal passage, indicating that she had probably been raped.

We could see from our briefings that close contact was being maintained between the Cannock, Aston and Bloxwich Murder Incident Rooms, with a view to co-ordinating the different systems and looking for common factors. So far there were none save the A.34. Nor had the scientists come up with any immediate answers, though they were working around the clock in their Birmingham laboratory on a mass of material taken from Mansty Gulley.

House-to-house enquiries were proceeding in the countryside and villages between Penkridge, to the north west, and Littleton, to the south east, of Mansty Gulley, and the man who had found the bodies—a local man who was a suspected poacher and had a history of violence—was being put through the mill as a possible suspect. Our hearts lifted. But by the next briefing he had been cleared.

For the first couple of days my partner and I worked as part of the "House-to-House" team, thrashing the Cannock and Penkridge areas for possible sightings of the murderer or his vehicle while people's memories remained fresh. Time is the enemy; it is vital that maximum pressure is applied in those first hours and days to the area of most immediate interest. Then, as publicity in the news media rises in a crescendo of horror, outrage and speculation, locally and nationally, there comes the deluge of information from the public. Again, time is the enemy as the officer in charge fights to deploy and re-deploy his manpower to cope with his various and ever-changing priorities. On the one hand, getting information from and around the scene; on the other, ensuring, by regular press conferences and personal appearances on radio and television, that his investigation is the main talking-point in every home, pub, club, shop and work-place in the land. He must achieve this, for it will be days or weeks, or even months, before everyone is interviewed, and he must put all he can into keeping the murder in the forefront of people's minds until we can get to them.

One of the earlier "Actions" given to me and my partner in our house-to-house phase was to do a door-to-door enquiry at a small row of cottages in a field close to a colliery near Cannock. It was a strange place. The single row of about a dozen terraced cottages—each with its outside lavatory at the bottom of its yard—was so compact and so isolated in its otherwise empty field that it looked as if it had dropped from the sky. My partner started at one end and I at the other, each of us with his clip-board of questionnaires, and my first call just about typified the weird character of that tiny community.

The lady who answered the door was in her early thirties, thin, hungry-looking, with a sunken face, which was deathly pale under her long, wispy hair. "''allo luv," she said in her broad Cannock accent.

"Good morning," I chirped. "Detective Sergeant Molloy, from the Cannock Murder Room. Can I come in, love? I've got a couple of questions I'd like to ask you."

She turned and led me into a living-room that must have seen better days, and she sank wearily into a settee. I stood, and turned to a blank questionnaire on my clip-board. It was the standard house-to-house form: a "master-sheet" giving the names and ages of all occupants of a house, to which one added separate questionnaires for each of them, covering such basic topics as personal details and such specific matters as knowledge of the deceased, knowledge of and visits to the scene of the crime, whereabouts during the material times and who could verify the movements given, and a space for any useful information the subject might have to offer.

I opened my questioning: "Who lives here, love?"

"Well," she began, stroking her chin as if having to think deeply. "There's me, and me man, and the daughter, and her bab [baby] . . . 'Er was let down by 'er feller, see . . ."

"Your husband," I interrupted, wishing to start at the beginning. "What's his name?"

"Er . . . um . . . er."

"His name, love. What is it?"

She racked her brains. She "er'd" and she "ummed", and she thought a bit more. And then she had an inspiration. Pointing to the mantel-shelf she said "There's a letter up there. That's got his name on it."

Well, I now had his initials and the family surname at least. Or so I thought. "So, he's S. Foster. What's that stand for, love?"

"Sam."

I wrote it down. "Thanks. And what's your Christian name, Mrs. Foster?"

"Oh I'm not Mrs. Foster sir. We ay married. My name's Sadler."

I wrote that down, too. "Now, what about your daughter? The one whose fellow let her down. What's her name and where does she work?"

"Oh, 'er name's Gardenia and 'er's in St. George's [mental hospital, in Stafford]."

I wrote it down. "And her child? What about the child?"

"Oh," she said sadly, "'er's in the backward school, over the back there. 'Er's seven."

Pausing only to ask the usual questions about the house next door, so that I should be well-armed in the event of any attempt at evasion or cover-up there, I closed the interview as gently and kindly as I could, declining the cup of tea she offered me when I saw the state of the cracked cups on her living room table.

When my partner and I met at the middle of the terrace and compared notes, the penny dropped. All our interviews had been much the same. "In-breeding," he said. "All in the row. And a bit of incest for good measure."

Well, it figured, and I just had to take his word for it, since he had worked the area as a uniformed constable and if anybody should know, it would be him.

*   *   *

One came into one's own as a detective on the more general "Actions". Here was the best possibility of coming face-to-face with the murderer and being the one upon whose instincts the whole operation could depend. "We are as strong as our weakest link," as one outstanding murder investigator used to say. "We can have the best Incident Room system in the world, working full blast and as smooth as you like, but let one of them buggers out there come face to face with him and not have a feeling about him, and we're sunk."

"*As strong as our weakest link.*" They were the words that were whispered at the back of your mind whenever a door opened to your knock.

And the variety of instructions on those "Action" forms was boundless:

"Interview Smith of Walsall, owner of a Jaguar car, registration number ABC 123, seen on various dates parked on Cannock Chase."

"Interview Brown of Cannock, said by Chadwick to be a strange one, who takes an inordinate interest in little girls and could be the murderer."

"Interview Dennis, said to have been interfering with little girls locally."

"Interview Blakely, convicted in 1962 of indecent assaults on children; served 2 years, released 1964, last known address Walsall."

"Interview Craddock of Bloxwich, seen by Mrs. Ball to stop his Volkswagen car registration number ABC 456 in Green Lane, Bloxwich, and speak to a girl about nine years."

"Interview James of Wolverhampton, who took blood-stained clothing into Acme cleaners in Walsall around time of disappearance of Diane Tift."

"Interview man known as Dave, uses Green Rock pub, Bloxwich; witness Johnson says he was a bundle of nerves when watching news item on TV in pub about finding of bodies."

"Interview Lake of Walsall, seen by neighbour spraying his car green over original grey in lock-up garage three days after finding of bodies."

"Interview Grey, last known address Blakenall Estate, said by Goodwin to have left the district at time of disappearance of Diane Tift and not been seen since."

The list was endless, and the reception one received to the knock on the door ranged from the welcoming to the hostile, and from the clearly innocent to the deeply suspicious, while the sensations of oneself and partner upon leaving ranged from the happy, to the ambivalent, to the feeling that here was one to get your teeth into. Always there was the feeling that the next door might be opened by the killer, and always one had at the back of one's mind the boss's words to all his door-knockers on all his briefings: "Your instinct is my most powerful weapon. That's why you work in pairs. If the 'bell rings' in a man's mind when he's on his own and he begins to question his instinct, the odds are that he'll convince himself he was wrong. But when the 'bell rings' in two minds at once, that's when I'll hear about it. And remember this. If the 'bell rings', never ignore it. You're all experienced detectives and you've all got a nose for a wrong 'un. So if you have the slightest misgivings about anybody you interview, let me know; bring him in if you wish. That's what we're in here for and that's what you're out there for.''

When you knocked on the door, you heard those words at the back of your mind, the adrenalin flowed and you were ready for anything. True, those instincts could become jaded with familiarity or with exhaustion born of long hours, but we were young, we were hard, we knew our jobs, and we were enjoying every second of it. This was what police work was all about, and the problem was not to keep us at it for twelve and fourteen hours a day, with a forty mile drive home at the end of it, seven days a week, for months on end, but to persuade us to go home!

"Interview Arnold of Walsall, whose Jaguar car was seen on Cannock Chase several times during the material period." We had hundreds of them. Cannock Chase is, of course, a highly popular place for courting couples . . . and married men with their lovers. And a typical "car on Cannock Chase" enquiry would proceed thus:

I would knock on the door of a large house standing in its own grounds on Walsall's Broadway, the nearest thing in the area to a Stockbroker Belt. The door would be opened by a very confident young man of some very well-paid profession or business. "Good morning sir," I would say. "I'm Detective Sergeant Molloy from the Cannock Murder Room." I would consult my "Action" form: 'You are the owner of a black Jaguar saloon car, registration number ABC 789?''

"Yes."

"We have had information that your car was seen parked on Cannock Chase, in a lane on the Penkridge side of the A.34, close to the spot where the bodies of the two murdered girls were found."

He would reply, nonchalantly: "I don't think so, officer. I can't think that I've ever had occasion to go there."

"Well," I would say, drawing my finger over the message on the "Action" form, "we have a witness who actually wrote down the make and number of your car, on three separate dates, and he's quite sure about it. What he says is that you had a blonde lady in the car with you." The hint of a sly smile would crease my face ever so slightly: "I take it your wife is a blonde, sir?"

And then the colour would literally drain from his face as he stepped forward into the porch, closed the front door behind him and dropped his voice to a whisper: "Look . . . I'm sorry, officer . . . it's very awkward you see . . . I mean . . ."

I would now smile reassuringly: "Of course, sir. Would it be more convenient to you if you called in at the Murder Room . . . say three o'clock tomorrow afternoon? If you'd care to bring the lady along as well, it would save us a bit of time. And you know how busy we are . . ."

It didn't always go exactly like that. There *were* occasions when the subject was not so co-operative; occasions, perhaps, when one would find it necessary to talk it over with the gentleman's wife . . .!

* * *

Perhaps our most memorable "car on Cannock Chase" interview was one that we should really not have been involved in at all. On our regular visits to the Cannock Murder Incident Room to deposit statements and questionnaires and to collect fresh "Actions", I had noticed one form, in the basket for a part of the county not normally covered by us, which remained in the basket while others came and went. It referred to a man I shall call Holman. What struck me was the slip of paper pinned to it, on which was written "KIV Member of Police Authority". It lay in that basket for an unusually long time, and one day I asked the officer on the "Action" desk why? "What," I asked, "does KIV mean?"

"Keep In View."

"Never heard of it."

"Oh, it's an old one. They've used it ever since I joined."

"Must be a County expression," I said, with the superiority of the City man. "So why has it lain here so long?"

He laughed. "Oh that's Councillor Holman. He's on the County Council and the County Police Authority and a right bastard he is. They're all frightened of him. Nobody will go to see *him*".

I looked at my partner, "Big Roy" Ashley, and he looked at me. We both smiled. "Sounds like one for us," he said.

We picked up that and a number of other "Actions" for the same area and went to see Councillor Holman, but when we knocked on his door and he answered, I was surprised to see, not a ogre of seven or eight feet, but a prosperous-looking fellow with a beer gut and the look of one who was used to having his own way.

"Good morning. I'm Detective Sergeant Molloy from the Cannock Murder Room . . ."

"Murder room? Murder room? What the f---ing hell has that got to do with me?"

I saw now what they meant by "KIV Member of Police Authority." I'd met guys like him before: petty local politicians whose importance was swollen by their involvement with the Chief Constable as the overseers of the administration of his police force. But I bit my lip: "Yes, the Murder Room, Mr. Holman. Could we come inside, please? Just a few routine questions . . ."

"No you f---ing well can't. Who sent you to see me?"

"The Murder Room."

"Gold, you mean. That bloody idiot from the Yard. Has *he* sent you?"

It wasn't easy. I'd given many another a smack in the teeth for less, but I kept a tight rein on my temper. After all, he could push me *too* far, and I'd show him the whip hand in the end. "Detective Superintendent Gold is my boss, yes, but he doesn't write out every enquiry we come out on. I have this instruction that tells me your car has been seen several times on Cannock Chase and that . . ."

He could contain himself no longer. He raved liked a madman. Four-letter words poured from him as he cursed my boss as one who "couldn't detect a bad smell" and who shouldn't be wasting his time in Cannock, but should be in Walsall or Birmingham, where it was obvious that the girls had been murdered. I still managed to remain calm and countered his torrent of abuse—when I could get a word in edgewise—with an explanation of how, even if his presence on Cannock Chase was perfectly legitimate, he, like hundreds of others we had interviewed, might nevertheless have seen something which might help us in our enquiries. He would also, like everyone else, be required to account for and verify his movements on the days when Margaret Reynolds and Diane Tift had disappeared. That was why we had been sent to see him.

But there was no stopping him, and finally, after ordering me fluently, if unsuccessfully, to get off his property, he fired what he clearly thought would be the broadside that would sink me: "Don't you know who I am?" he roared. "Don't you know who you're f---ing talking to?"

"Well I know you have something to do with the Police Authority," I replied disingenuously.

"Something to do with it? Something to do with it? I'm the f---ing chairman! I run the f---ing thing! Who the hell are you? Where are you f---ing stationed? I want your name, rank and number and I'm going to get on to your Chief Constable. I'm having no more of this f---ing nonsense!"

But now it was my turn, and I fired off my own not insubstantial armoury of ripe language in such a manner as overwhelmed even this bullying swine, of whom the local men were clearly terrified: "Oh you won't know me," I roared. "I don't belong to your ***** police force [after all, I was still a member of the Stoke City force] and I don't give a ***** about you, its Chief Constable or the rest of your ***** Police Authority. Your car was on Cannock Chase and I'm ***** well going to find out why. If I don't find out here and now, your feet aren't going to touch the ***** ground until you hit the cell in Cannock Police Station."

My six feet six ex-Grenadier Guardsman partner (I am only six feet three!) stepped forward menacingly, but I put out my right arm to block him while I finished my tirade: "You can stuff your ***** Police Authority. What the hell were you doing on Cannock Chase?"

He was stunned. No one had ever spoken to him like this before. I had taken his breath away. "Well?" I shouted. "What's it going to be?"

It took a while for him to collect himself, but I saw him recover his old self and prepared to apply my ultimate sanction. I clenched my fists and looked at him grim-faced. His jaw tightened and he took a deep breath as he stepped back and opened the door wide. "You'd better come in," he said. "But I haven't got much time to spare, mind."

We entered. "Right, Mr. Holman. Your car—a Rover isn't it? Registration number XYZ 123?" He nodded. "Well your car was seen on Cannock Chase, up near Mansty Gulley, on three occasions around the time the two girls' bodies were dumped there. What were you doing there and who was with you?"

He was, of course, perfectly entitled to be on Cannock Chase and he eventually satisfied us on all counts, though there was naturally some embarrassment over the lady who had been with him there. But then the storm broke again: "Right, Mr. Holman. Thank you very much. Now we'll just put that into a written statement . . ."

He exploded: "Statement? F---ing statement? What are you talking about, statement?"

"We have to have everything in statement form, signed."

"Who says?"

"My boss says." Which was enough to precipitate another tirade against The Man from the Yard.

I waited for him to draw breath. "I need a statement, Mr. Holman."

"Well, I'm not f---ing making one. Go and tell your f---ing boss that I'm not making any statement and that I'm reporting him to the Chief Constable. I've told you everything. You're satisfied. That's that."

I had the answer to that: "OK, so we go back to Cannock and I tell Mr. Gold that I've seen you, that you're a perfectly respectable, if foul-mouthed, citizen and that I have had an explanation from you with which I am completely satisfied. Mr. Gold will say, 'Well done, Sergeant. Can I have a look at his statement?' 'No sir,' I will say. 'I haven't taken a statement.' 'Well, **** off back and take one,' he'll say. So I'd come and knock on your door again and we'd have all this palaver all over again. So what's the point? I might as well have your statement first as last, so make up your bloody mind, here and now."

He made his statement. He signed it. We even shook hands as we parted. For one thing is certain: he had got away with it for far too long. He might have been a powerful man in his council chamber, but on our ground he stood no chance. What is more, if someone had tried much earlier speaking to him in the language he understood, we might never have had so much trouble with him. And I couldn't help reflecting: the only other real difficulty I could remember anyone having in carrying out an "Action" since I had first become part of this enquiry, was that of the officer who was refused entry to the house in Walsall when we were looking for Diane Tift, because he didn't have a Magistrates' warrant. *And that character helped to run a police force too!*

*   *   *

Although much of what we were doing was repetitive, now and then we would pick up an "Action" that had some real meat in it. As the weeks went by, and Detective Superintendents Cyril Gold and Harry Bailey got to know the calibre of the men on their team, my partner and I began to receive calls to the Inner Sanctum and to be given "Actions" which looked particularly promising and which, in their opinion, needed special CID skill and experience. Now we *really* felt part of the investigating team.

We were out in our car when the call came: "4.CS.17. 4.CS.17. Are you receiving?"

I picked up the mike. "4.CS.17, receiving. Go ahead please."

"4.CS.17. Go at once to Cannock. See Detective Superintendent Gold. Matter is urgent. ETA please?"

I looked at my watch, and then at my partner, who was driving. "How soon?"

"You just watch me. Ten miles. Tell 'em eight minutes," he answered, throwing the gear lever into third and roaring the speedometer up to eighty.

"ETA eight minutes. Over and out."

We were just a little out of breath as we entered the Detective Superintendents' office. "You wanted us, sir?"

Cyril Gold shot to his feet, holding an "Action" form: "This woman's got in touch with the Divisional Chief Superintendent at

Stafford. Wouldn't talk to anyone else. She says her husband's our murderer and she's got the evidence to convict him."

I grabbed the paper and my partner's six feet six inches leaned over my shoulder to read it.

"No need to check the index before you go out on this one," said the Yard man. "She's a new name and there's no record of the family car either. She will only meet you in her car in some place remote from town. It's now [he looked at his watch] three twenty. She's going to ring in from a call box at three thirty, so you can make your own arrangements with her. Mr. Bailey and I will be waiting to hear from you. Let us know immediately you've made your initial assessment. You can have first crack at the husband if you like, but if there's the slightest doubt, bring the bugger in."

"Right, sir. Leave it to us. We'll contact you from a phone box."

She was right on time with her phone call, and I made arrangements to meet her in her car in a lane near Penkridge. She was there when we arrived, and I walked over to the car. "Mrs. Martin?"

She was a bundle of nerves. She looked frightened to death. "Who are you?" she asked, white-faced and trembling. "What do you want?"

"You're Mrs. Martin, I think. I'm Detective Sergeant Molloy and this is Detective Constable Ashley. We're from the Cannock Murder Room and I think you've got something you want to tell us."

She had. When she had settled herself with me in the back seat of our Squad car she began to tell me. "My husband is the man you're looking for. He's the man who killed Diane Tift, I can prove that. And if he killed her he must have killed the other one as well, mustn't he?"

I nodded. "I imagine so, Mrs. Martin. But what's your proof that he killed Diane Tift?"

"The handbag. The little pink handbag. You know, the one that was in the paper."

My heart missed a beat, because every man jack of us had been looking everywhere for that handbag—and for Margaret Reynolds' little green umbrella—wherever our enquiries had taken us. "The handbag? Do you know where it is?"

"I know where it *was*. It was in the glove-compartment of my husband's car."

"That one?" I asked, pointing to the one in which she had travelled to our rendezvous.

"No, his own. A Ford. I was in it with him the day after Diane Tift disappeared, and I happened to open the glove-compartment and there it was."

"Is it there now?"

"No. I asked him about it and he said Mary, his niece, had left it in there. I took it out and had a good look at it, and then I put it back. When I sneaked out to the garage that night to have another look, it had gone. I've searched all over, but it's gone."

"And *was* it his niece's?"

"No," she said. "That's just it. I didn't let on to anybody, but I asked her quietly if I could look at her little pink handbag and she said she hadn't got one. I asked her if she was sure and she said she was. And then, when I saw the picture of little Diane's handbag in the paper and on the telly, I knew immediately it was that that I'd seen."

But there was more. There was a catalogue of suspicious behaviour on the part of her husband, and of outlandish sexual proclivities, that, taken together with his interest in little girls and, above all, that pink handbag, pointed to a suspect of the first magnitude. If it were all true.

I had to find out, so I persuaded her to go with us to a police station well outside Stafford (she would not go to Cannock), where we could question her further and get it all down in writing. But first I made my phone-call to Cyril Gold and Harry Bailey: "If this woman is telling the truth," I told them, "he's *got* to come. We're going to Stone. We'll talk some more and I'll come straight back to you."

It was incredible. I finished up with a statement that would have convicted the Holy Father himself. Even her description of the handbag was spot-on: that shiny pink plastic, with those shiny white plastic diamond-shaped pleats across its flap. It was perfect. But something was nagging at me. It was something impossible to describe; just a detective's suspicion that something is too good to be true. I talked to her some more, and then some more. I talked to her for another couple of hours . . . of her husband's treatment of her, of his sexual perversions, of her own life and the children she could not have. And a thousand other things, for it had slowly begun to dawn on me that I had a nut-case on my hands. I knew the cure for that.

When someone is deranged by an obsession, he or she can look and sound perfectly sane in the beginning, and will be able to keep it up for a very long time. But the longer one converses, the greater the obsession will become and eventually the disturbed mental state will surface and the story stray into the grotesque. The secret is to keep talking.

By the time I had finished with that poor woman, she was telling me how her husband was bombarding her through the bedroom wall with electric rays from a machine she had not yet been able to find, but which he obviously kept secreted somewhere around the house. I had seen it so many times before: the persecution complex, the sexual perversions which were the product of a repressed and tortured mind, the Valium prescribed in vast quantities by a doctor who could think of nothing else, and the odd visit to the "nerve specialist."

It was so sad, but it was goodbye to Glory so far as we were concerned. There was nothing more to do but see the "Action" out to its conclusion, which was an interview with the man (on a pretext which he would never even remotely connect with his wife), which led to his total elimination from our enquiries.

The sad thing is that, when one is involved with a sensational murder investigation, the world is full of "nutters". We even had to open a "Nutters" file (although we obviously called it something else) to cope with all the letters and phone-calls that poured in from clairvoyants, water-diviners, mediums and just plain weirdos. Mediums will have messages from the murder victim, or from famous murderers, executed on this earth but determined in the next world to make amends by helping to find others of their kind. Others will receive messages through Ouija boards or through upturned spirit glasses, or even through visions. One even gave us the time and date on which our murderer's Boeing 707 had left Heathrow for New York!

Do we ignore them? Not on your life! Woe betide the detective whose mind is not open to everything the world throws at him during a big murder investigation, for those who know, those who have been through this kind of thing so many times before, know that once in a lifetime the "nutter" will have the answer. I once arrested a man, charged him and had him convicted of killing his wife. *And the first person to tell me he had done it had received the message through a session with the spirits "on the other side", using an upturned wine glass!*

*   *   *

It was now the beginning of March, 1966, and we had been working on the Cannock Chase murder investigation for seven gruelling weeks: fourteen hours a day, seven days a week. We seemed to be getting nowhere.

Every morning of every day, Detective Superintendents Cyril Gold and Harry Bailey brought us up to date and shared with us what they could of their own feelings about how things were going. The consecutively-numbered "Actions" had now reached their thousands; house-to-house and "cars seen on Cannock Chase" questionnaires dwarfed even that, and the card index had swollen by the tens of thousands, to fill many hundreds of drawers. Index clerks huddled over their desks, writing their cards and pushing them over to the indexers, who ever-so-carefully placed them in the right sections in the right order. "One card out of place and we'll never see the bloody thing again," they were constantly told by "System" expert, Detective Sergeant Eric Bailey, who prowled that Incident Room as a guard dog prowls its scrap-yard.

Statement-checkers pored over every word of every statement, picking out points that merited further investigation and passing them on to the "Action" clerks for "actioning" out to people like Roy Ashley and me. The "Classified" index clerks picked out the details of every single factor in the statements and put them where they might come together with others as common factors: in the motor vehicle index, or the streets, personal descriptions, occupations, "screams heard on Cannock Chase", or "cars seen on Cannock Chase", or the many hundreds of other sections of that multi-headed index.

Telephone clerks answered their battery of telephones and wrote out their messages on forms that would become "Action" forms; typists rattled away in the seclusion of their own room amidst the clatter of the Gestetner, which spewed out the dozen copies of every one of those thousands of statements, while others sorted and stapled them, and still others spread them through the growing forest of four-drawer filing cabinets. Oh for a computer! But this was 1966, and no one had even thought of writing a computer programme for a Murder Incident Room System.

It all seemed to be leading nowhere, though an outsider would never have sensed such a thing, looking around that hive of activity, or seeing the enthusiasm of the crowd at our morning briefings, or experiencing the confidence that emanated from our leaders and pervaded the whole place and everyone in it. If confidence and enthusiasm alone could win battles, that one would have been won long ago. But we were losing. Time was passing, and though the mountain of paper grew remorselessly, the material it contained grew less and less relevant, more and more routine. In the end, as we all well knew, it was all waste paper without the one statement that clinched a man's guilt, or the confession that acknowledged it.

But we worked on with a will, and the world held no other goal for us but that of finding the killer of Diane Tift and Margaret Reynolds.

*   *   *

One day I was sitting in the room in which we outside-enquiry men milled around, finished off our paper work and made our telephone calls. I had an "Action" before me and was ringing a factory manager, making an appointment. I sensed someone behind my back. It was Detective Superintendent Cyril Gold. "Pat," he said. "Mr. Lockley [the Assistant Chief Constable (Crime) of Staffordshire] is in my office. He'd like a word with you."

ACC Tom Lockley, lanky, big-handed, friendly, and an old detective who was a legend in his time in Staffordshire, strode forward to greet me. He held out an enormous slab of a hand and gripped mine fit to burst it. "Nice to meet you again, Sergeant. See . . . the last time we met was in Newcastle Police Club, wasn't it? When the North Staffs. Crime Squad was formed. A couple of years ago?"

"Yes, sir. It's nice to see you again," I said, remembering the night when we had responded to a message that the ACC of Staffordshire would like to meet us in the club and buy us a drink.

"Well, Sergeant, I'm here to put a proposition to you."

"Sir?"

"Yes. You know we're in the throes of a reorganisation, don't you, what with the formation of the West Midlands Force on the first of April and the loss of part of the south of our County?"

I did.

"Well, I'll come straight to the point," he said. "We're reorganising into new divisional boundaries, with a new rank structure and we've found ourselves short of a DI [Detective Inspector]. We've been watching you, my lad, and the Chief has sent me down to tell you that if you'd be prepared to transfer from the City to us, we'll make you a DI straight away."

My brain reeled. I had been a Stoke City man for sixteen years and it had never occurred to me that I should ever be anything else. Three years a Sergeant and all but five months of that a Detective Sergeant, I thought I had reached the pinnacle of my career. A Detective Inspector? There was only one of them in the Stoke-on-Trent City Police, and he traditionally either died or retired at age-limit in the job.

Dumbfounded I might be, but my instincts served me then as well as they have served me at other turning-points in my life and career, and I accepted his offer without hesitation.

"What about your wife?" he asked. "You'll want to talk it over with her, of course."

"I don't need to, sir. It'll be as big a shock to her as it is to me, but I know what she would want me to do. You can tell the Chief Constable I accept."

He threw out that big hand again and gripped mine. "Good man. We look forward to having you in the force."

My mind was still whirling, and among a thousand other things it touched briefly on what might be the consequences of my recent brush with the Chairman of the County Police Authority over the sighting of his car on Cannock Chase, now that I was to become a member of his force! But the ACC's words cut across my thoughts: "We have to find a DI for the new Regional Crime Squad branch office at Burton-on-Trent, but we thought you'd be ready for a change so we're putting Detective Inspector Stewart there and you can replace him in Stone Division."

I couldn't believe it. My colleagues often talked about "Molloy's Luck", but this was ridiculous. If he had asked me where in the County I would like to be stationed, I would have said Stone, a town which contained the headquarters of the County division adjoining the southern end of Stoke-on-Trent—right on the doorstep of my old force.

"Thank you, sir," I said, mentally pinching myself to make sure it was all true.

It *was* a shock to my wife and our three children, but the move came about, though not without sadness on my part at leaving the force in which I had been so happy, and not without some friction between the hierarchy of the two forces over the allegedly "back-door" way in which my transfer had been brought about. But fortune favours the bold, and I took my good fortune in both hands.

I parted from the Cannock Murder team with great sadness, too. I would dearly have loved to be there when fortune smiled on them, but it was not to be. I shook hands with Cyril Gold and reserved my place at the mammoth party that would surely follow the locking up of his murderer. We did see each other, several times, between the first of April, 1966, which was the date of my promotion, and the 19th of June, the day on which he retired from the Metropolitan Police Force. But we never did have that party, for he left Cannock a disappointed man, leaving behind him the first undetected murders of his thirty-year career.

* * *

62 *Not the Moors Murders*

The mothers of Aston mourn Margaret Reynolds. *Express & Star*

A sad farewell to Diane Tift from her school friends. *Express & Star*

Dominoes and Door-knockers 63

At last I had something of my own. I was the head of a Divisional Criminal Investigation Department, with a team of my own and with the freedom to organise things more or less in my own way. One thing I was resolved to do was to see that if ever a crowd of Regional Crime Squad men descended on my division to help with a large-scale murder investigation, they wouldn't need to play dominoes while they waited for me to get organised. I had studied "The System" thoroughly during my two months at Cannock, and I put together an Incident Room kit— with everything we needed to get the show on the road, from blank questionnaires to paper-clips—and then taught my boys how to operate it. We did have a murder or two, and we did bring out that Incident Room kit, and the only dominoes we and the Crime Squad played from then on were in the local pubs at meal-times.

I was still in regular touch with the Cannock Chase Murders because, like every other division in the force—indeed every police

A farewell drink in a presentation tankard, as the author (fourth from left) leaves the Regional Crime Squad and the Cannock Murder Team, on promotion to Detective Inspector. His Crime Squad partner, "Big Roy" Ashley, is behind his right shoulder.

force in the country—we had a regular flow of "Actions" from the Cannock Incident Room, of the kind that did not justify sending out men of the murder team and that could more conveniently be done by local CID officers. We also had (again like most other divisions and forces) what might be called successful "spin-offs" from the Cannock job . . . suspicious incidents involving men in cars and young children, which turned out to have nothing to do with the Cannock Chase Murders but nevertheless resulted in convictions for indecent assault, rape or child abduction. Many such cases were brought to light and their perpetrators brought to justice solely through the intensity of the Cannock Chase Murder Investigations and the public awareness generated by the massive and continuing publicity they were receiving.

I visited the Cannock Incident Room at regular intervals, under Harry Bailey's policy (he was now a Detective Chief Superintendent and head of the County CID) of gathering his senior officers together for briefings. Such briefings served the double purpose of helping us brief our own men who were doing "Actions" for Cannock and of tossing the problem around amongst a gathering of experienced detectives to see if any new ideas might surface.

The Cannock Incident Room was now merely ticking over. True, there was plenty of paper-work flowing through it, but it had acquired the character more of a neat and tidy processing system than of a vehicle that knew where it was going. In the way "The System" does when it is on a loser, it was taking in irrelevancies by the hundred, neatly processing and packaging them, and as neatly filing them away without taking its operators one inch nearer finding out who had done the killings. Not one of the thousands of people who had come forward in an effort to help us had been able to contribute anything in the way of a definite pointer. The mountain of waste paper grew apace, but the essential evidence remained as elusive as ever.

A kind of numbness comes over such an investigation, a numbness which stands between the natural refusal of the police to state publicly that an investigation has died on them, and their obligation to keep administering the kiss of life to a dead duck.

Though no one from top to bottom of the organisation would have admitted it for one moment, that was where the Cannock Chase Murder Investigation stood in the summer of 1967, eighteen months after the finding of the bodies in Mansty Gulley.

It was the end of the road.

CHAPTER THREE

A JOB AND A HALF

They say everyone remembers where he or she was when hearing the news that President John F. Kennedy had been assassinated. Nearly every man and woman in the Midlands in the summer of 1967 also knew where he or she was on the afternoon of Saturday 19th August. Thousands of men, for example, knew they were at a league soccer match, because it was the first Saturday of the season. Others had their own reasons for remembering . . . not least the shock of hearing that what everyone in the Midlands had feared since the earlier enquiries had virtually petered out had happened again.

I know where I was that afternoon. I was sitting at home in Stone, twenty miles away from the Cannock Murder Incident Room, on week-end leave from my six months course at the Police College, studying some papers in preparation for a class-room exercise . . . and I was listening to the radio. At three o'clock there was a news flash which froze my heart: *"News is coming in of the disappearance of a seven year old girl from Camden Street, Walsall. About half an hour ago, at half past two, she was seen to get into a light-coloured saloon car, and to be driven away by a man. She has not been seen since. West Midlands Police have set up road blocks, and say they are keeping an open mind on the possibility that the girl's disappearance may be connected with that of two others nearly two years ago, whose bodies were found on Cannock Chase."*

I would have given anything in the world to have been able to get into my car and join the team that I knew was at that moment being called together to help the West Midlands Police to set up an Incident Room in Walsall and embark on what might be another murder investigation. I felt paralysed and helpless. Had I been back on my division I might have had a call in the next few minutes, but even if I had not, I could still have gone down there to see how they were getting on. But I had another four months to go at the College, and I would have to remain a frustrated bystander.

*   *   *

Seven year old Christine Darby was a happy little thing, who always contrived to look as neat and tidy as the humble, terraced home where she lived with her unmarried mother and her grandmother, in the older, working-class, part of Walsall. Her dark, straight and fringed hair framed a pretty, ever-smiling face, and, like most children in and around Walsall, she had been well-drilled in the perils of speaking to strange men and accepting lifts in their cars. But who can know how the minds of little children treat such things; who can know what goes through the minds of those whose station in life has dictated that they will probably never set foot inside a car in their lives? Who can predict the effect on even the most carefully-instructed child of a once-in-a-lifetime invitation to feel the luxury of a deep, soft seat in the carpeted warmth of a car?

Around lunchtime on that Saturday, young Christine was out playing in Camden Street with her friends in the warm sunshine which punctuated that showery August day, when, at about half past two, a group of them walked around the block formed by Camden Street, South Street, Junction Street and Corporation Street.

Christine's playmate, eight year old Nicholas Baldry, a near neighbour, was with the group and by her side when what he described as a light-coloured car drew up at the pavement's edge. Information gleaned later by the police would suggest that the car had been following them slowly for a little while before it drew up alongside them. At all events, the driver stopped, wound down the window on the passenger's side and spoke to the children. In the words of young Nicholas, a bright little lad who made a better witness than many an adult, "The driver, a man, leaned over and said, 'Could you show me the way to Carmer Green please?' We all said, 'Up that way,' and pointed up towards Carmer Green. The man said to Christine, 'Could you get in and show me the way, please?' The man opened the passenger's door. He did not get out of the car. Christine got into the passenger's seat. She shut the door and he backed up into Corporation Street and went down towards the traffic lights . . . Christine laughed when she shut the door. That was all we saw and we ran straight down the road and told Mrs. Darby."

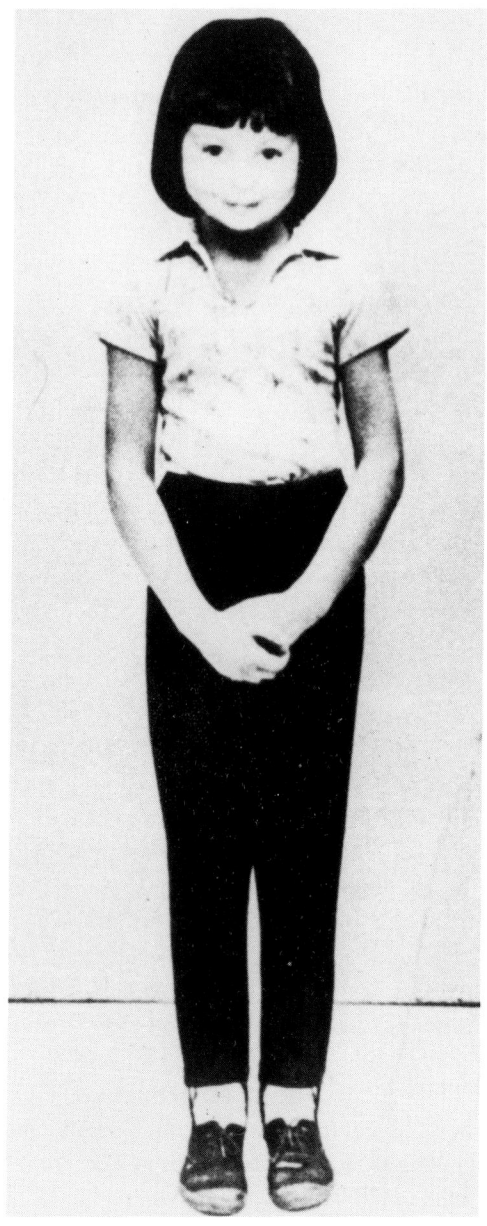

"Seven year old Christine Darby was a happy little thing": a composite photograph showing her as her abductor saw her.

Express & Star

Camden Street, Walsall: children still play in the sunshine, shortly after the abduction of Christine Darby. *Express & Star*

No wonder the children reacted so quickly to Christine's departure. *Carmer Green was in the opposite direction to that taken by the car.* What is more, young Nicholas Baldry and his friends were about to give the police their first meaningful clue as to where her abductor might have come from. For "Carmer Green" is the local vernacular for "*Caldmore* Green". No outsider would have pronounced it that way. He was either resident in the Walsall area, or he was a native of Walsall living somewhere else.

The boy's description of the car was not so helpful. It was light grey, he said, like the Ford Consul usually parked in their street, and the driver was in his thirties, with "darkish coloured hair". He was clean-shaven, fairly thin, and was wearing a white shirt, without a tie.

The significance of the abductor's pronunciation of Caldmore Green would be a matter for the detectives to follow through later. For now, the implementation of the pre-arranged, joint-force, road check plan had to receive the highest priority.

After the discovery of the bodies of Diane Tift and Margaret Reynolds on Cannock Chase, and with the fear that the same thing could happen again at any time, the Staffordshire, West Midlands and Birmingham City Police Forces had prepared an elaborate plan designed to quickly seal the immediate locality where a child had been abducted or accosted, and then throw out another cordon to block strategic points on main roads further afield, with the final back-up of a deployment of police vehicles on all the main approaches around the perimeter of the eighty-five square miles of forestry and heath-land which is Cannock Chase. It was known, rather prosaically, as "The Stop Plan".

Unfortunately, there was a lapse of at least twenty-two minutes between the abduction and the 999 telephone call to the West Midlands Police Operations Room—time enough for the abductor to have taken his victim anything from ten to fifteen miles from the centre of Walsall before the deployment of police vehicles in their "Stop Plan" positions could even begin. Thus, as dusk began to fall over the hive of activity which was the Police Incident Room in Walsall Police Headquarters, and the streets around Camden Street swarmed with door-knocking police officers, it was plain that "The Stop Plan" would play no part in detecting this particular crime.

By the end of the day, though, the picture of little Christine's abduction was beginning to fill out with other "sightings" which might be significant. One witness told the police about a grey-coloured car she had seen hanging about a nearby primary school during the past couple of weeks; another said she had seen a grey-coloured Morris Oxford car in Camden Street while she was actually watching the children at play between 2.15 and 2.30. But no one had noted a car number, and no one other than her playmates had actually seen Christine with the car and driver.

As the days passed, more "sightings" would be logged, at places further afield, some of them very promising, some less so, and some clearly mistaken or irrelevant, but all carefully recorded against the time when, it was hoped, they could be tested against what was really known to have happened that day. As it was, the pattern of sightings beginning to take shape had already begun to point the finger once again towards Cannock Chase.

* * *

Something would have to be done about searching Cannock Chase. The minds of some very experienced senior police officers pondered that question late into that Saturday night in the Staffordshire County Police Headquarters in Cannock Road, Stafford, itself on the northern edge of the Chase. They faced a daunting prospect.

To begin with, Cannock Chase is vast. It covers at least eighty-five square miles, and around a third of its area is planted with thick groves of fir trees, under which, at that time of year, was a dense thicket of brambles and ferns growing to a height of six feet and more. For the rest it consists of heath and moorland, dotted with old mine-shafts and excavations, sand pits, clay pits, bogs and swamps, and old wartime military training grounds pitted by infantry fox-holes and shell craters.

One thing was certain: there were no precedents for organising a search of this magnitude. Even the back-aching search of the Yorkshire Moors two years earlier for the bodies buried by Myra Hindley and Ian Brady held no lessons of manpower or time-scale, for they had been to some extent localised by the identification of places shown in photographs found in the couple's homes and by high level photography of ground disturbances by RAF Vulcan bombers. No one had yet attempted a "line-sweep" of such difficult terrain as this, with a breadth of at least ten miles, and there was no other way of doing it in the absence of anything to help narrow down the search area. They were working on "guess-timates" and one wildly optimistic "guesstimate" made late at night in that headquarters conference room was that it would take five hundred men something like a couple of months!

Underestimate it might be, but it was still bad news, for a child's body would not remain in one piece for long in a place swarming with foxes, weasels and carrion crows. One expert told the police that it would be stripped to a skeleton within days, and the bones dispersed by foxes and such within a fortnight. But something had to be done. And quickly.

*   *   *

It was now Sunday morning, and Christine Darby had been missing for around twenty-one hours. Police activity in Walsall was intense and the hitherto almost moribund Murder Incident Room at Cannock had sprung into renewed life, under the direct control of the head of Staffordshire CID, Detective Chief Superintendent Harry Bailey.

Indications being pieced together by the hundred-strong team of West Midlands police officers working their way from house to

Part of Cannock Chase's 85 square miles of forest, heath and moorland.
Staffs. Police

A Job and a Half

house around Camden Street and up the A.34 trunk road were that the child might have been taken in the direction of Cannock—an ominous portent that what had happened to Diane Tift and Margaret Reynolds might have happened to her.

By Sunday morning, the summer showers that had marred an otherwise warm and sunny Saturday had passed from the Midlands and the sun shone in a clear blue sky, as the first elements of what would become a massive police search began to work their way across Cannock Chase. Six officers of the Staffordshire force's mounted section were riding in an extended line eastwards from the A.34 trunk road (which traverses the Chase longitudinally), and one of them—PC Arthur Ellis—was riding his horse along the road which intersects the A.34 at right angles (at Pottal Pool cross-roads), and crosses the Chase from Penkridge (in the west) to Rugeley (in the east). It was 11.15 am, and PC Ellis had ridden nearly half a mile eastwards from the cross-roads when he saw a piece of cloth hanging on the branch of a fallen tree to his left, above the fence that bounded the road. He dismounted, picked the cloth from the branch and found that it was a pair of child's knickers. They had been soiled by faeces, and Ellis felt they had not hung there for very long.

For some reason it took nearly twenty-four hours for the knickers to arrive at the Darby home in Walsall to see if they could be identified as Christine's. When they did arrive there, they were identified at once by the child's grandmother, who recognised her own stitching in a repair and was able to produce the spool from which she had taken the cotton.

Lady Luck comes in many guises and gives her favours sparingly, but she was looking kindly on the police that day, for here was a focus for a search which would offer far greater odds on finding something than could any general ''line-search'' of such a wilderness.

Whether Christine's kidnapper had deposited her knickers there simply to tease the police or as a signpost so that he could get some perverted thrill from an early finding of the body, would be a question long debated among those seeking to identify him. But the Staffordshire Police were ready to seize upon any chance. Men had

"PC Ellis picked the cloth from the branch and found that it was a pair of child's knickers". *Staffs Police*

worked through the night, marking out search-sectors on large-scale maps. They had drawn up their manpower requirements; they had caused senior officers in the divisions and surrounding forces to be called from their beds to arrange for a concentration of men on the Chase and for mobile canteens to feed them, and they had laid on all the vehicles and equipment that would be needed for what they anticipated would be an operation lasting several weeks.

Having the timely pointer provided by the knickers, the Chief Constable of Staffordshire, Welsh Rugby Cap and wartime fighter pilot, Arthur Morgan Rees, personally assembled his men at the Pottal Pool crossroads. At his signal, three hundred policemen moved out eastwards, within touching distance of each other, every tenth man unrolling a large ball of "binder twine" and fixing it to the trees as he went. It was the only way in which any kind of control

Pottal Pool Cross-roads, looking east towards Rugeley: the searchers gather at the edge of the forest. *Express & Star*

could be exercised over a search in such a forest as this, and by the end of the search, a total of *fourteen miles* of binder twine would have been reeled out, while the size of the search teams would have more than doubled.

The parallel lanes marked out by the men carrying the binder twine—in the manner that soldiers carrying mine detectors mark out their clearances—moved steadily forward, as the searchers probed the undergrowth with their sticks and rakes, handing back anything they found to the Scenes-of-Crime specialists bringing up the rear. Ahead of the line went what might be called the skirmishers—men armed with white tapes to mark out guidelines.

Meanwhile, if any further proof were needed that Lady Luck was really out and about that Monday, she performed again, at one o'clock in the afternoon, when a forestry worker, working his way through the forest which bounds the north side of the Penkridge to Rugeley road, some three miles further on towards Rugeley, found a child's plimsoll. It lay in the bracken just a few yards into the trees, as if it might have been thrown from the road. That, too, was identified as her grand-daughter's by a now totally distraught seventy-one year old Henrietta Darby.

It was another pointer, now at a place where a motor vehicle could have been driven some distance from the road into the heart of Cannock Chase and even into the rides and firebreaks of its dense forest.

Nightfall brought the search to a halt. At around eight o'clock, the men were called in and dismissed, but police activity elsewhere continued unabated—in the residential areas bordering Cannock Chase, in the streets from where little Christine Darby had been abducted, and in the Incident Rooms at Cannock and Walsall, where men and women by now thoroughly experienced in such matters were handling the flood of information that had begun to come in from a public fully alerted to the fact that the police needed their help in yet another child murder investigation.

In the Police Headquarters at Stafford, just up the road from Pottal Pool cross-roads, the lights burned late again, for the planners had set their sights beyond this day's work, and even

A Job and a Half

Chief Constable Arthur Rees (second from left) and the head of his CID, Harry Bailey (second from right), assemble their search teams.
Express & Star

*   *   *

beyond tomorrow's, which had already been mapped out and organised in all its logistical detail.

*   *   *

Tuesday dawned, and, by eight o'clock, sixty-six hours after the disappearance of Christine Darby, Chief Constable Arthur Rees had deployed his search teams again. This time there were *seven hundred and fifty of them:* five hundred police officers from the three contributing forces, two hundred troops from Whittington Barracks in nearby Lichfield, and fifty airmen from the RAF Maintenance Unit at Stafford. The drill was to be the same: the whistles sounded, the now much-extended line moved slowly forward, heads down, sticks probing, and those parallel lines of binder twine pushed on, further and further into the depths of the forest.

For nine hours that line moved forward, fuelled by countless gallons of tea brewed by mobile canteens, and by five o'clock that afternoon—the time they were supposed to finish for the day—they had pushed a broad front some two and a half miles from their start point of the previous day. They were at a location known as "The White House", to the north of which stood a tract of forest known to the Forestry Commission as "Plantation 110".

The senior police officers and the commander of the army contingent (Major Nesbitt of the Staffordshire Regiment) conferred. "My men would like to go on," said the Major. "There's another three hours of light, and I suggest that if we could clear that area over there [he pointed his stick towards Plantation 110], we would

ACC Stanely Bailey briefs the first outside enquiry teams at the Murder HQ in Cannock. *Express & Star*

have a natural start line for tomorrow morning." It was an offer the police could not refuse, so the long thin line of searchers was formed up again, the binder-twine bales were loosened and, at the blast of a whistle, the line moved forward into Plantation 110.

The army Major's suggestion must have been whispered to him by Lady Luck, who was clearly still around, for exactly forty-five minutes later, Private Michael Blundred halted, gave a shout and held up his right hand—the prearranged signal that he had found something. Another whistle blast stopped the whole line.

The tragedy was complete, for there in Plantation 110, covered by ferns which had been broken and bent over her, lay the body of seven year old Christine Darby.

*   *   *

She lay on the ridge between two furrows, at the foot of a tree, and, in the classic position of a rape victim, her arms were outspread, her legs were apart with the knees raised, and she was naked from the waist down, apart from her clean white socks, the soles of which were so clean that she had obviously been carried there. A glance at her genital area was enough to tell anyone what she had been through in her death throes, for she had been severely torn and had bled profusely.

As the word passed in whispers along that far-stretched search-line, a silence fell over the forest. But only for a moment. Police officers cannot afford grief over the victims of crime, nor anger at those who could do such things. Not yet. There was work to be done, discipline to be observed, and the detailed, painstaking process of a murder investigation to be followed through, with luck through to a Court of Assize, where any errors due to judgements being clouded by emotion would be ruthlessly exploited by a defending barrister dedicated to securing an acquittal of whoever might be accused of this foul deed.

*   *   *

Soldiers of the Staffordshire Regiment form up and take their arm's-length dressing for the search. *Express & Star*

"A silence fell over the forest": Christine Darby's body is found, covered by broken ferns (right foreground). *Staffs. Police*

A Job and a Half

Experienced police officers never jump to conclusions, but there was murder in the air from the very moment Christine Darby stepped into that car in Camden Street, Walsall. From the moment he heard that her knickers had been found ten miles away on Cannock Chase, Chief Constable Rees knew in his bones that he had a murder on his hands, even though a kidnapping had occurred in an area covered by another police force. For the law says that, in the absence of any evidence to the contrary, a murder is assumed to have been committed at the place where the body is found. So, following his normal practice when a murder investigation promised to be long and difficult, he had made a telephone call to the Commissioner of the Metropolitan Police at New Scotland Yard, asking him to send a Detective Superindendent of his Murder Squad to help his own head of CID find young Christine's killer.

It took only five hours for the man on the top of the Murder Squad's "call-out" list to be contacted, to pack his bags, and to travel with his right-hand-man (a Scotland Yard Detective Sergeant) the hundred and forty miles to Stafford. The Chief Constable's decision to send for him on the off-chance proved to have been an inspired one, *for at the very moment Private Michael Blundred of the Staffordshire Regiment was standing frozen with horror, looking down on Christine Darby's body the Yard man's train was pulling into Stafford station!*

*   *   *

Detective Chief Superintendent Harry Bailey was standing on the platform as the London train drew to a stop. A swarm of passengers alighted, but he had no difficulty in identifying the short, stocky man in the mac and trilby who walked along the platform with a companion who was laden with a holdall and the large, distinctive document case—the famed "Murder Bag", that contained the basic ingredients of "The System".

The three men shook hands warmly. "Ian Forbes," said the bull-necked, broad-shouldered Scot, whose gruff, no-nonsense

Aberdonian manner contrasted just a little with the smile that creased his jowls. "And you'll be Harry Bailey," he said, extending his hand to the County CID chief. "Good to meet you, Harry."

Harry Bailey shook the Scotsman's hand: "Good to meet you, Ian. We could do with a bit of help. We've got a job and a half on here, I can tell you."

The Yard man laughed. No grim faces here. Policemen usually reserve them for the cameras. Grim faces are the physical expression of emotional involvement, and, though the public expects to see murder investigators looking grim, no detective worth his salt allows himself the luxury of feeling as emotional as he looks. He knows it will only cloud his judgement, and he knows that if he doesn't keep his equanimty and, even more to the point, his sense of humour, in even the most distressing of cases, he will as likely as not make a foolish mistake. So Forbes laughed. "A job and a half? Well . . ." [he put his hand on the back of his assistant, Detective Sergeant Tom Parry, and pushed him forward to introduce him to their host] ". . . there's three of us to one of him, so we've got the odds on our side, haven't we Harry?"

So saying, the leading lights of the Cannock Chase Murder Investigation team walked along the station platform towards the greatest challenge of their professional lives.

*   *   *

Fifty-three year old Ian Forbes was the epitome of the hard-nosed, front-line detective in what most people would regard as the finest detective force in the world, and his experience in the thick of the Capital's crime war was unequalled.

Born in the village of Lumphannan, twenty miles west of Aberdeen, and starting his working life at the age of fourteen with the very minimum of formal education (as did many policemen of his day, including the author), Forbes had joined the Metropolitan Police Force at the end of 1938, and become a detective (albeit an "Aide to CID" to begin with) on the tough streets of the East End

A Job and a Half

within days of completing his initial training. Four and a half years later, and with a lot of CID experience under his belt, he was caught up in the Second World War.

It was in keeping with his reputation for physical toughness and for always being in the front line of the battle against crime, that he should become an infantryman—and a Scottish infantryman at that. He joined the Seaforth Highlanders and fought his way from the beaches of Normandy through to the Nazi surrender on the North German Plain. He came out of the army a Lieutenant . . . and, like many other policemen, returned to his force as a constable!

From 1946 on, it was front-line detective work all the way, to the place where he really made his name, to Scotland Yard's "Flying Squad"—the legendary "Sweeney"—where physical toughness, the ability to get right to the heart of the most villainous of London's villainy, and high qualities of leadership were absolutely indispensable. He had a fund of stories of hard-fought battles with the cream of the Capital's criminals.

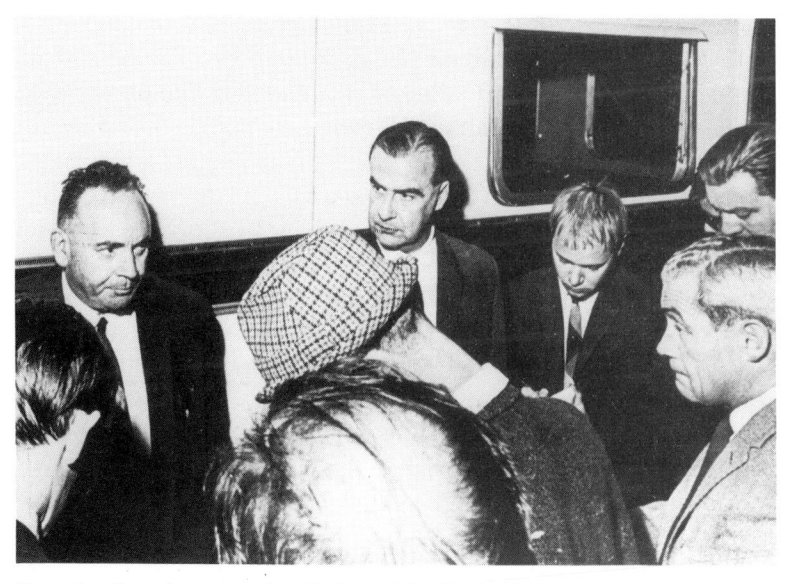

Detective Superintendent Ian Forbes of the Scotland Yard Murder Squad (left) arrives at the scene and meets the press. *Express & Star*

Within eighteen years of returning to his force as a constable, Ian Forbes was a Detective Superintendent, and two years later, as a member of the Yard's famed Murder Squad, he was in the thick of it again, dealing with a spate of inter-gang shootings and violence in the East End of London. For bringing that gang-war to an end—in the year before embarking on the investigation of the Cannock Chase Murders—he received the Queen's Police Medal for Distinguished Service. Now, with a couple of sensational provincial murder investigations under his belt as well, he was taking on the series of abductions and child murders that had thwarted the best efforts of a lot of experienced police officers for nearly three years.

The Commissioner of Police of the Metropolis could not have sent a better man to Staffordshire.

*   *   *

The three detectives were driven in a Jaguar car from Stafford Railway Station to the Police Headquarters a couple of miles away, but even as they arrived in the Chief Constable's office, the phone was ringing and they were whisked straight off to Cannock Chase.

Carefully, with the minimum disturbance to the ground around her, they squatted on their haunches to take as close a look at the violated body of little Christine Darby as "scenes of crime" discipline permitted. They took a cursory look, too, at the area within a radius of about twenty yards of the body, seeing nothing of note, but observing that the only disturbance or damage to the vegetation was to that which had been broken and bent over it.

Very shortly after the discovery of the body by the young soldier, Christine's black trousers had been found, a few yards on the other side of a gap (or "Ride" as they learned to call it) which traversed Plantation 110 from top to bottom, twenty-six paces from the body. It took the investigation no further, but it was one more reason why that whole area would need to be subjected to the fine-tooth comb treatment of what is known as a "finger-search".

Police photographers were already busily clicking away, and among the most fascinating of the hundreds of photographs they would produce of the work done in that forest would be those which showed Plantation 110 before and after Detective Chief Inspector Bob Stewart and his team did their "finger-search". The "Before" shot would show an almost impenetrable jungle. The "After" shot would show every inch of that ground exposed to an incredible degree . . . as if someone had gone over it with a razor! Just one of the less glamorous, less sensational, sides of a murder investigation; just one of those back-aching aspects of detective work that rarely get into the newspapers.

Now dusk was falling over the forest and the Home Office Pathologist, who had to come about sixty miles from his base at Sheffield University, could not arrive before dark, so the portable generator was being connected to the floodlights around that half-naked body, which would have to remain cruelly exposed until he could examine it where it lay.

It may seem strange to some that work at the scene should have to be halted for several hours merely to allow a pathologist to look at the body, but no pathologist can make total sense of his post-mortem examination of the victim's body without beginning his examination at the spot where it was found.

One of the greatest truisms in the detective's book of quotations is that you have only one go at your scene. It can never be recreated in the aftermath of a failure of scenes-of-crime discipline. Hence the dozens of photographs taken of the body and its immediate surroundings before anyone even approaches it, and the photographs which record every stage of the examinations made by pathologist, scenes-of-crime officers and forensic scientists. It all begins here. No greater disaster can befall a murder investigator than that his scene should be disturbed or contaminated or that the priorities of Photographer, Scenes-of-Crime Officer, Pathologist and Forensic Scientist should not be observed to the letter.

*   *   *

The "finger search" for clues: before and after.   *Staffs. Police*

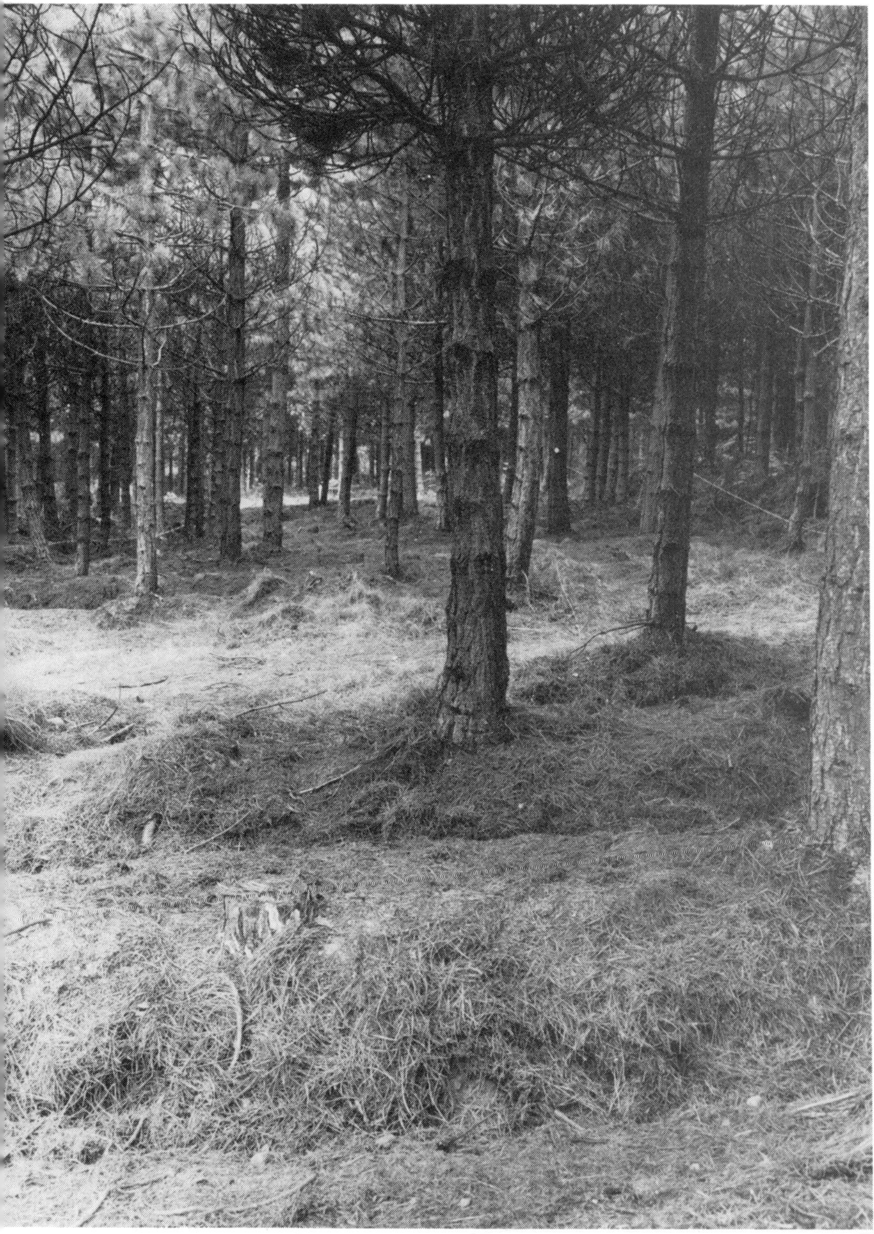

Every region has its list of Home Office-retained pathologists who can be called upon to examine bodies involved in suspicious deaths, and the Coroner for the area where such a body is found is the man who will determine which of them shall be employed. In a case of suspected homicide he will, of course, have regard to the views of the senior CID officer in the case, and there will inevitably be an element of "horses for courses" when the choice is made. In this case, Detective Chief Superintendent Harry Bailey had no doubt who he wanted to do the job, and the Coroner agreed.

Doctor Alan Usher ran the Department of Forensic Pathology at Sheffield University and was regarded as one of the country's leading forensic pathologists. He covered an area which included the northern part of Staffordshire and I had last met him when he was called to investigate the mummified body of a child, in the attic of a house in Leek. I was in the attic when he looked at it, picked it up . . . and immediately announced that we could all go to the nearest pub for a pint, since there was no point in investigating the death of an *orang outang*!

But this time the game was deadly serious, though one would have found it hard to guess so from his manner, for he was a genial, friendly character, with boundless energy and humour, who would joke his way through the grimmest of experiences, while leaving not the slightest doubt as to the meticulous professionalism of his approach. Like policemen, pathologists cannot afford to become emotionally involved with death and violence. Hence, all the forensic pathologists of my acquaintance have been good-humoured fellows, sometimes to the point of eccentricity, and prone to adjourning to the nearest pub to discuss the implications of their discoveries at the scene and in the mortuary.

At 11.25 that Tuesday night, Doctor Usher got down to his preliminary examination of Christine Darby's body under the glare of police floodlights that lit up the lower branches of Plantation 110's tall fir trees with a ghostly green glow that served to heighten the drama being played out in that dense and now forbidding forest. He noted the damage to the child's gaping and torn private parts, and the blood that stained the grass and pine needles beneath. Among the normal post-mortem staining he would expect to find on a body that had lain in such a spot for three days he detected something abnormal: there were "petechiae" on the skin of the face and forehead, pin-point sized marks produced by the bursting of the blood vessels under the skin . . . a sure sign of asphyxiation, reinforced by the fact that the face was discoloured and the tongue protruded slightly through the teeth. It was something which would be reinforced still further, later that night in the mortuary, where he would also find petechiae on the child's eyes and bruises on her left cheek consistent with the application of pressure by an assailant's hand across her nose and mouth.

That death had been due to asphyxiation by suffocation was obvious to him, as was the evidence of a violent sexual assault, and it was fair to assume—for the time being at least—that she had been brought to the spot, sexually assaulted and murdered within a very short time of her abduction in Walsall. On this question—the "Time of Death"—only the most fool-hardy would pretend to anything but an approximation, for an estimate can be made only on the basis of very detailed examination and laboratory testing, and even then, given the innumerable variables involved in the equation, it will be largely the product of instinct and experience. The timing of a death from the examination of a body is a somewhat inexact science, to say the least.

In the case of Christine Darby it was a combination of the opinion formed by Doctor Usher and the laboratory work performed by a forensic scientist that gave the police investigators the answer. Doctor Usher noted the presence of fly larvae and maggots about the eyes and nostrils; John Joseph Merchant, Senior Experimental Officer at the West Midland Forensic Science Laboratory in Birmingham, was able to deduce from his long experience in such matters that death must have occurred from two to three days previously, since fly eggs hatch in a given time at a given temperature . . . in two to three days at the temperature of fifty degrees Fahrenheit known to have obtained around young Christine's body.

Sexually assaulted, suffocated, and dead for three days. It was

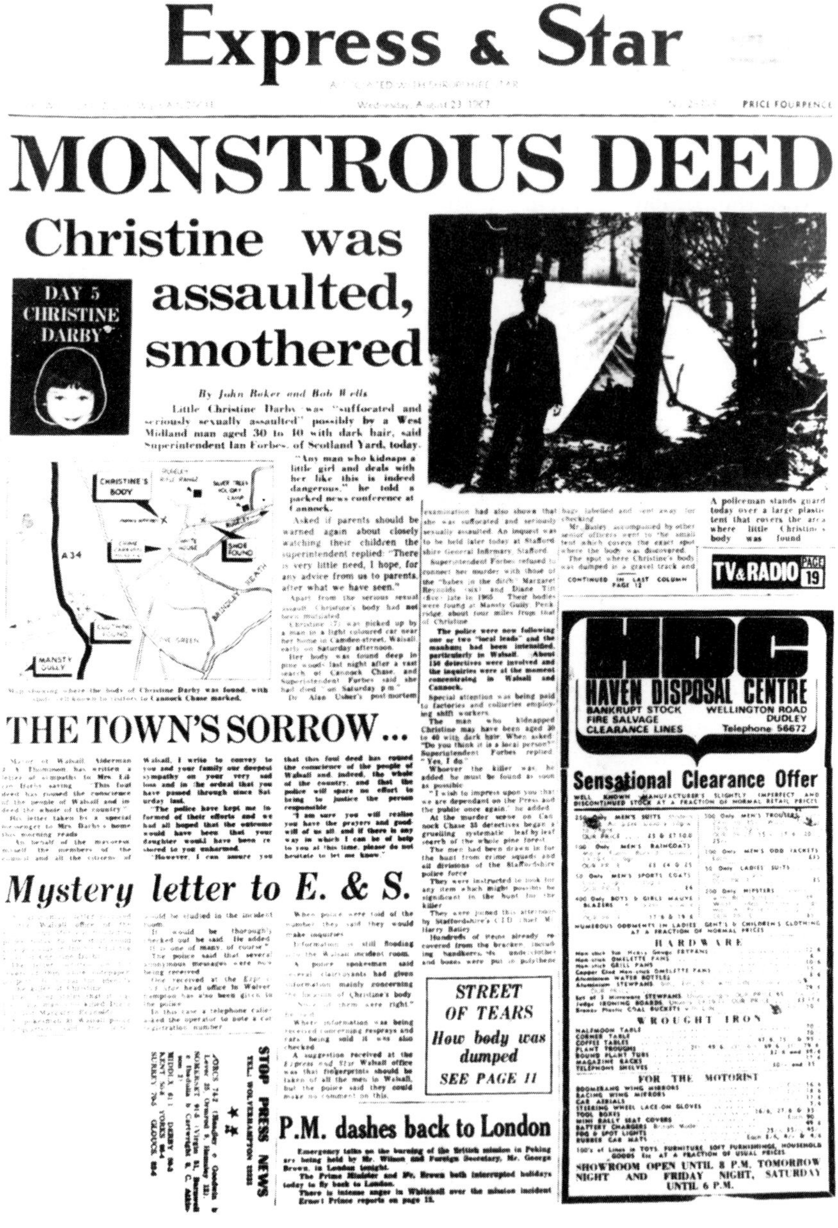

really no more than the detectives could see for themselves, but it was a start; an authoritative start which, they could only hope, would be built upon to their advantage in the many hours of laboratory work which both the pathologist and the scientists would have to do before their definitive reports could be completed.

CHAPTER FOUR

LIFE'S LIKE THAT

On Ian Forbes's first full day in Cannock he took stock of the task facing him, and a formidable task it was: There was the forest to be searched; several hundred, perhaps several thousand, people to be traced who had been picnicking and courting that Saturday afternoon on the most popular picnicking and courting spot in the Midlands; every one of the hundreds of motor vehicles that must have been present on Cannock Chase that afternoon to be identified, traced and their occupants interviewed; all the work already being done by the outside enquiry teams and the Incident Rooms staffs in the West Midlands, Birmingham and Staffordshire to be continued and intensified; the whole population of the Midlands to be moblised to report to the police every suspicious action, person or vehicle they might have observed on and around that day in the ten miles or so between Camden Street, Walsall, and the place where Christine's body had been dumped by one who, on the strength of his pronunciation of Caldmore Green, was probably a native of Walsall.

On top of all the other huge tasks facing him, Forbes would have to supervise the linking of five massive indexing and filing systems to the one which now promised to outstrip them all, in a search for the common, linking factor which would hold out the only hope of success.

It was a big enough task to face even a man who came fresh to it from a good night's sleep, but Forbes, his partner, and Harry Bailey, had worked through the night to the conclusion of Alan Usher's post-mortem examination, and it was over breakfast that the three men discussed its implications. For the two detectives it was then a quick wash, shave and clean shirt and off back to Cannock to get the rest of the investigation under way.

*   *   *

It would be the job of Ian Forbes's right-hand-man from the Yard, Detective Sergeant Tom Parry, to see to the detail of getting

Life's Like That 93

the Incident Room System into top gear, while Forbes's own top priority, after introducing himself to his investigation team and its Incident Room back-up staff and making a brief appearance before a growing horde of press men, would be to have a better look at the scene and tell the search teams exactly what they were to look for and how they were to go about it. Amazingly, he and Harry Bailey were back among the pine trees of Plantation 110 by ten o'clock that morning.

It did not take long for them to find the tracks that indicated the presence of a motor vehicle in the "ride" close to the spot where Christine Darby's body had been found. It did not take them long, either, to realise that they could thank Lady Luck for the find, for had there not been showers of rain on that otherwise sunny Saturday, not even the heaviest vehicle would have made the slightest impression on the concrete-hard earthen surface of that "ride".

The tyre marks were fragmented, visible only at intervals, but they extended from the top of the "ride" (where it emerged into

Fragmented and indistinct tyre tracks are found near the body.
Staffs. Police

open heath-land), to a point about 140 yards into the plantation, where they stopped, level with where the child's body had been left by her killer. As compared with tyre tracks found in another, parallel, "ride" and obviously left by a tractor or some other heavy Forestry Commission vehicle, they were light and of a narrower wheel-base, suggesting that they might have been left by a car. But this would be a question to be addressed by experts, and the police officers contented themselves with having the tracks photographed while they waited for the experts to arrive.

They decided that it was a job for the best in the field, so, in addition to the Forensic Science Laboratory's tyre expert, the detectives sent for a man who knew as much about the tyre business as anyone in Europe. That man was Mr. Joseph Beattie Wilson, technical manager of the British branch of the Pirelli Tyre Company, who had given invaluable help to Harry Bailey in an earlier murder investigation.

Joseph Wilson arrived on Cannock Chase on the Thursday (24th August) and, while he was unable to identify the make of tyre from the tyre pattern, he was able to conclude from the width of the tracks that they had been made by a family-sized saloon car. Further than that he could not go—at least in relation to the make and model of the car. But he *was* able to tell the detectives something of crucial importance: "There was no clear evidence of the vehicle having made marks on its return journey in a position different from those entering," he said, "and I would conclude that the driver was one of considerable skill and experience, in that he had reversed the car with little or no deviation. I would similarly infer that only one car had been in the ride since the previous rainfall [on the day Christine Darby was abducted]. *I subsequently checked that the ground when dry was not capable of accepting impressions from the tyres.*"

There was no getting away from it. Frustrating though it was not to be able to identify the make of the tyres (which were of a common ribbed pattern anyway), one thing could be said with something approaching certainty: these were the traces left by the car which had brought Christine Darby to her brutal death. Only one car had entered that "ride" and that same car had gone back the way it had come, for the bottom end of the "ride" was blocked by a fallen tree, as was every other "ride" in that plantation, to keep out picnickers' cars and reduce the risk of fire.

The next job was to find that car.

*   *   *

By now reporters and camera teams of every branch of the local and national news media were swarming around Cannock Police Station, Cannock Chase and the streets of Walsall, stung into action by what was in those days the most dramatic announcement that could be made in any crime story . . . that "The Yard" had been called in to assist with a provincial murder investigation. They were the words that in those days guaranteed a news media interest far in excess of anything that could be generated by a local CID chief in even the most sensational of murders, for the phrase "Calling in the Yard" still had an almost magical connotation that only the build-up of experience and expertise in the newly emergent Regional Crime Squads would eventually dispel.

If the news media wanted a figure to focus upon, they could not have been presented with one better than Detective Superintendent Ian Forbes. He was larger than life. His gruff Aberdonian manner and stocky build betokened a strength and toughness that the news media and its public likes to see in a murder investigator, while his frankness and blunt directness of speech was a refreshing novelty in a police service that had yet to be dragged out of its traditional "no comment" response. What was more, his ability to speak the language of even the most lowly of the men he now commanded, and his impatience with those "admin bastards" who, rightly or wrongly, were seen as getting in the way of the working police officer on the ground, made him an instant success as a leader. His men came to idolise him; they would work around the clock and jump over the edge of the proverbial cliff for him. In a situation where men have to be driven hard, even to the point of exhaustion, for days, months and even years, that is no mean achievement.

I saw many leaders during my thirty-four years police service, some great, some not so great, some indifferent and some downright bad, but neither I nor any other police officer who met him ever encountered one quite like Ian Forbes!

The immediate problem was Cannock Chase: the search, and the tracing of every person and every vehicle known to have been there. The line-search of the forest had now been concentrated into something more detailed than a search for a body. It would be a search for any tiny clue, so it would be a slow and laborious one, and though it produced nothing of long-term significance to the investigation it did produce eloquent testimony to the popularity of the Chase among courting couples and men and women conducting secret liaisons with the wives and husbands of others. The number of stained and discarded items of women's underwear found there reached close on five hundred!

The "finger-search" of the area immediately surrounding the body produced many amazingly tiny finds, but, again, nothing of evidential value. It had been a hands-and-knees, shoulder-to-shoulder search of startling thoroughness, but the organiser of that search was then given an even more lengthy and exhausting task—that of tracing every motor vehicle that could possibly have visited that part of the Chase. He succeeded to an equally remarkable degree.

Plotting the "sightings" on a vast map on a wall of the Cannock Incident Room, Detective Chief Inspector Bob Stewart, Detective Sergeant Malcolm Bevington and their team used a flat-headed map pin for each one, the head of the pin being colour-coded to show the time of day and whether its driver had been traced. In fixing his or her own position on the map, each driver would also fix the positions of other vehicles he or she had seen. They in their turn would be traced and each of their drivers would be asked to fix the positions of others, and so on, and so on, until the almost incredible total of nearly six hundred pins crowded their eight feet by twelve feet, 25 inch to the mile wall map. For each driver and each of his or her passengers, there was a witness statement in the file, and for each statement, a card in the central "nominal" index and several others in the "classified" indexes—under such headings as "car makes", "car colours", "car types", and "cars seen on Cannock Chase".

Incredibly, too, the investigation team traced almost every car represented by those six hundred map pins. The one exception was

Life's Like That

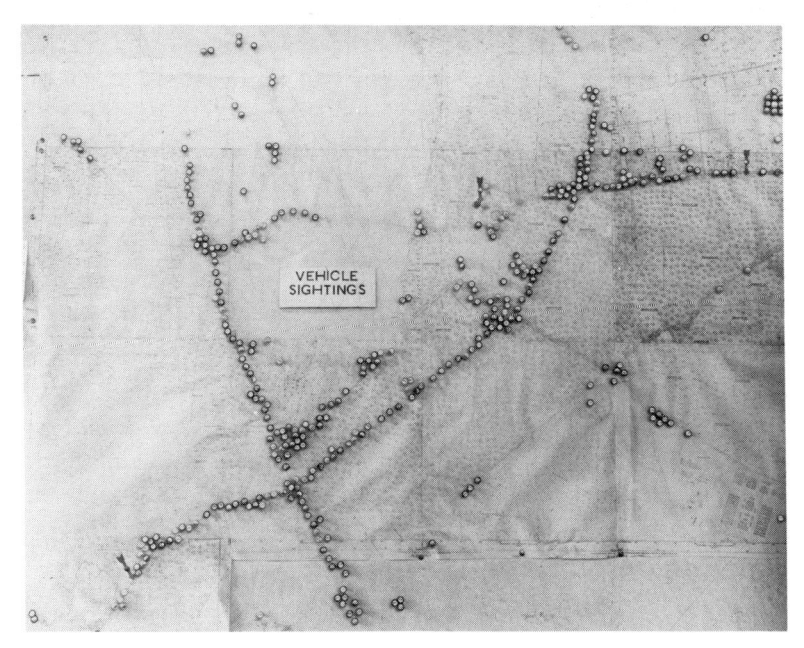

Detective Sergeant (now Det. Chief Supt. and head of Staffs. CID) Malcolm Bevington, checks out the Cannock Chase vehicle sightings from the Incident Room wall map. *Staffs. Police*

a blue-coloured Volkswagen "beetle". That car did not get on to the map until a week after the finding of Christine Darby's body, and only then when two people who had been mushrooming on the Chase close to Plantation 110 came forward to say that they had seen a man walk from the "ride" close to which the body had been found and get into the blue Volkswagen car. They said it was about four o'clock that Saturday afternoon, and they were even able to give part of the car's registration number. If they were right, here was a man who might be the murderer. If he were not the murderer, he might well have seen him. So the highest priority was accorded to the tracing of that blue Volkswagen car and its driver.

If he were not the murderer, why had he not come forward voluntarily? After all, by this time some 14,000 leaflets had been handed out to people actually met on Cannock Chase by an army of police officers employed on a vast operation of check-points and interviews on the days following the discovery of the body. The leaflets, which bore on their reverse side a plan of the Chase, showing Plantation 110 and the location of the body, appealed to anyone who had been near the spot that Saturday afternoon to come forward, whether or not they felt they had anything to contribute to the investigation. That identical plan was shown on the front page of every daily and weekly newspaper in the Midlands, while BBC and Independent Television brought it into every home in the country. Why, then, had the driver of that Volkswagen not come forward?

The answer came several days later, after officers from Cannock had made enquiries of every Volkswagen distributor in the Midlands and had made a permutation of registration numbers in several local vehicle taxation offices. It came when police officers went to the home of Victor Warren Whitehouse in Hednesford, within sight of that part of Cannock Chase which contained Plantation 110.

*   *   *

Victor Whitehouse spent a very uncomfortable few hours in Cannock Police Station sampling the rough edge of Ian Forbes's tongue, for he was to all intents and purposes a prime suspect for the murder of Christine Darby. Until, that is, he was able to satisfy his interrogators that there was a simple—if quite astounding—reason for his failure to come forward. Yes, he had been there with his car at the time claimed by the two witnesses. He knew Cannock Chase like the back of his hand, having walked almost every inch of it in the past twenty-five years or so and he was an almost daily visitor to the place. He certainly never failed to walk miles over the Chase at weekends.

"Then why the hell has it taken you so long to come forward when practically every tree on the Chase has a map pinned to it, with an appeal for everyone to come forward who was at the spot marked X that Saturday? You couldn't fail to see the damn thing, if not there, then in your newspaper or on your TV screen. Everybody in the country must have seen it by now. So why the hell didn't you come forward?"

"I'll tell you why," said Victor Whitehouse. "I had seen the map . . . but I was nowhere near the spot marked X."

"But the witnesses saw you there."

"They did not. Not there. If you wish, I'll go up to the Chase with you now and show you where they saw me."

He did . . . and he took them to the "ride" at the top of Plantation 110, the "ride" which passed within yards of the spot where Christine Darby had been violated and murdered and where the tracks of her murderer's car could still be faintly seen, extending nearly a hundred and forty yards into the forest. And then he pointed to the X on the map. *Whoever had drawn it, he said, had put the X in the wrong place, and since he had been nowhere near that place, he thought he would have nothing useful to contribute!*

Thus did a slip of the pen nearly rob Harry Bailey and Ian Forbes of perhaps their most crucial witness, for though they had lost a suspect, they had found a man who might well have seen the murderer's car, and the murderer standing alongside it!

Victor Whitehouse, a tall, fit-looking man of tweed suits and stout walking brogues, was, as befitted one who loved the countryside and its wildlife, a man of keen observation and retentive memory. Though slow to commit himself, when he did so he spoke thoughtfully, and impressed as one who did not take any such commitment lightly. Thus he spent hours and even days working out with the police just what he *had* seen.

The Wolverhampton Express & Star helps in the appeal for information.

Express & Star

He had, he said, walked out of the forest fire-break, as described by the two mushroomers, but as he did so he had seen ". . . a car backed into a 'ride'. It was a slatey-grey colour, backed in about fifteen yards down the 'ride' to my right. I remember the radiator grill was the full width of the car and it had a mesh grill. I am not absolutely satisfied about this, but if I was allowed to give this some thought and see several types of cars I think I would recognise it.''

He was given that chance with a number of cars of the 1600 cc range—Fords, Austins, Morrises, Standards and Vauxhalls—placed in the exact spot he had pointed out, and after looking at all of them and thinking long and hard, he chose one and said he was absolutely certain that that was the car he had seen. It was a light-grey coloured Austin saloon, the A.55 or A.60 "Farina" model, between which there was no difference in appearance that mattered. Unfortunately, as is so often the case, he could remember nothing of the car's registration number.

He was, however, also able to describe the man who was standing by the open door of the car and appeared to be its driver: about forty years of age, about five feet ten inches tall, with a smooth complexion, either ruddy or flushed, and dark hair, which was either very short or flattened, smooth and brushed back. He was wearing a dark jacket, possibly a blazer. "The man was on the far side of the car from me," said Whitehouse. "He was standing sideways towards me, but as I got nearer he turned towards the front of the car and I saw him full face. He looked at me. I think I would recognise him again if I saw him."

It was the first real lead of the entire investigation, for, apart from the eight-year-old boy in Walsall and one or two indefinite sightings between Walsall and Cannock, this was the first time that anyone had been able to connect a man and a car with any one of the four child abductions now being investigated.

In the meantime—in fact on the very day that Victor Whitehouse was brought to the police station—someone else came forward with a story of a car on Cannock Chase near Plantation 110. She was Mrs. Jeanne Mary Rawlings, from Wolverhampton, who had been out picnicking with her husband at the lower end of the plantation.

Her husband was rummaging in their car boot at the time, so he saw nothing, but Mrs. Rawlings described a car which came slowly down the side of the forest, from the direction of the spot where it had just been seen by Victor Whitehouse. It passed within a few feet of her and was driven by a man who was alone. Her father had had one exactly like it, so she had no doubt at all what kind of a car it was. *She, too, told the police it was a light-grey coloured Austin A.60 "Farina" model saloon.*

When Mrs. Rawlings was asked if she might be able to help a police specialist to construct an "Identikit" picture of the driver, she said she would do her best.

* * *

So, after nearly three years of building a mountain of paper-work that had produced virtually nothing in the way of a vehicle or a face on which to hang a definite line of enquiry, the police now seemed to have both. But how big a task were they facing? "Trace every grey Austin A.55 and A.60 'Farina' registered in the Midlands," ordered Forbes. "And check on the owners' movements at the times of the disappearances of Margaret Reynolds, Diane Tift and Christine Darby." Teams of detectives were put into the Vehicle Taxation Offices (these were the days before the centralisation of records on the Swansea computer) to extract the relevant files. This, it is emphasised, covered only the Midlands, but even so it took several weeks' work in the offices at Stafford, Stoke-on-Trent, Burton-on-Trent, Wolverhampton, Smethwick, West Bromwich, Birmingham, Solihull, Coventry, Walsall and Dudley, to go through *one million three hundred and seventy five thousand files—and to identify more than twenty-five thousand grey Austin "Farina" A.55s and A.60s*!

Thus did the Cannock Chase Murder Investigation team—with the help of every police force in Great Britain—embark on the most extensive vehicle check of its kind ever undertaken.

* * *

Life's Like That 103

So much for the car. What of the search for the man driving it? Here began another potentially mammoth task, with the production of two independently-taken "Identikit" impressions based on the descriptions given by Victor Whitehouse and Mrs. Rawlings. The two "Identikit" pictures were almost exactly the same, so a newspaper artist and cartoonist, Lewis Williams of the Birmingham Mail, was asked to take the process a step further by filling out the one-dimensional lines of the "Identikit" pictures into an artist's impression, first in black and white and later in colour. It was an innovation in Britain (though much-practised in the United States) and Lewis Williams's colour picture was to become famous on some forty-thousand posters which found their way into every corner of the British Isles, as well as into every country in Europe and, eventually, to the four corners of the world.

That picture was also to make British newspaper history, when, on 25th October, the Daily Express put the weight of its huge circulation figures behind the investigation by publishing Britain's first-ever coloured front page. It included the artist's picture, and a coloured photograph of an un-named man who had realised he resembled the poster picture and had volunteered to be photographed with a grey Austin car as his contribution to the publicity campaign.

A publication landmark was also created at New Scotland Yard, where the Police Gazette—the official medium for the circulation of crime and wanted persons—published its first-ever colour supplement . . . printed from the block used to print Lewis Williams's artist's impression of the Identikit picture, loaned to the Yard for the purpose by the Birmingham Mail.

The coloured front page of the Daily Express contained a quote from Ian Forbes summing up his appeal to the public: "We are convinced," he said, "that the man who murdered Christine Darby is the man in the Identikit picture and that it is a good likeness. His is a face well-known to someone—probably to several people. He is being shielded—either by a relative who knows of his guilt but is prevented from coming forward by misguided loyalty or fear, or by people who recognise a resemblance in an acquaintance but cannot bring themselves to believe that the person could be a

104   Not the Moors Murders

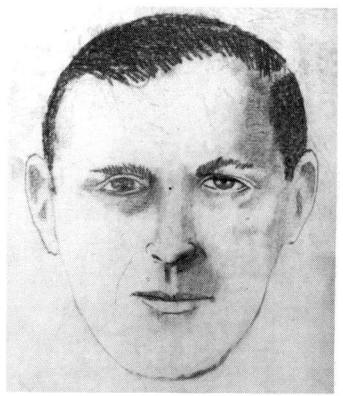

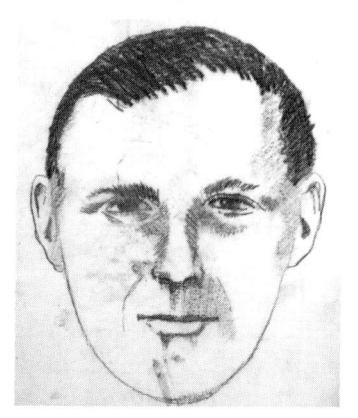

Step by step, *Birmingham Post & Mail* artist Lewis Williams transforms the black and white "Identikit" outline into a coloured portrait.
Staffs. Police and the late Lewis Williams

Life's Like That

STAFFORDSHIRE CONSTABULARY
WANTED FOR MURDER
OF
CHRISTINE ANNE DARBY

MAN, born 1927 to 1932, 5ft. 10in., medium build, broad shoulders, hair brown, (greased, brushed back with slight parting), oval face, straight nose. May frequent licensed premises.

Was in possession of a grey A.60 or A.55 Austin Cambridge car.

Any information or suggestions as to identity to Incident Post, Cannock Divisional Headquarters (telephone No. Cannock 4347) or any Police Station.

Printed by the Receiver for the Metropolitan Police District, New Scotland Yard, S.W.1.

Staffs. Police

A volunteer from the public helps re-construct Victor Whitehouse's sighting of suspect and car in Plantation 110.   *Daily Express*

child-killer. The innocent—and many innocent men may well resemble the picture—have nothing to fear. But no child is safe while the man guilty of the murder of Christine Darby goes free.''

By the time the Cannock Murder Investigation Team had finished with that picture, there could hardly have been one person in the whole of England, Scotland, Wales or Ireland who had not seen it, and, if only for the massive avalanche of calls from the public which it precipitated, the poster and the news media campaign based on it have to be judged one of the greatest ever.

What kind of a risk was Forbes taking in relying on the accuracy of the picture to the extent that he did; in putting all his eggs into one basket? The answer is "A Big One", for human memory is notoriously fickle and identifications made on the basis of fleeting encounters are notoriously unreliable. If the picture turned out to be a true representation of the man seen near Plantation 110 (and no one would know until the police found him), Forbes could be onto a winner. If not, the result could be catastrophic. If the man arrested and charged with the murder did not look a bit like his "picture" it could well knock a murder charge right out of court.

The publication of an Identikit (or its present-day counterpart, the more rounded "Photofit") impression is a risky business at the best of times and the wise detective will allow it only after the most careful consideration. For one thing there is the nature of the Identikit (or Photofit) itself. *It is not a photograph.*

A "Photofit" impression is simply a collection of facial features, framed by a face which gets as close as possible to the witness's recollection of the person he or she saw. If, as in the case of the Cannock Chase "Identikit", those facial features are but six in number—the hair-line, a slightly-creased forehead, the eyebrows, the rather prominent cheek-bones, the somewhat bulbous nose, and the fact that the teeth showed slightly through one side of the mouth—that is where the attention needs to be concentrated. One can teach that to a police officer, but one can never expect the public at large to appreciate such fine points of identification. To them it will be a photograph. It will channel their vision, and if the suspect they have in mind does not look like what they think is the criminal's "photograph", they will not report their suspicions, now matter how great they might be. They will not understand the essential difference between a photograph and what they are really looking at. Thus, to make a Photofit impression public is to take a calculated risk, one of the primary calculations being how desperate you are to find your man.

As with the man, so with his car. Human memory is no less fickle when it comes to identifying motor vehicles, so if, after tens of thousands of A.55s or A.60s had been traced and eliminated, a suspect turned up with a different make of car and was charged with the murder, Victor Whitehouse and Mrs. Rawlings could well find themselves being called to give evidence for the defence!

The Daily Express publishes its first ever coloured front page.

Daily Express

Life's Like That 109

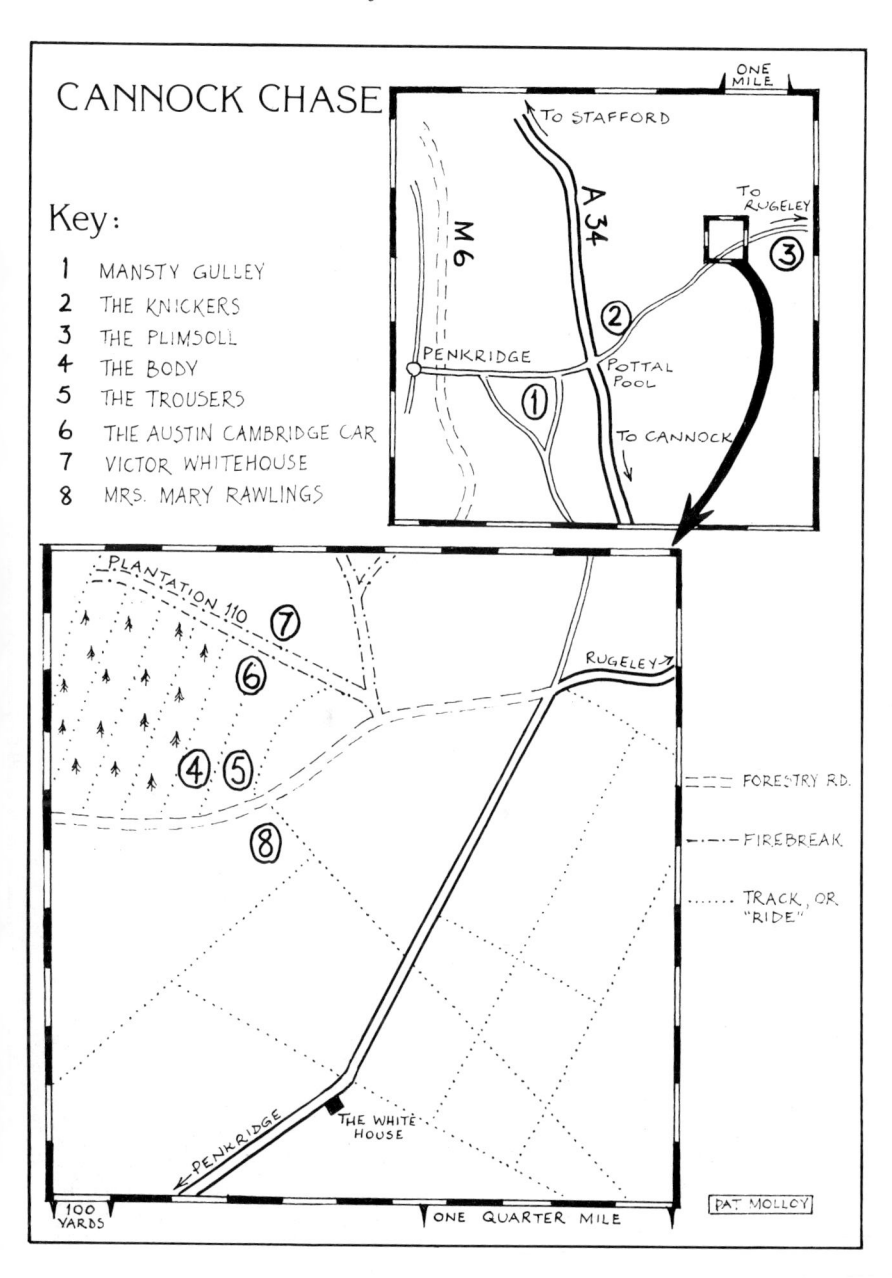

CANNOCK CHASE

Key:
1. MANSTY GULLEY
2. THE KNICKERS
3. THE PLIMSOLL
4. THE BODY
5. THE TROUSERS
6. THE AUSTIN CAMBRIDGE CAR
7. VICTOR WHITEHOUSE
8. MRS. MARY RAWLINGS

ONE MILE

TO STAFFORD
A 34
M 6
TO RUGELEY
PENKRIDGE
POTTAL POOL
TO CANNOCK

PLANTATION 110
RUGELEY →
= = = FORESTRY RD.
— · — FIREBREAK
· · · · · TRACK, OR "RIDE"

← PENKRIDGE
THE WHITE HOUSE

100 YARDS
ONE QUARTER MILE
PAT MOLLOY

When it comes to decisions as crucial as this, it will be down to one man, and he will get the credit or the blame. I, and any other detective with experience of extensive murder investigations, can testify to the burden of responsibility that this represents. It was the biggest gamble of Ian Forbes's career.

*   *   *

With publicity comes information from the public—in this case a veritable avalanche—and the Incident Room system required to process what soon became an almost overwhelming deluge of telephone calls, statements and questionnaires, itself became so vast that no police station could accommodate it. By good fortune, though, the Department of Health and Social Security had just vacated a spacious, open-plan pre-fabricated building a couple of hundred yards away from the centre of Cannock, and it was there that "The System" was given the space for rapid expansion it so badly needed.

The Cannock Murder Room is established in a pre-fabricated building recently vacated by the DHSS. *Staffs. Police*

Life's Like That

The Cannock Murder Room in full flight: Ian Forbes standing, right.
Express & Star

"Occupations": one of the 50 or so classified indexes in the Murder Room's "Paper Mountain". *Staffs. Police*

Since Cannock was ten miles from Walsall, where police activity was equally intensive, it was decided that the Walsall Incident Room should continue to operate, though linked closely with that at Cannock. After all, they were in two different force areas and the Walsall Incident Room had been operating, at varying levels of intensity, since as far back as December, 1964.

Direct telephone lines were installed between the two Incident Rooms, and so was a closed-circuit TV system that enabled operators in each of them to view documents stored in the other. Every possible effort, short of actually merging the indexes and files, was made to integrate the two operational bases. Total integration of the "systems" was, of course, out of the question, in view of the outside chance that more than one murderer was at work in that part of the Midlands.

By now more than two hundred police officers were operating out of the two Incident Rooms, piling paper by the hundredweight onto an already towering mountain, in an operation that seemed to be settling down into a smoothly efficient—if hectic—routine. The days stretched to weeks and the weeks to months, while suspects trooped through police cells (forty-four in Cannock alone, not counting the sixteen "Peeping Toms" who found themselves locked up there); hundreds of witnesses trooped through police station interview rooms, and thousands of others were seen by police officers in homes, offices, work-places, pubs and clubs in the Midlands and throughout Great Britain.

The twenty-five thousand grey Austin A.55s and A.60s dredged from vehicle records in the Midlands swelled to thirty and forty thousand as the net was spread through other licensing centres, through the motor trade's network of car distributors and to the manufacturers themselves.

The artist's impression spread throughout the country, and the section of the "classified" card index headed "Man resembling Identikit" rapidly spilled over into a second drawer, and a third, and a fourth, as thousands upon thousands of reports were received and processed.

The inevitable "Nutters" file also swelled as mediums, fortune-tellers, ouija-board and spirit glass operators, and all manner of people claiming psychic powers besieged the Incident Rooms with their suggestions, while the equally inevitable cranks wrote and telephoned anonymously claiming responsibility, threatening further murders or identifying others as the killer. Inevitably, too, disgruntled wives by the score tried to dispose of their husbands by pinning the crimes on them.

It is the "Cranks" who deserve a special mention here, for it was such a one who so disastrously deceived the investigators of the so-called "Yorkshire Ripper" murders. The reason for it opens up another crucial aspect of any protracted murder investigation, namely the need to maintain absolute control over the output to the news media. In any properly-run major crime investigation there can be only one "police spokesman". In the "Yorkshire Ripper" investigations just about every Tom, Dick and Harry in the several police forces involved who could push himself in front of a camera and a microphone did so, and was responsible for the *débâcle* that broke the health and probably hastened the death of the fine old Yorkshire detective who was made to carry the can for it.

In Yorkshire, Assistant Chief Constable George Oldfield and his team were taunted by a man with a "Geordie" accent who bombarded them with recorded messages and letters, confessing to the murders, describing them in some detail, and telling where and when he would strike again. Those tape-recordings and letters received massive publicity and the public was told that the police believed them to be genuine, *with the consequence that no man who did not have a "Geordie" accent was regarded as a good suspect, no matter what else might have brought him under suspicion.*

Of course the world now knows that the "Yorkshire Ripper" did *not* have a "Geordie" accent. What is not so widely known is that no-one suspected that the hoaxer's tape-recordings and letters were not genuine until a senior police officer had spent *six whole weeks* studying the massive police news-media output, only to find that there was not one iota of the detail contained in the spurious claims that could not have been acquired from newspapers, TV or the radio. The effect that this discovery had on the progress of the "Ripper" investigations was nothing less than catastrophic, and the public outcry caused by its disclosure was immense. Which was why those, from highest to the lowest, who had so vociferously supported George Oldfield in his acceptance of the tape-recordings and letters as genuine, deserted him in droves, and the career of a distinguished policeman came to a sad and bitter end.

In the Cannock Chase Murder Investigations, despite a flood of cranky claims to responsibility and threats of further killings, no such problem ever presented itself. It could not. There was only one "Police spokesman": Ian Forbes himself. And if anyone engaged on the investigation needed to check a crank's letter against the news-media output, he had only to search through Detective Sergeant Tom Parry's meticulous record of his "Guv'nor's" press briefings and interviews, and his burgeoning and always up-to-date press cuttings file, to do so.

*   *   *

The massive police effort being put into the Cannock Chase Murder Investigations, and the massive attention it received in the news media also touched a nerve in the public at large that generated a widespread and unprecedented consciousness of its responsibility to protect its children. Never before had school gates been so crowded with parents and their cars at the beginning and end of the school day; never before had children been made so aware of the dangers of speaking to (let alone accepting lifts from) strange men, and never before had the streets been so empty of young children, even in broad daylight and at week-ends. A pall of fear hung over the Midlands, and never had there been such widespread sensitivity to the existence of men who take an inordinate interest in little children. Hundreds of them were reported for hanging around schools during playtimes, and woe-betide any man who, no matter how innocently, stopped his car and asked a child for directions. His number would be taken and his feet would hardly touch the ground before he would see the inside of a police station. Not even innocent fathers picking up or dropping off their own children were immune from such attentions!

*   *   *

As 1967 drew to its close, with nearly four months having passed since the discovery of Christine Darby's body, the three-year-old Cannock Chase Murder Investigations had already established their place as the most extensive in history. Yet the passage of time had served to increase rather than diminish their dynamic, and Detective Superintendent Ian Forbes was now leading a nearly three-hundred-strong team that was motivated as never before in the experience of those either working on it or seeing it in action. If ever a leader had taken to heart Clausewitz's dictum that *"Material resources are merely the wooden handle of the weapon; morale is its cutting edge"*, it was he. Forbes had never heard of Carl von Clausewitz, but he knew the meaning of that statement just as surely as if he had written it himself.

He and his team deserved better, but New Year's Day, 1968, would see the investigations entering their fourth year, and the Cannock Chase Murderer still walking as free and elusive as ever.

*   *   *

All through the autumn and into the winter of 1967 I watched, frustrated beyond measure, as events unfolded only twenty miles from my home. At the Police College, time crept by, the trees shed their leaves, the frosts came, thin brushings of snow whitened the Hampshire countryside under leaden skies. And my spirits were as grey as the weather.

Six months was a hell of a long time to spend away from home and police work and many was the time that I sat in syndicate room or lecture theatre and found my thoughts wandering away to where my colleagues were slogging relentlessly on against unpleasantly long odds. What wouldn't I have given to be there with them?

I made the best I could of it, eagerly scouring every newspaper, never missing a radio or TV broadcast, seeking out my pals during weekends at home to get myself up to date from the inside. I even met Detective Superintendent Ian Forbes one night, while he was visiting my local police club bar.

My CID boss, Harry Bailey, introduced us and I relished the opportunity of seeing in the flesh the man about whom I had heard so much and at whose side I would have given anything to be, in the thick of the investigation that I had seen in its early days from the ground floor. We had a great night in Stone Police Club, Ian Forbes downing his Chivas Regal whiskies, me swimming in pints of draught Guinness, and everyone listening to his ideas on where it was all leading and enjoying his diversions into his roistering past in London's underworld. His earthy humour and his even more earthy language ("My voice doesna' carry," he would growl mischievously when he saw the shocked expressions around him) had the place in uproar, and I could see what my own men and my ex-Crime Squad colleagues had been talking about when they described his morning briefings. They must often have been riotous, for they always sent a crowd of happy and enthusiastic police officers into the outside world, daring it to throw its worst at them for as long and as hard as it chose.

What struck me above all was his confidence in the path he had chosen. "Are you *sure* you're not putting too much into the Identikit and the Austin Cambridge?" I asked him, trying to get the feel of the thing I had hitherto got only second-hand, and knowing what I did about the frailty of human observation and memory. "Are you really sure? Aren't you taking a big risk putting everything you have into them?"

"Son," he said, relishing the fresh glass of Chivas Regal he had taken from the half dozen lined up for him on the bar counter, "bring yourself down and see us when you get the chance. Read what I've read. Come up and walk the Chase with me. Just to get the feel of it." He grinned slyly, dipping his chin into his short bull neck in the way that spread his jowls and characteristically curled up the left side of his mouth. "Aye. Just get the feel of it, and then you'll be as sure as I am, I know. You see, son, [I was all of fifteen years his junior!] it's the *feeling*, isn't it? You know the feeling, I know you do. Just come and see that 'ride'. Only one car went down and the same car came back up. Down to drop little Christine, and back to tidy himself up before he came out onto the road. Just have a word with Victor Whitehouse and you'll be sure as well. He saw him, and he'll know him again when we bring them face to face, I'm sure of it. It'll come. The bastard's out there somewhere, Pat, and we're getting closer to him with every day that passes."

I knew just what he meant. No one can explain it, no one can quantify it. It is not merely recording what witnesses tell you, it is talking to them and getting the feel of them as people; absorbing the atmosphere of the scene, and immersing yourself in the whole affair just as if you had been there, seeing and hearing it all happen, as only an experienced detective can. Instinct is one word for it, I suppose, and I had already learned that a well-honed instinct (as distinct from guesswork and theorising *à la* Sherlock Holmes), is something that the experienced detective ignores at his peril.

"Come down and see us," he said again, as he turned to answer a question from behind him. "Get that college lark out of your system and when you get back for good, come and have a look at us. And then you'll be as sure as I am that the bastard in that picture, and his grey Austin Cambridge, are out there somewhere, and we'll have 'em as sure as night follows day."

At the end of the evening I shook hands with Harry Bailey and Ian Forbes beside the chauffeur-driven Jaguar that was to take them home, which, for Forbes, was The Hollies Hotel in Cannock. I wished them luck, and as my wife and I walked home I didn't have to voice my thoughts to her. She could read them like a book.

*   *   *

My College course was now almost at an end. It was Wednesday the 20th of December, at around six in the evening, and I was taking a pre-dinner couple of pints in the bar in Bramshill's Tudor mansion. "Message for you, Mr. Molloy," said the barman, putting down his telephone. "They want you to ring your Chief Constable straight away."

The call was not unexpected. I had been on pins for a week or two, knowing that in the reorganisation which was to take effect on the 1st of January, 1968, on the amalgamation of my old force with the Staffordshire County Police (as part of a nationwide programme of police amalgamations), my county division was to be broken up and I would, so to speak, become redundant. My

College course would end with the commencement of the Christmas holiday and sooner or later I would have to be told to which new division I was to be posted. Where that would be I hadn't a clue.

I went straight out to the payphone and made a reverse-charge call to the police headquarters at Stafford. "County Police headquarters," chirped a female voice.

"Chief Constable, please."

"Sorry sir, the Chief Constable's gone."

"But I've just had a message to ring him urgently."

"Sorry, sir, but I'm afraid he's gone and there's no one about. Everybody's gone."

"Well, damn me."

"And who are you, sir?"

"Detective Inspector Molloy. I'm at the Police College."

"Oh yes, Mr. Molloy. I have a message for you."

I hardly dared to ask. "Oh, thank you. What is it?"

"You've been promoted Chief Inspector, sir. Congratulations."

"Thank you. From when?"

"From a week on Monday—the 1st of January."

The rate of my heart-beat began to increase startlingly. "Uniform or CID?" I asked querulously, for it could have been either.

"CID."

I swallowed hard with relief. "Where?"

"Cannock, sir. You'll be in charge of the Divisional CID."

I don't know exactly what I said, but if she hadn't been a hundred miles away I would have thrown my arms around her and kissed her. Promoted by a telephone operator! And given the very post I would have given my right arm for . . . *right at the heart of the Cannock Chase Murder Investigation, ranking next to its leaders, Harry Bailey and Ian Forbes*!

After phoning my wife I went for dinner, and then back into the bar, where my colleagues celebrated my news with gusto. My fellow CID men on that course of mainly uniformed officers knew exactly how I felt about being sent to the scene of the most challenging murder investigation ever to lure a detective. A form of masochism it might be, but every detective in the college bar that night envied me my luck. What a turn-up. But life's like that. Isn't it?

CHAPTER FIVE

THE N.F.A. FACTOR

I walked into Cannock Police Station at eight forty-five on Monday morning, the 1st of January, 1968. I had, of course, met everyone before—my civilian staff as well as my detectives, with whom I had worked on the earlier murders—and I received many congratulations on my promotion, and words of welcome on my return to Cannock, three months short of two years after leaving Yard-man Cyril Gold's door-knocking team. That experience had not only made introductions unnecessary, it had also given me a good start so far as knowledge of my new territory was concerned. So, by the end of the morning I was able to leave the Divisional Headquarters and walk up through the town centre to the Cannock Chase Murder Incident Room.

Detective Chief Superintendent Harry Bailey, Yard Murder Squad Detective Superintendent Ian Forbes, and Forbes's assistant, Detective Sergeant Tom Parry, gave me a hearty welcome, and I stayed there until well into the evening immersing myself in the office lay-out, in the already massive files and indexes, and in the paper-flow patterns of "The System". It was huge. In the Christine Darby system alone there were already around three dozen four-drawer filing cabinets, nearly three hundred card-index drawers, a long, specially constructed two-tier wooden rack for the scores of "Action" books, and twenty or thirty long trestle tables, stacked with card-index drawers and labelled and fitted out as desks for the telephone, "Action"-writing, "Action"-allocation, card-writing, card-indexing, statement-checking, house-to-house index, correspondence sections, and the score of other functions which figure in "The System's" paper-flow chart.

At the far end of the room stood three trestle tables spread with Criminal Record Office files and piles of papers bearing the official crest of the Metropolitan Police. It was the corner occupied by Tom Parry, who watched over that whole bustle of activity as a bird hovers over its young.

The N.F.A. Factor

All this was housed in the spacious, open-plan main room of the building, over which loomed Bob Stewart's great, pin-spattered map of Cannock Chase, which showed how he and his team had so painstakingly eliminated from the enquiry every vehicle but one. Standing in stark isolation from six hundred other flat-headed map pins was one placed alongside a large cardboard arrow. The arrow pointed to a pin showing the location of Christine Darby's body. The pin alongside it represented a grey Austin A.55 or A.60 "Farina" model car. That car stood in isolation for the simple reason that it was the only one which had penetrated the forest. Every one of the others was plotted on the main roads, the broad gravel public roads which criss-crossed the Chase, the areas specially laid out for picnickers or the open heath-land which lay between the forestry plantations

There were two small adjoining rooms, one of which was labelled "Exhibits Room", and was stacked with carefully-labelled boxes and plastic bags containing several thousand exhibits relating solely

"Standing in stark isolation": The pin (alongside the arrow) denoting the only untraced car. *Staffs Police*

to the murder of Christine Darby. These were items gathered from Cannock Chase and elsewhere which might or might not be required for production as evidence in a criminal trial. The other room was labelled "Officer-in-Charge Investigation", and it contained the desks of Harry Bailey and Ian Forbes, the two men who sat on top of that paper mountain, in an eyrie to which everything of any real significance would rise from the huge, largely irrelevant, mass below. Here they read every single one of the many thousands of "Action" forms and statements passing through the system, making their own comments and ordering further "Actions" to be made out wherever they felt that there was an unanswered question. It was a burden that could never be shirked by the men at the top, despite the fact that subordinates at several other levels of the system would already have been through them, and it was a task for which time had to be allotted on every day that came, however difficult that proved to be, so as not to allow an impossible back-log to accrue.

It was in that room that I received my first full briefing, after which I wandered around, asking questions of the Incident Room staff, poking into the system at random to find instructive examples of what was passing through it, and studying the file of "Material" statements that had been extracted for use as evidence in the happy event of the murderer being arrested.

My day ended in The Hollies Hotel, the "home base" of Ian Forbes and Tom Parry for their stay in Cannock. It was packed, as it always was throughout their residence there, by people flocking to meet the man everyone in the Midlands was looking to for the answer to the mystery that had cast such a cloud of fear over the area. The night grew hectic, as many other nights would in The Hollies before we were through. Ian Forbes's "assembly line" (as he called it) grew apace, with the tumblers of Chivas Regal whisky sent to him from all corners of the crowd. And the stories poured out of him, late into the night.

How the distillers of Chivas Regal whisky must have blessed Ian Forbes's long stint in Cannock, for everyone seemed to go on the stuff (myself excepted, of course, being strictly a beer or Guinness drinker). In fact the local Chivas Regal "rep" made such an impression with his sales figures that his bosses promoted him. What happened to his successor after Forbes departed God only knows!

*   *   *

My full orientation into my new job (or jobs, because I had a divisional CID to run as well) took several days. Thereafter I divided my time according to the changing demands of the two responsibilities, but a routine soon began to take shape: I would be working twelve hours most days, dividing my time between the police station and the Incident Room, and then, going "off duty" (if there ever was such a thing in that situation), I would end most evenings in the company of Forbes and his sergeant, since, as the head of Cannock Division CID, I was their "host". It was a long, long day.

At around four on the afternoon of Friday the 5th of January, I walked through the Incident Room and into Ian Forbes's office. "Glad you've come in, son," he said. "I want you to go down to the ITV studios in Birmingham." He looked at his watch. "Better go now. Ask for Reg Harcourt. He wanted me, but I'm too bloody busy here and I've got to go down to Walsall later. You're going on television."

"Doing what?" I asked, shocked a little at being thrown so peremptorily into something of which I had not even the remotest experience.

"The big Walsall house-to-house. They're doing a feature on it after the six o'clock news—'Midlands To-day'. And you're on."

"What do I say?" *After all, I had only been there four days!*

"Ye'll think of something by the time ye get there," he said with that mischievous laugh of his.

There was no time for more, and the thoughts had to tumble through my brain on the three quarters of an hour drive down to Birmingham.

The "Big Walsall house-to-house" was an operation that had received a good deal of thought over recent weeks. Given the pronunciation by Christine Darby's abductor of Caldmore Green as "*Carmer*" Green it was a logical step to take, even though it would mean going over some of the ground already covered in this and the earlier investigations. But it required much thought and planning because of the magnitude of the task. At a conservative estimate there were at least *fifty thousand* houses in the Borough of Walsall, and with well over two hundred police officers fully committed already to outside enquiries, mounting this operation would call for a substantial increase in manpower. So, when Her Majesty's Inspector of Constabulary gave the go-ahead, the word went out to the Chief Constables of Birmingham, the West Midlands, West Mercia, Warwickshire and Coventry calling for their contributions to the team of two hundred which would have to be put into Walsall to interview every male person there aged between twenty-one and fifty.

Whereas many house-to-house operations are conducted on the basis of the voters' lists alone (a dangerous practice in view of the need to work on name and address lists which are absolutely up to date) a physical reconnaissance of its streets and properties had already been carried out in Walsall, and all the questionnaires had been printed and batched ready for distribution to the enquiry teams. The operation was due to be launched on the afternoon of Monday 8th January, with a briefing of the two-hundred-strong team at Walsall by Ian Forbes.

The Cannock Murders were news-worthy at any time, but the news-media sat up sharply when it was announced that we were about to embark on the biggest single house-to-house enquiry in history! Hence my journey to Birmingham through the afternoon rush-hour three days before it was due to be launched.

*   *   *

I met Reg Harcourt at the ITV studios and was offered a drink, which I could have knocked over in one go at that moment, but I declined: "Let me get it over with first," I said, unable to hide my apprehension at going before a TV camera for the first time in my life.

They took me to the make-up studios, where they removed from my chin the dark shadow that had hitherto defied even the closest shave. Twenty minutes or so before we were due to go "on air", Harcourt and I went down to the studio and sat facing each other on the two chairs that constituted the only furniture on a vast expanse of studio floor. During my thirty-four years police service I had many heart-stopping experiences, and over the years since that first terrifying moment in Birmingham's ITV studios, I have faced many TV cameras—live and recorded—but that first time ever on television is imprinted on my memory as clearly as any of the biggest moments of my life.

My heart thudded as if trying to burst its way through my rib cage as the TV camera was trundled silently in front of us. "We're going out live," said Harcourt comfortingly, "and when you look into that lens there'll be *four million* people watching you from the other side of it!"

I nearly died. The hands of the clock seemed to be going around faster than any I had ever seen before, compressing in frightening fashion the time left for me to get prepared for my ordeal. My desert-dry throat croaked nervous and (it seemed to my anxious ears) totally inadequate answers to the questions my interviewer rehearsed from the clip-board on his knee. Then, as the hands of the clock sped to the appointed time, my shaking began to ease, my heart-beat somehow recovered, and a quick swallow of water put my voice back into gear as I managed to compose myself before coming face-to-face with those four million viewers glued to their sets on the other side of that menacing camera lens, waiting for words of wisdom from me.

Reg Harcourt made his introduction, with a brief summary of the Cannock Chase investigations to date, and with a reference back to the item in the preceding news bulletin on the impending launch of our mammoth operation. Then he turned to me: "Pat Molloy; you're a Detective Chief Inspector with the murder team . . ."

"Yes."

"Could you tell me and the viewers just what this new phase of your investigation means in terms of furthering your search for the Cannock Chase killer?"

I could, and I did. I had recovered in the nick of time for what turned out to be a friendly and unchallenging interview, and so far as one can judge one's own performance before a TV camera I was quite happy with mine. But I was a novice and I wasn't ready for one of the oldest tricks in the TV interviewer's book. The seconds were ticking off fast to the close of our interview, when Reg Harcourt, timing it to perfection, threw me the big one . . . the unrehearsed one . . . the one that had to be answered instantly or be embarrassingly interrupted by the programme presenter, bringing the interview to an end and leaving the interviewee (me!) suspended in mid air and obviously floored.

"Well," he said, "the enquiries into the murder of Christine Darby have been going on for over four months now, and the investigation as a whole for three years. What makes you think you've got any chance of catching the killer after all this time when all your previous efforts seem to have to come to nothing? Do you really think you stand any chance now?"

"Yes," I almost snapped back. "I think so. I think we'll catch him . . .'

My brain spun; a million thoughts raced through it. Think? Think? Four million people watching me say "*I think* we'll catch him". Only "think"? What confidence will that give them in the police? Think? Is that what they expect to hear from people hunting a killer who has put them in fear of losing their children?

The words came out as if someone else was speaking them, but I straightened myself up and did my best imitation of someone throwing out his jaw with determination as I heard them: "Think?" I heard myself exclaiming. "Oh no, don't you worry. We'll get him all right. He's out there somewhere and we'll get him. I *know* we'll get him!"

It was all over, barring my fury at being set up in the way I had with that carefully-timed unrehearsed last question. But my anger was short-lived. He had his job to do after all, and it was a lesson I would have had to learn at some time or other anyway, for with the expansion of local television reporting, police officers at all levels would find themselves thrust more and more before the TV cameras and called upon to explain themselves to the viewing public. The old days of "no comment" were passing swiftly. And then there was the liquid hospitality in the studio Green Room . . .!

I re-joined Harry Bailey and Ian Forbes in The Hollies, back in Cannock, where they and a crowd of customers had watched the interview. Forbes slapped me on the back as he ordered me a pint of Guinness. "Great! Bloody great! Confidence . . . that'll show 'em."

"The Chief thought so too," said Harry Bailey. "Phoned me straight after the broadcast."

Everyone else in the bar seemed to have been equally impressed, judging by the way my own "conveyor belt" of drinks grew during the course of that evening. But my show of confidence in that interview, my words of certainty, would return to haunt me, for as the months passed, still with no arrest to show for all our massive effort, they would be thrown back at me time and time again, in good-natured, but still stinging, taunts in bars all over the Midlands!

* * *

The heavy grey sky which brought the darkness of night to the Midlands as early as two o'clock in the afternoon of Monday, 8th January, 1968, promised at least a foot of snow. The street lights of Walsall and the lights inside its police station burned brightly. Inside Walsall Police Station around two hundred police officers, muffled in thick layers of clothing, sporting every variety of headgear, and clutching questionnaire-filled clip-boards, packed the gymnasium for their briefing by Ian Forbes.

In front of a huge map, his bulky figure looked as broad as it was high, and the voice, the manner, and the tightly-throated Scots accent in which he addressed them could (unless it was my imagination) actually be seen to be drawing hidden reserves of stamina and determination from his audience.

Even as he uttered the first words of his address, the first large flakes of the winter's heaviest snowfall were already reflecting the police station lights as they drifted lazily past the windows to lay what would become a foot-thick carpet of white over the town.

"Ladies and gentlemen," said Forbes, "we should have done this job a long time ago, but there's a limit to what can be done all at the same time. Some of you have been with us from the beginning, and you will appreciate that the demands of the investigation so far have prevented us from taking Walsall apart in the systematic way in which you are going to do it now."

He pointed to a poster bearing the artist's impression of our suspect, and to an enlarged photograph of a grey-coloured A.55 Austin Cambridge car. "This is the killer," he said, "and this is the kind of car in which he took little Christine Darby up to Cannock Chase and murdered the poor little mite. The bastard's out there in those streets somewhere. He pronounced Caldmore Green as "*Carmer*", and nobody but one who was born or has lived in Walsall would have done that. If he's still here, then one way or another one of you people is going to come face-to-face with him before you've gone very far."

The audience stirred and muttered as the implication of that statement sank in. Then Forbes's voice rose and stirred them still further, as he hammered the message right in: "Those of you who have worked with me have heard me say it many times: we are as strong as our weakest link. I, as the man in charge of this investigation, am only as strong as the weakest one among you out there. There are going to be no weak links here. Your instinct is my strongest weapon and if your nose tells you there's something funny about anybody who answers a door to you, don't take it upon yourselves to clear him, *bring the bastard in*!"

This is what they wanted to hear. "Forget complaints against the Police," said Forbes. "Any complaint against you is a complaint against me . . . and they can kiss my arse! Bring the bastard in . . . that's what Harry Bailey and I are here for. We'll sort 'em out."

It was a rousing performance, and as the snowfall thickened to a brilliantly-reflective white cloud outside those windows, the Walsall "House-to-House" team's morale and fighting spirit grew apace.

They would, Forbes told them, be working in pairs, under team-leaders who would sort them out after he had finished speaking. The addresses shown on their "Master Sheets" (the sheet that bore the address and a space for listing every member of the household —lodgers and visitors as well as family) could be depended upon to be there, and not demolished to make room for Council tower-blocks or new roads. The rest was up to them. The name and details of every occupant of the house must be listed on the Master Sheet, and a questionnaire attached to it for each male member of the household aged between twenty-one and fifty. There were now three dates (the dates of the abductions of Margaret Reynolds, Diane Tift and Christine Darby) for which those men would have to account for their whereabouts, and for which they would have to provide a record, a witness or some other means of verification.

Every person in every house would have to be interviewed, even if it took a dozen return visits to one household to do so.

Men who were in the household on any of the material dates but had moved away—to no matter where in the world—would be traced and their whereabouts explained and verified, even if the job had to be done by the police in Timbuctoo!

"Assume that you are likely to be lied to, or something is going to be concealed from you, in every house you are going to visit. And prepare yourselves by asking the people you are interviewing in one house for details of those you are going to speak to in the one next door . . . and of those living in one you have just left on the other side, just in case they have been lying to you. Most important of all, take your time with your interviews. Don't rush. Fifty thousand houses is a hell of a big job, but if we are not going to do it properly we might just as well not do it at all."

"Any questions?"

A hand shot up: "What hours shall we be working, sir."

The Yard man grinned, narrowed his eyes and shot back "Ye'll come when I tell ye, son, and ye'll go when I send ye. And if any admin man back at your home station jibs at any claim ye make for overtime or subsistence, refer the bastard to me and I'll settle *his* ***** hash for him!"

The cheer which greeted that remark brought the briefing to a fitting end, and after being split up into their separate groups and spoken to by their group leaders, two hundred policemen and women turned up the collars of their anoraks and their sheepskin coats, pulled their headgear about their ears and trudged out, heads down, into the snowstorm.

*   *   *

The section of the Walsall Incident Room which was to process the questionnaires as they came in from the house-to-house operation consisted of a Detective Inspector, two Detective Sergeants, a Detective Constable, three uniformed Woman Police Constables and three girl Cadets. Theirs was a potentially crucial job, for any one of those questionnaires could contain the name of the murderer. They had therefore to be checked against the central "Nominal" index, which would refer them to any other material which might previously have come into the system on a particular person. In this way, the existence of several entries on the same man, some of them perhaps contradictory, should cause that man to be put under the spotlight of a much closer examination.

The fact that there were three separate dates should serve to make this kind of examination even more reliable as a guide to a particular subject's possible significance. As a simple illustration, one could consider a man who was known to have been a commercial traveller working the Aston district of Birmingham on 8th September, 1965, when Margaret Reynolds disappeared, as one worth talking to at some length; if he also happened to have been working in the same capacity in the Bloxwich area of Walsall on the 30th December that year, when Diane Tift disappeared, one would spend even more time on him. But if he were also not able to account for his movements on the day Christine Darby was murdered, and was known to have owned a grey A.55 Austin Cambridge car at the time, he would then be a man of very considerable interest, not to say a red-hot suspect.

This was what "The System" was all about, and the House-to-House Administration Team in the Walsall Incident Room received its own little lecture from Ian Forbes that afternoon on the subject of an investigation being "as strong as its weakest link". How they handled the questionnaires that would soon begin to pour in, he told them, could turn out to be the key to the whole frustrating mystery. Woe betide us all if there was any weakness in *that* part of our Incident Room set-up!

We returned to Cannock through that snowstorm to resume our studies in the Incident Room, and the desultory conversation on the way back underlined the feelings of all of us. We had embarked on what might turn out to be the most crucial part of the three-year-long investigation, for if our murderer had already passed through "The System", unrecognised among the hundreds of thousands who had been cleared, this should flush him out. Nothing, therefore, was more vital to the whole investigation than that the Walsall House-to-House Enquiry should be conducted with meticulous care from the first knock on the first door in the town to the filing of the very last questionnaire.

*   *   *

It was in February that I suggested to Detective Chief Superintendent Harry Bailey that now the machinery of "The System" and the Walsall House-to-House operation had settled into a smooth-running hum that required few adjustments of the throttle, he and I might sit down and go again over some of the ground that "The System" had already covered in its search for "The Common Factor". Everyone acknowledged that we might already have interviewed the murderer among the thousands of men already in the system, so some kind of re-run might offer the chance of turning up something that had been missed along the way.

Why not begin, I suggested, with what was thought to be the very first incident in the series—the rape and attempted murder of the little girl by "Uncle Len" at Bentley, near Bloxwich, way back in December, 1964? In comparison with the indexes and filing systems relating to Margaret Reynolds, Diane Tift and Christine Darby, that one must be quite small. Why not go through it again with a fine-tooth comb, re-trace every "Action", check again on every man cleared in relation to that incident, and then pass his name through the three subsequent systems to see if any of them turned him up again and, perhaps, put a question mark over his first clearance?

He thought it a good idea, so we set about finding out where to lay hands on the material. To our surprise it was not in the Cannock Incident Room nor its counterpart at Walsall. In view of the fact that the old Walsall Borough Police Force, which had dealt with the crime, had since been amalgamated into the newly-formed West Midlands Force, with all the upheaval that that involved, it took us a few days to trace it, and it was eventually found buried in a storeroom somewhere in Walsall and sent to us at Cannock.

Harry Bailey and I couldn't believe what we were seeing. The books, documents and index cards were all contained in a large television carton, and looked as if they had been shovelled up and thrown in! We found to our horror that it had never been re-analysed and related to the three later systems.

I began with the "Action" book, a lined foolscap book into which every incoming message had been written and endorsed as to the action taken on it. One would find, for example, information from a member of the public suggesting that X, the owner of car Y, might be the man they were looking for. The message would be entered verbatim, with the time and date of receipt, and the next columns would show to whom the "Action" was given and what the outcome was, with the date and the name and number of the officer who had carried it out. That, at least, was the theory.

There were several hundred such "Actions", and in my spare time over the following week or two I went through each of them, extracting those relating to all the men cleared and then checking them in turn through the Margaret Reynolds, Diane Tift and Christine Darby systems, all of which were in the Cannock Incident Room. In some instances I wanted to know the basis on which a man had been declared "cleared" . . . and immediately ran into problems.

In several of those cases the names of the officers who had carried out the enquiries were absent, and the word "cleared" was not backed up by any other documentation. So who had done the enquiry? How thoroughly? What kind of an explanation had he or she been given? To what extent had it been verified? Finally, to what degree had the subject been "cleared'? Was his alibi watertight, or was it suspect, or did he have none at all? Had he been marked "cleared" simply because the officer had done all he could think of doing, (or all that his supervising officer had sent him back to do), and it was felt that they had come to the end of the road and could never know for sure? It is, of course, a fact of life that many people challenged to explain their movements on a day several months before would not have the slightest idea where to begin, and, though innocent of the crime under investigation, be unable to prove it beyond doubt.

In one or two cases I was able with some difficulty to identify the officer who had carried out the "Action" and to speak to him, but even then the passage of three years had inevitably dimmed his memory to the point where little or nothing could be added to the entry in the "Result" column of the "Action" record. In others, it was impossible to know how much reliance could be placed on it, and it would be impossible after three years to do the enquiry again and achieve a more satisfactory result.

It was now that the later systems should have come into their own, so I next checked every one of the men cleared of the Bloxwich attempted murder through the card indexes of the other three systems, and in the nature of things, with the intensity of the two years or more of investigations in and around Walsall which they represented, most of them turned up again in one or more of the indexes. This time, though, it was possible to get back to the statements or questionnaires which formed the basis for the later "clearances". The problem here was that whereas some alibis were of the "cast-iron" variety, most were not; most ranged from "Alibied by wife only" to no alibi at all, the subjects in those cases usually having been cleared on the basis of several interviews and even then often with serious misgivings. It was a case of "reaching the end of the road" and having to file the matter away.

The trouble was that while there were dozens of dubious "clearances" in the heap of books and documents that represented the earliest of our systems, there were thousands upon thousands in the later ones. It began to dawn on me what a potentially fatal flaw was built into our system. Weak or strong, an alibi leading to a clearance finished up in one place . . . in the central "Nominal" card index. Assuming that one day, however far distant that may be, we ran completely out of steam, with every "Action", every House-to-House questionnaire, every statement "cleared" (if only after many return visits and interviews), every man in our records would have been eliminated from the enquiry. *And there would be no residual index of, say, "Unsatisfactory clearances" to which we could return for another go.*

The number of people in our single, central index must now be approaching a million, and to think of going through them all again, and back through the statements and questionnaires to which they related, with a view to creating such a residual index, was to contemplate the impossible. With the best will in the world we had come too far for that.

But we persevered with the re-check, noting the items about which we remained unhappy, yet ending up at the bottom of that battered television carton without feeling any nearer an answer. Then we started to do the same with the Mansty Gulley index. We worked for two solid months at it, in between doing our other jobs, but again we came up with nothing new; again we came up against what I began calling the "NFA Factor" (NFA—No Further Action —the way everything was marked in the end) which remained as intractable as ever, despite the existence in these cases of an abundance of documentation to show why they had been marked "NFA".

There was no getting away from the weakness inherent in our lack of a residual index to cover dubious clearances. When an enquiry (be it on an "Action" or on a House-to-House questionnaire) had been taken to the point of exhaustion, it had to be terminated and there was nothing to do with it but mark it "NFA", and nowhere for it to go but the central index. Once in there it was regarded as closed, and there was no means of differentiating between a dubious clearance and the many hundreds of thousands of genuine and proper clearances if one wished to go back and take a second look. For all practical purposes they were lost for ever.

Thus did the possibility begin to haunt us: what if he were already in there and we had missed him? What if the massive Walsall

House-to-House operation failed in its primary aim of throwing him up again for reassessment? Worse still, *what if he struck again and another child lost her life, only this time because our "System" had ingested and failed to recognise the man we called The Cannock Chase Murderer?*

*   *   *

Many of Ian Forbes' sayings had become by-words among his now three-hundred-strong Cannock Chase Murder Investigation Team. There were sayings like "We are as strong as our weakest link", and "It's all right, my voice doesna' carry", and "Any complaint against you is a complaint against me". But perhaps the outstanding one was "In a murder ye can get away wi' murder!" In other words, if one were to keep a man suspected of a minor burglary in custody for several days without charge, one must not be surprised if there were an outcry, and quite properly so. Keep a man in for several days because he is suspected of having committed the Cannock Chase Murders, and . . . who would complain except the man himself?

It is a fact that (even to-day, twenty years after the Cannock Chase Murders, at a time when there seems to be less public confidence in the police), whenever the news-media announces that "a man is helping the police with their enquiries" into a crime that has aroused wide-spread public anger, nearly everyone assumes they have got the right man. Hence the scenes reminiscent of lynch-law which often occur outside magistrates' courts when an alleged child killer (who is supposed to be innocent until proved guilty!), is brought through angry crowds of parents for his first court appearance. Such is the public's confidence in its police force, even to-day.

So, "In a murder ye can get away wi' murder", said Forbes, who authorised the detention at Cannock alone of forty-four men whose explanations had not satisfied his outside enquiry officers. Come 1984 and the passing of the Police and Criminal Evidence Act, with its infinitely tighter restrictions on arrest and the length of detention and its insistence on immediate access to solicitors—the death knell to any attempt at serious interrogation—and none of this would have been possible. Sixteen years on and the national crime detection rate would be seen to drop by an alarming seven percent as a direct result of the passing of this Act and its handcuffing of the police. But, though bound by the Judges' Rules, the Magistrates' Courts Act and the sanction of *Habeas Corpus* in our handling and interrogation of suspects, we were, thankfully, not subjected to such crippling impediments as are our successors in the job to-day. This was 1968, and the violent or professional criminal had not yet received what most detectives now call his "Criminals' Charter", giving him even more power to thumb his nose at the forces of law and order. Forbes could still say to us "In a murder ye can get away wi' murder". No one could say that to-day.

Some of our suspects were in for a couple of hours and some for two or three days, and the suspicions against them ranged from their habits of hanging around primary schools and ogling little girls, to their previous convictions for child rape or indecent assault and their continuing suspicious behaviour. Where such men could not satisfactorily account for their whereabouts on the murder dates, the interviewing officers, following Forbes's exhortation not to take it upon themselves to clear anyone of whom they harboured misgivings, but to "bring the bastards in!", did just that.

One of them stands out clearly in my memory and best exemplifies the need for this final sanction to be available to the officers on the ground. It was about seven o'clock one January evening when I answered the telephone in the Cannock Incident Room. "Station Sergeant here, sir," said the voice. "What's happening about Peter X?"

"What do you mean 'What's happening?'"

"I was just wondering when he's likely to be released, sir."

"Christ! Is he still inside? I thought he'd gone."

"No sir, he's still in the cell. Mind you, he's not complaining, and we've kept him fed and watered, but I was just wondering, sir . . ."

"Hold on," I said. "I'll have a word with Mr. Forbes."

Peter X had been brought in by two experienced detectives who had not liked the look of him on account of his previous convictions for indecency with children, his hanging around school playgrounds, and his failure to satisfy them as to his movements. At the police station he had had a thorough going over by Harry Bailey and Ian Forbes, and further enquiries had cleared him to their satisfaction.

He should therefore have been released by now. The plain truth is that we had forgotten about him!

I went in to Forbes's office, where he had his head down over the latest batch of statements. "Sorry to interrupt, sir . . ."

He raised his head and looked at me with a puzzled frown as his brain cleared of the statements he had been reading and readjusted to take in what I was saying. "Peter X," I said. "He's still in the cooler and the Station Sergeant's getting a bit concerned. I thought the bugger had gone, but he's still there." I looked at my watch. "We've had him forty-eight hours."

His frown deepened. "Tell them to fetch the bastard up here. I'll have a word with him."

Peter X was escorted into Forbes's office about fifteen minutes later, and Forbes looked at him as though he were something loathesome. "Right," he growled. "Ye can go. We've finished with ye."

Not content with such a summary dismissal, the man protested: "What, just like that? Just turned out with no explanation as to why I've been kept locked in a cell for two days? Am I to be charged or not?"

I thought Forbes was about to spring on him. "No ye're not" he said grimly. "So ye can go."

"But what about my rights? Have I no redress? How can you do what you've done to me and then turn me out without explanation or compensation?"

Forbes had an answer to that all right: "I'll tell ye what to do," he said. "Just take a walk down the road to the centre of Cannock and tell the first people you meet there that ye've been in custody for two days on suspicion of murdering Christine Darby, and they'll ******* lynch ye! Now **** off!"

He did. But he was in custody again somewhere else within a matter of weeks, charged with several child rapes, *for which he was eventually sentenced to life imprisonment.* So who was right about his detention at Cannock, the child raper or the policeman? And he was not the only one whose detention was vindicated by a subsequent conviction for sexually assaulting children. The Midlands were crawling with such people.

*   *   *

The weeks turned to months, the paper-mountain grew higher and there were times when one felt swamped by it all. As I would occasionally say to the Incident Room staff, "Do you know, we've created a monster here. One day its going to open its big mouth and swallow us all up." It was meant as a joke, but there were times when I wasn't so sure!

The door-knockers flogged away in the streets of Walsall, and the "Action" teams ranged far and wide, while every police force in the Kingdom put officers full-time on doing follow-up enquiries for us and interviewing the owner of every grey-coloured Austin A.55 or A.60 car that could be traced from Vehicle Taxation Offices or the car manufacturing and distribution trade.

We had special lines of enquiry for all army, navy and air-force units, for commercial travellers' associations, for mental hospitals, for prisons, for factories and for every other conceiveable institution or organisation that might harbour the kind of man we were looking for. Forbes's regular briefings, at which he never failed to throw the question open to the floor, brought out suggestions for further lines of enquiry, while the blackboards which stood in both Incident Rooms for all and sundry to put up other suggestions, were filled up regularly.

The interest of the news-media remained high, and not one day of the entire investigation passed without a briefing by Ian Forbes of as many or as few press men as cared to turn up. If he felt their interest might be waning, he would think up some new headline for them. He was a master at the media game, and I watched him with some fascination, learning all the time how the press can be harnessed to a murder investigation so as to ensure that it is always the leading topic in home, bar-room and everywhere else where people gather. What I learned from him (and profited from in future murder investigations of my own) was that the police and the press share a common objective: the reporter wants a good headline so that he can keep himself on the front page, and the front page is just where the police want their investigation and their appeals to the public to remain for as long as possible.

It could, of course, boomerang occasionally, as when we received a letter from an irate Commissioner of the South African Police, with whom Britain had neither an extradition treaty nor the benefit of liaison through Interpol. By the Spring, uncompleted questionnaires from the mammoth Walsall House-to-House operation were being sent not only to all parts of the United Kingdom, but also to all parts of the world. When a morning press-briefing seemed to be struggling for something new, therefore, the passing of an enquiry (however routine) to a foreign country was guaranteed to spark off a fresh headline.

"Anything new this morning?" asked one reporter.

"Oh, yes," replied the Yard man. "Our House-to-House in Walsall has come up with an interesting one . . . a chap who's gone out to South Africa. We're in touch with the South African Police to have him interviewed."

The reporters scribbled furiously, their interest now fully rearoused. No matter that the enquiry was purely routine, and necessary only to render the questionnaire tidy enough to be filed away as "cleared". This was something special, and the headline duly appeared: *Cannock Murder Net spreads to South Africa. Hunt for Walsall man . . .*'

Thus the irate letter from the Commissioner of the South African Police. "I have read with astonishment," he declared, "an article in the Rand Daily Mail [evidently picked up from a British newspaper] to the effect that my officers are scouring the Johannesburg area, 'hunting' a man suspected by the British police of the Cannock Chase murders . . ."

The Commissioner, like virtually every other police chief in the world, was of course well aware of what was going on around Cannock Chase, but this one had floored him. What he was not to know was that a perfectly routine enquiry had found its way direct to his Johannesburg CID officers without passing across his own lofty desk. He was angry, but, I assume, placated by the letter we sent him apologising for the over-enthusiasm of the press and thanking him for all the valuable assistance given to us by his officers, which, we were confident, would continue.

The reply we received to a house-to-house questionnaire sent to another African police force was even more of a shock. It was in the form of a telex message from the Commissioner of Police in Ghana. "Subject Cannock Chase Murders," it read. "Re Charles X, born Y, home address Z Street, Walsall, Staffs, UK, subject of house-to-house questionnaire, to be interviewed re whereabouts on material dates. This is to inform you that the interviewing officers formed opinion that he resembled the picture in your Wanted Poster. Subject taken into custody and committed to Accra prison . . ."

"Christ," I said as I read the telex and pictured our man being flown in chains from his civil engineering site several hundred miles up country, and now lying in a stinking, vermin-infested tropical prison cell in a police state like Ghana. "We'd better answer this one quick, sir, before they behead the poor bugger." We did, and he lived to tell the tale!

CHAPTER SIX

TROUBLE DOWN BELOW

It was in the Spring of 1968 that I picked up the first rumblings that all was not well in the Walsall Incident Room. I was having a drink with some of the boys who had finished their day's door-knocking. One of my own CID men, Detective Constable (now Detective Sergeant) John Till, took me aside and told me: "Boss, Walsall's going to let us down for sure. There are house-to-house questionnaires being marked NFA and being filed there that should never be. He's going to be missed, if he hasn't been missed already. For God's sake get something done about it or we might just as well set fire to the whole bloody system."

I asked him to explain, and what he told me made me freeze. *The "NFA (No Further Action) Factor" had hit the Walsall House-to-House administration with a vengeance.* Men bringing in questionnaires and telling the desk officer that they had taken a particular enquiry as far as they could and were still unhappy about the man, were simply being told to go back and see him again . . . and again, and again. Remembering Ian Forbes's declaration that the final interrogation of such people would be carried out by him and Harry Bailey, they had reminded the desk officer of it. To no avail. "Go back and see him again," they would be told.

"There's no point," they would reply. 'We've seen him half a dozen times already and it's time somebody else had a go."

"Then you've taken it as far as you can," the desk officer would say. "Leave it to me," And that would be the end of it. A highly dubious "NFA" would be written on the bottom of the questionnaire, the cards (one for Walsall and one for Cannock) duly endorsed, and the whole unresolved suspicion buried in our mountainous filing system. Furthermore, since the questionnaires themselves remained in Walsall, those of us in the main (Cannock) Incident Room who wished to check back on a man had only the card to refer to (though a questionnaire could be sent up from Walsall if it were thought worthwhile), and the concern expressed by the interviewing officer might never become known to us.

If John Till was right, then the "NFA Factor" had reached crisis proportions. Not satisfied to rely on only one such complaint, I made it my discreet business to find out how many others shared it. And I was appalled. So much so that I told Harry Bailey and Ian Forbes. I thought the latter was going to explode. "I'll have the bastard out now!" he roared. "And you can go down there and take over."

"Not on your bloody life," I replied. Not that I was averse to tackling anything the job threw at me . . . even going where angels feared to tread. I could quite easily have gone down there, taken over and upset everyone in sight without turning a hair. But the malaise was not going to be cured as simply as that. If it were to be tackled as radically as it needed to be, it was a case for major surgery, not for the sticking plaster that would be represented by my taking over as the key figure in the Walsall Incident Room.

A great deal of damage had already been done and it could really only be repaired by the re-examination of every one of the tens of thousands of questionnaires already filed away at Walsall, in order to resurrect those so wantonly and unjustifiably marked "NFA" and cleared. In practical terms an impossibility.

That there were some "political" problems (for want of a better way of describing elements of inter-force rivalry) between the two police forces mainly involved in those investigations (Staffordshire and the West Midlands) was already apparent to all of us, as were some personal animosities at the higher levels. And—*though, as ever, there was nothing but comradeship and total integration among the men and women carrying out the enquiries on the ground*—those "political" problems higher up were the cause of there being two Incident Rooms. They seemed to be working well and to be linked effectively, but it was all an illusion.

In murder investigation as in, say, military operations, there can be only one headquarters, only one centre of command and only one operational commander. In criminal investigation, you can have two, three or even more Incident Rooms, but all must be subordinate to the main one and everything in them must be duplicated there, creating one central system, again under one operational commander.

If the investigation extends to more than one murder in more than one force area, this is even more crucial, as was so clearly demonstrated in the "Yorkshire Ripper" murder investigations, in which this need for a central grip on things was also disregarded, with disastrous consequences.

In the Cannock Chase Murder Investigations there was a debilitating division of command and control as the result of this "political" compromise, at the root of which lay the fact that Birmingham and Walsall were in one police area and Cannock in another. For one thing, there were among the constituent forces of the West Midlands Police (which had but recently amalgamated) those who had never "called in The Yard" and felt that to do so was to be seen to bow to the superiority of the Metropolitan Police. To "call in The Yard" there would have been looked upon as something akin to throwing doubt on one's virility.

Needless to say, the Chief Constable of Staffordshire, Arthur Morgan Rees, did not share that view, as he showed again in 1975, when twenty-year old Lesley Whittle was kidnapped in Shropshire by the man dubbed by the news media "The Black Panther", who left her naked body hanging by a wire around her neck in a sewer in Kidsgrove, Staffordshire. The Shropshire force had not "called in The Yard". Staffordshire did, and caused a rift in the hitherto excellent relationship between the two forces that took years to heal.

While Ian Forbes (strictly speaking, in Staffordshire to *assist* Harry Bailey), was seen by the public and everyone serving under him as the man sent from London to *head* the Cannock Chase murder investigation, he was also a Superintendent among Chief Superintendents and even Assistant Chief Constables and, in practical terms, out-ranked. He was (figuratively speaking) a stranger in a foreign land, and while he was one of the most popular and effective leaders of men I have ever encountered, and while his relationship with Harry Bailey could not have been bettered, it is equally true that at the higher level there were times when he trod on egg shells and came into conflict with his "superiors" in the other forces. This was not uncommon, of course, and, among their other attributes, Scotland Yard Murder Squad detectives had to be masters of diplomacy, a skill in which I would class Ian Forbes as their leading exponent.

All in all, then, while those not versed in such things could be excused for thinking that Forbes's experience and skill would give him the "clout" to assert himself as the "Supremo", in reality he, tough and uncompromising though he was in his investigation and leadership, sometimes had to tread lightly. As all too often in such situations, compromise was the order of the day, however detrimental it might turn out to be to the cause of operational efficiency.

The compromise reached here was not what either Harry Bailey or Ian Forbes would have wished. They could only pray that the weakness it had implanted in their investigation would not grow to fatal proportions. What I had had to tell them raised the awful possibility that it already had.

*   *   *

Changes were made in the Walsall Incident Room in the hope that officers unhappy about individuals they were interviewing could be certain of having their enquiry vigorously taken up by more senior investigators. But the magnitude of the task of going back over all the many thousands of questionnaires already filed away put that idea right out of court, at least at that stage of the game. No doubt the ending of the huge Walsall house-to-house operation without its throwing up a decent suspect would necessitate the re-examination of everyone with a less than satisfactory clearance—a mammoth task given the fact that the "System" did not differentiate between good and poor alibis—but for now we would have to be content in the knowledge that the wound had been staunched and to pray that our man had yet to be interviewed.

The great slog continued. But it was by no means "all work and no play", for Harry Bailey and Ian Forbes knew too much about leadership to allow that to be the case. Irrespective of the burden of responsibility they shouldered for the pursuit of the murder investigation and of the volume of work they had to get through each day, they made it their business to relax with their team whenever and wherever they could. They would turn up unexpectedly in bars they knew they frequented at the end of their long days, and Forbes would demonstrate, to the unending incredulity of all who worked with him, that phenomenal memory of his. "John!" he would exclaim delightedly to a young detective constable. "Ye're back, man. How did the wife get on with her operation? Did you manage looking after the kids all right while she was away? Is she back on her feet yet?"

The man would be amazed, yet his boss really did recognise him and know all about his domestic problems. In fact it was in accordance with Forbes's strict policy of looking after any of his people in that kind of situation that the young detective had been given time off, no doubt without any formal record being made of it, so that his Annual Leave entitlement would be unaffected. Had "John" not been sent home, he could not with the best will in the world have been expected to work at one hundred percent effectiveness with problems like that on his mind, and Forbes was not a man to risk that kind of "weak link" in his chain. When "John" came back with all his problems resolved, he would be one of the keenest, most energetic and most loyal workers to be found in that team.

Forbes knew every one of his men and women by name and recognised them instantly, though he might not have spoken to them for weeks. I know from personal observation that this was no pretence, either, as it was with Napoleon who used a similar device to ingratiate himself with his troops. He would point to a private soldier far along the ranks and ask his officer for a potted history of him, so that when he reached him he could astound him by appearing to remember him from some far back campaign. "My God," the humble soldier would say to himself, "my Emperor recognises *me* out of his whole army. *Vive l'Empereur!*"

I have known many senior police officers to practise the same kind of subterfuge, but in Forbes's case it was a matter of a genuinely photographic memory, and there are still hundreds of people in the Midlands to-day who would vouch for the fact. As for his style of leadership in general, it would be a fair bet that every police officer who served under him at Cannock and Walsall still looks back on those days as the most enjoyable and challenging of his professional life. It was leadership *par excellence*!

*   *   *

By May of 1968, the hunt for the killer of Christine Darby had been going on for nine months. The great Walsall house-to-house operation had nearly been completed, insofar as most of its 54,000 houses had been visited and their occupants spoken to, except for several hundred men of the age range in which we were interested who had left home or lodgings for one reason or another and who had yet to be traced.

Our attempt to track down every Austin A.55 and A.60 "Farina" car ever made and interview its owner had reached a point where something like 34,000 had been eliminated and 10,000 or so remained to be located.

Every one of a score of lines of enquiry had been pushed almost to exhaustion, with the number of people recorded in our central card index by now approaching the million-and-a-half mark. Save for our continuing and worrying reservations about the "NFA Factor", every one of them had been eliminated from the investigation.

Not that we were running out of work, or likely to, for it was reckoned that if we did not receive a single further item of information, there was enough work outstanding to occupy a team of officers (perhaps reducing to forty or fifty as time went on) for at least the rest of 1968!

Where was it all leading to? Our paper mountain now exceeded in size anything that had gone before in any investigation anywhere in the world. Suspects galore had been brought in, interrogated and released, yet we were left without a single name at which we could point the finger of suspicion. What was more, our murderer (or murderers?) seemed to have gone to ground, for despite many false alarms there had not been one further attempted child abduction. At this rate we would peter out as the Margaret Reynolds and Diane Tift investigations had petered out, without anything to show for our pains and with the awful suspicion that he was in our system somewhere and we had missed him.

Trouble Down Below

Could it be that the only chance we now had of catching our murderer was if he should try again and fail? The possibility that he should try again and *succeed* was one almost too dreadful to contemplate. But contemplate it and prepare for it we did, as we had to.

"Doldrums" is not quite the right word to use, considering the long hours and hard work still being done by our outside enquiry teams and their Incident Room support staff, but whatever state we were in on the afternoon of Saturday 21st May, 1968, we were shaken out of it just as surely as if someone had put a bomb under us!

*   *   *

The bombshell exploded at around 4.30 p.m. that Saturday when a telephone call was received at Walsall to the effect that two little girls had been abducted in *Bloxwich* and taken away by a man in a Morris 1000 car.

The girls, aged five and two, were picked up almost outside their home in Stag Crescent, in full view of their friends and a number of adults. The man must have been mad! In that climate of fear, even simple reports of missing children were treated as possible abductions and everyone in the Midlands had been conditioned to react swiftly to anything remotely suspicious where little girls were concerned.

Mad or not, the driver of that Morris 1000 car had enticed those two little girls into it and driven away with them. An all-cars radio message sent hundreds of police vehicles to road-blocks, check-points and pre-arranged patrol areas all over the Midlands. Twenty-three police cars alone were deployed around the perimeter of Cannock Chase, sealing off every main entry and exit.

Our well-practised "Stop Plan" was in place within minutes, primed this time with the registration number of the abductor's car. It was a text-book example of what we had planned for, and within an hour the car was intercepted at Aldridge, some six miles east of Walsall and south-east of Cannock.

The thirty-three year old driver still had the girls with him, unharmed. They were the daughters of some friends of his, he said.

No we are not, said the girls, who, young as they were, were able to tell the police officers that the man had gagged their mouths with sticking plaster and sexually assaulted them by interfering with their private parts. He denied it. But the girls showed the officers the roll of sticking plaster he had used (it was in the glove compartment) and their abductor was immediately arrested.

The TV and radio news-flash of the arrest and its circumstances hit the Midlands like a thunderbolt: "Two girls aged two and five were abducted from Walsall at about four o'clock this afternoon by a man driving a Morris 1000 car. The car, still containing the children, was found about an hour later in Aldridge and a man has been arrested. *The man leading the hunt for the Cannock Chase killer, Detective Superintendent Ian Forbes of the Scotland Yard Murder Squad, is understood to be on his way to Aldridge to interview him.*"

The effect was instantaneous: A horde of newsmen and TV camera teams descended on Aldridge Police Station, and, when the news broke, the building was quickly surrounded by a great crowd of people come to see—and lynch if possible!—the Cannock Chase Murderer.

The news spread like wildfire through the investigation team. The Incident Room erupted into a flurry of activity as arrangements were made for the allocation of the many enquiries and records searches that would be necessary if the man in custody at Aldridge were to be charged with the Cannock crimes. Men were called in to be re-assigned to the new tasks, and we felt on top of the world as Harry Bailey and Ian Forbes got into their chauffeur-driven car to be taken to Aldridge to interview the prisoner. As they departed, we at the murder headquarters went to work with a will, in the certain knowledge that, when this was tied up, we could expect to embark on the biggest celebratory booze-up of our lives.

The world outside was already celebrating as every television channel in the country screened news-flashes of the arrest. For, while couching their accounts in language designed to keep just within the laws which require a man to be regarded as innocent until proved guilty, all of them managed to convey the news that the long-running hunt for the Cannock Chase killer was over!

*   *   *

Busy as we were at Cannock, the hands of the clock moved agonisingly slowly around to seven, eight, nine o'clock, without a word from Aldridge. Telephone calls to the police station there revealed nothing more than that Harry Bailey and Ian Forbes were still talking to the abductor, and though the world outside was already celebrating, the Incident Room resembled a waiting room in a maternity hospital where a father-to-be awaited news of a delayed and difficult birth. Not a word reached us through those four tense hours.

Then, to our amazement, at around ten o'clock, the door opened and in walked Harry Bailey and Ian Forbes. We crowded around to get the news and to congratulate them. "Well," I said to Forbes, "have we got him?"

His expression should have told me. "No we haven't ******** got him," he growled, as he threw his trilby hat across to the hat-stand in the corner of his office . . . and missed.

Hope dies hard in a situation like that. "But it *must* be him," we chorused, shaken to the core. "It's got to be him. There can't be two of the bastards picking kids up from the streets in Bloxwich."

"Well there's one bastard less now," said Forbes, his face brightening as his old spirit returned and the man back in Aldridge was cast into his mental dustbin. "It's back to the grindstone, boys. But not to-night. Come on, let's go for a pint!"

The people of the Midlands did not shake it off as easily as that, and on the abductor's appearances on remand at the local magistrates' court, they turned out in their hundreds to shout abuse at him and threaten his life. The news media also refused to believe the coincidence. Crime reporters dug deep into their stores of innuendo and news editors strained desperately at every legal leash to be the first to carry the biggest crime story of the century: even the BBC was fined for committing a breach of the restrictions placed by the law on the reporting of magistrates' court committal proceedings! In fact the news media did just about everything they possibly could to link the stories; everything, that is, short of actually calling the prisoner The Cannock Chase Murderer.

But Ian Forbes was right. There *was* more than one man in the child-abduction business in the Midlands!

When the Aldridge child abductor appeared at Stafford Assizes and was given two years probation for indecently assaulting his five-year old captive, Christine Darby had been dead for exactly a year. He had not killed her, but for all the work done in our monumental year-long investigation (on top, of course, of that done in the earlier investigations), we were not one step nearer finding out who had.

Ian Forbes had broken all Scotland Yard Murder Squad records by remaining on a provincial investigation for longer than anyone had ever done, and he and Tom Parry were showing unmistakeable signs of wear and tear from their year away from home and all the long hours, the hard work and the socialising it had entailed. Parry, in fact, had become a father during this stint away from home, and had hardly seen his new baby more than half a dozen times. It was now nine months old!

On the anniversary of Christine Darby's death, the Commissioner of the Metropolitan Police decided that a year was long enough and that he would have to have his men back. Not that the investigation would come to an end on that account. Forbes had been sent to assist the Head of the County CID, Harry Bailey, who would continue the investigations along exactly the same lines until every last line of enquiry had been exhausted.

It was time for Ian Forbes to write his report. On the 19th of August, 1968, he and I sat down (me at a typewriter) to draft it. I would say that it was one of the saddest experiences of my whole thirty-four year police career, drafting those seventy-four pages in which were condensed everything that had gone into the mountain of paper that was our Incident Room System; all the long hours of leg work that, inevitably, had brought a weariness to even the strongest of us; all the cars traced and eliminated in the biggest car-check in history; all the door-knocking in the world's biggest ever house-to-house operation; all the questioning, re-interviewing, verifying and heart-searching that had gone into clearing (to some degree or other) every one of the nearly one and a half million people represented by those drawers full of index cards.

All of this ended up in that seventy-four page report, where it was spelled out in all its awe-inspiring detail, and where Ian Forbes, his faith in his identikit picture and his Austin Cambridge car entirely undiminished, told his Commissioner: "This investigation is still alive. What enquiries remain are in the hands of experienced local officers, and should developments occur in the future, the necessary steps will be taken."

And the saddest words of all: "*It is regrettable that in spite of the efforts of all concerned, the killer has not been traced.*"

Forbes was given a series of send-offs more befitting the departure of a victorious general than that of an unsuccessful murder investigator, and our final farewells on the morning of his departure were said quietly, so as not to disturb the hangovers that hung like a pall over the occasion. "Keep at it lads," he said, as he got into his car for the drive back to his home in Wembley. "We'll have the bastard, don't you worry. I'm on the other end of a phone and ye'll only have to call me once. I'll be back."

Sadly, we waved goodbye. Then, like the police officers we were, we shook off our sadness and got back to the business of finding the Cannock Chase Murderer.

CHAPTER SEVEN

ROCK BOTTOM

By mid-October, two months after Ian Forbes's return to London, the Cannock Chase Murder Investigations were drawing to a melancholy end, and not a few of us had doubts about Ian Forbes's judgement in putting everything he had into the Identikit picture and the grey Austin car. Not that anyone on the outside would have guessed, given our show of total confidence, the consistently high morale and energy of all who were still working on the investigations, and the tone of the police statements to the news-media. But the reality was inescapable. We were running out of steam and would hardly see the year end before coming to a halt at the end of the line, still with nothing to show for it all.

As the work-load had decreased, so had the number of officers working on the investigation, to the point where around forty of us

Harry Bailey (left) meets Ian Forbes in London for one of their periodic conferences, after the latter's return from the Cannock Chase Murder Investigation to duty at Scotland Yard.   *Express & Star*

were now employed finishing off outstanding "Actions", doing the few fresh ones that were coming in, and handling the flood of "sightings" of our Identikit man (from Land's End to John O'Groats) which swept in with every mention in the newspapers. Detective Chief Superintendent Harry Bailey, whose daily visits to the Cannock Incident Room had gradually fallen away to weekly and then fortnightly (and those only token visits in view of the dwindling paper-flow), had taken up the reins again as Head of the County CID. I, as Head of Cannock Division CID, was supervising the now tiny Incident Room staff (whose hours had been cut back to 9 am to 5 pm) and the residual outside enquiry team, with Harry Bailey always at the other end of the telephone should I wish to call upon him in the event of anything worthwhile beginning to develop.

With the Walsall house-to-house enquiry also approaching the point of exhaustion (with around thirty-five thousand men already interviewed), with just a trickle of completed questionnaires coming back from other police forces in Britain and abroad, the Walsall Incident Room had been closed and I had merged the two systems as nearly as they could ever be. With the completion of the new divisional headquarters building at Cannock, we had moved out of the pre-fabricated building at the other side of town, and put everything into the police station basement.

I had been doing two jobs (working on the murders and running my busy divisional CID) ever since I had arrived in Cannock, eleven months before, but now I could do them both from one office, still working twelve hours a day, going down periodically to the basement to see the office staff and (in the evenings) to root among the paper mountain in what, it had to be admitted, was the vain hope of finding that elusive "Common Factor". Many was the evening I sat down there alone, surrounded by fifty four-drawer filing cabinets, three hundred card index drawers and nearly five tons of paper, under the low, concrete, basement ceiling, amid the dim pools of light cast by thickly-glassed cellar light bulbs. The desk lamp that illuminated my work there and made the rest of the basement seem so dark around me served only to increase the sense of isolation and to enhance the illusion that I was alone with the Monster.

That it should all come down to this, I would tell myself when I permitted such morbid thoughts to enter my head. That the efforts of hundreds, if not thousands, of police officers, should be reduced to a mass of waste paper. For such it was doomed to be if it remained inert and if it was beyond man's ability to go back and shake it all up in the hope that our murderer might yet fall out of it. But that would have taken an effort almost as great as that which had gone into putting it there. And there was no one left to do it.

The "NFA Factor" that we had identified when the Walsall house-to-house enquiry was at its height still haunted me. Was the answer buried in that paper mountain through some fault of our own? Was our man still somewhere in Walsall, and was his one of the more than thirty thousand house-to-house questionnaires which had been marked "NFA" and filed away there without there being any way of differentiating between the quality of the alibis that had put them there? Would he strike again? If he did, would another little girl lose her life?

A pall of fear hangs over the Midlands:
Wednesfield forms its own Safety Organisation to warn its children.

Express & Star

Rock Bottom 155

Bereaved mothers, Lilian Darby and Irene Tift (first and second left) join in the campaign for the restoration of capital punishment.

Express & Star

Though my facial expression never once betrayed it, a pang of fear struck the pit of my stomach every time we received a call from some Midlands police force that a girl had gone missing, or had been accosted, or was thought to have been abducted. Every such report (and there were many of them) was routinely passed to the Cannock Incident Room, and the Midlands "Stop Plan" activated. Every one of them was potentially a new Cannock Murder and my heart would sink.

We could still make the occasional small headline in the local newspapers, and get the odd mention in the Midlands TV news bulletins, but Harry Bailey's press briefings were now only sporadic and often in the form of prepared statements issued from force headquarters. When they did appear they would be couched in terms designed to assure the public that the enquiry was "very much alive", that "a strong team of investigators is still employed on the case", and that "the Head of the County CID is in regular touch with Ian Forbes at Scotland Yard, who is ready to return at a moment's notice".

Every police force has to go through such motions when a murder investigation is drawing inexorably and depressingly to a close . . . and every detective knows their true worth. Especially if he is the one who has to sit in contemplation of a great, sleeping Paper Monster, waiting for the dread moment when a killer strikes again and the beast has to be re-awakened.

*   *   *

It was on such a night—the one before "Bonfire" night in November, 1968—that, alone in the Incident Room, I received yet another call about the accosting of a young girl. I put down the telephone, slipped two sheets of carbon paper between three Telephone Message/Action forms, and put the whole thing into the typewriter. I typed the message from the notes I had made:

> "At 7.45 pm to-day, in Bridgeman Street, Walsall, a young girl (age not at present known) was accosted by a man in a car, believed Green Ford Zephyr with white roof. The man asked her if she wanted some money for fireworks and took hold of her arm to try and get her in the car. The girl broke away. Story believed genuine at this stage. Car number taken as 429 LOP. There was an independent witness. Cars are still searching the area and efforts are being made to trace the registration through Motor Tax. Driver described as about 5'10", well built, dark hair, wearing grey suit. Well dressed."

I checked the index, but the vehicle registration number was not on record, and I asked the Walsall operator to let us know the outcome. The Incident Room staff would be in touch in the morning if nothing more was heard that night.

In the bar later that evening I received a second telephone call. It came from a Walsall CID officer, who told me that the incident had been witnessed by a twenty-one year old married woman, who had evidently made a crucial mistake in her recollection of the car number, and that she had probably got the make of the car wrong too. They had done a permutation of the figures 429 and the letters LOP and this, coupled with the fact that the witness had been through the police car-identification book and had picked out a Ford Corsair of the same (green with white roof) colour scheme as she had described, had led them to such a car with the registration number 492 LOP. It was owned by a man who lived in one of a block of high-rise flats in Green Lane, overlooking Walsall Police Station.

It was not much, but enough to bring him in the following morning to be questioned and put up for identification. "Fine," I said to the Walsall CID man, "I'll do the usual. I'll send a team down to hold a watching brief for us. What time?"

"Around mid-morning."

I finished my conversation and put down the telephone. Drinking with me were Detective Sergeant John Farrall and his partner, Detective Constable Jim Speight, of our small County Crime Squad, who were still attached to the murder investigation team. "I've got a job for you two," I said. "Another accosting in Walsall. Pop down to the Incident Room and pick up the last action on the file . . . I made it out tonight, just before nine. Mark up the office copy to show that it's allocated to you. They're bringing a guy in around mid-morning, so go straight down there first job tomorrow. See how they get on and what you make of him."

*   *   *

I next saw Farrall and Speight at around half past three the following afternoon, when they came down to the basement Incident room to report back. Farrall threw up his hands in mock surrender. "Just hear us out, sir," he said. "Don't bollock us until you've heard us out."

"Go on," I said, at a complete loss for words anyway.

The two men could not contain themselves. "He's got to be ours, sir," said Farrall. "He's a ringer [double] for our Identikit. You ought to see him, sir. He's just got to be ours."

"And . . .?" I answered.

"And they've turned the bugger out. All the top brass were there. They just put him on an ID parade and when he wasn't ID'd, they turned him out. They got him a solicitor as soon as they brought him in. He had asked for him by name and we think they were scared of him. They dropped him like a hot potato as soon as the witness failed to pick him out, even though she had recognised him and told them so when she came out of the room. We didn't know what the hell to do, he's so much like our Identikit. We even toyed with the idea of arresting him ourselves when they released him and bringing him back with us, he's so good."

Like me, Farrall and Speight had seen many men who resembled our wanted poster and had been built up and let down by many promising lines of enquiry that had come to nothing. But they were so full of this one that I would have to give it some serious consideration. Ian Forbes had said it often and I knew it well enough from my own experience: our men's instinct was our strongest weapon. And here were two of the best on my team swearing that the man they had encountered was the Cannock Chase murderer. They could easily have done what had been done with hundreds of such "Actions" when the incident on which they were based seemed to have fizzled out: they could have reported the outcome and had it marked "NFA". But they hadn't. They had followed their instincts and come back to me, believing I would do something about it.

"Sit down lads," I said. "Let's work this out for a minute or two."

We went through the whole thing, stage by stage, objectively and unemotionally now that they had got their fear of my reactions out of their systems. So, what exactly *did* we have? To begin with, we had what was clearly an attempted child abduction. The ten-year-old girl the man had tried to get into his car had told the police that she was standing on waste land in Bridgeman Street when a car drew up in a dark corner of the nearby garage forecourt. The driver had walked over to her and asked her who had prepared the bonfire on which she was placing pieces of wood. "Me and my brother," she had answered.

"Do you want some fireworks?" asked the man. The girl did not answer. He tried again: "Do you want any rockets or Catherine wheels?"

This time she said yes and followed him to his car. He opened the driver's door and pointed to the front passenger seat. "The fireworks are over there," he said.

All the girl could see was an empty seat, but she noticed something about it to which a detective would attach very considerable significance: it was covered with a newspaper. To prevent the deposit of any fibres or other traces that a child had sat on the seat? Whatever the reason for the newspaper it was clear to her that he had no fireworks and she made a move to go. He grabbed her right arm and tried to push her into the car, but she somehow pulled away from him.

"I'll open the other door for you," said the man, walking around to the nearside of the car, while the little girl took the opportunity to walk away and sit on a low wall under a street light.

It was at this moment that the would-be abductor saw a young woman (who had come out of a chip shop across the road) watching him, and he got out of Bridgeman Street as fast as he could. In driving off the garage forecourt and on to the street, though, he had had no choice but to drive past the woman, and in doing so he bent his head forward, almost touching the steering wheel, so that she would not see his face.

A few questions of the child told the woman that she had witnessed an attempted abduction and, being conditioned like the rest of the population of the Midlands to pay close attention to such happenings, she did her best to memorise the number of the car . . . and almost managed it.

Whatever the problem with the make and number of the car, though, both victim and witness were agreed on its colours. It had a white or cream coloured roof and a green body.

"Anything else?" I asked, seeing another dead end looming up with the collapse of the identification parade. "Did he have anything to say while he was inside?"

The two men looked at each other, and Farrall took a deep breath. "You're not going to believe this, sir, but he told the arresting officer that the car he had before this was ... guess what?"

I was streets ahead. "Don't tell me it was a bloody Austin Cambridge."

"That," said the Sergeant, "is why we expected you to go berserk and throw us out for coming back without him. He did have a Cambridge ... a grey A.55. He's been interviewed about it. On a questionnaire, back on the first Midlands Taxation Office checks ... only a month after the murder."

"Well Jesus Christ!" I said slowly, as the implications of what he was telling me began to sink in. Then I threw the next question: "Alibied?"

"Alibied."

I was now reduced to monosyllables. "How?"

Speight interjected: "Wife. She alibied him then, and she alibies him now."

I had had bad dreams of this day; dreams of our "NFA Factor" rising up and hitting me straight between the eyes. It had had to come, and, painful though it would certainly be, it would have to be met head on now that it had. "*Alibied wife only*—NFA" was written across hundreds of thousands of cards in our index and all but one of those alibis would be no less genuine for that. But it was odds-on that there would be one to which, when it surfaced, we could begin to attach other factors. How many more we would find in relation to this particular fellow was, at that moment, anybody's guess.

I was on the telephone at once. I spoke to Norman Williams, the West Midlands Detective Inspector in charge at Bloxwich, who made it plain that he, too, harboured deep suspicions about the man and was equally unhappy about the speed at which he had passed through the hands of the police. "I'd like a chat with you Norman," I said. "There's too much of a coincidence here, what with his having had a grey Austin Cambridge and having the kind of car you're looking for for last night's job. What about coming over to see us? Come this evening and we'll have a couple of pints while we talk about him. We're going to have to go through this system of ours and find out just where he fits in, so I'll need your help at the Walsall end, because we'll have to make a few discreet enquiries there."

"I'll be over about seven," he said. "And I'll bring Con [Detective Constable Conrad] Joseph with me. He was one of the two who brought him in this morning."

My next job was to bring Harry Bailey up to date, so I rang his headquarters office. It was all, of course, mere speculation, so carefully do detectives have to distinguish between "evidence" and mere "suspicion", and we had been through this kind of thing many times before. But Harry Bailey shared the belief that his men's instinct was his strongest weapon, and he saw from the way I explained things how John Farrall and Jim Speight felt about this one. "Norman Williams is coming over to see me tonight," I told him, "and we're going to set about taking the system apart to see if it throws up anything useful. It'll take a day or two, and I'll let you know how we get on."

* * *

It was not until Monday the 11th of November, six days after Norman Williams and I had first spoken about it, that we were in a position to bring together everything we had dug up on the man. What we saw then confronted us in all its enormity with the failure of our system to identify one who should have been a prime suspect for the Cannock Chase Murders. *It had been digesting information on him from almost the very first day, all of four years before*!

Williams, Con Joseph and I met in the early evening, down in the basement Incident Room at Cannock, and spread our thick file of papers, in chronological order, across the tops of the filing cabinets.

I had gone back to the "Action" book buried in the old TV carton among the jumble of papers which represented the Incident Room System of the abduction, rape and attempted murder in Bloxwich. In that case the police were looking for a two-tone Vauxhall Cresta car fitted with a hand-operated spot lamp on the driver's door pillar. Our man had had such a car at the time. He had been interviewed about it, but his wife had told the police officers that he was at home with her at the material time. The Action had been marked "NFA".

We had found him in the Christine Darby files, too. He had been interviewed twice, the first time just seventeen days after that murder, on the first round of checks on owners of grey-coloured Austin Cambridge cars. On that questionnaire was noted the fact that his wife alibied him for the material times and that he had described his route home from work that Saturday as one which took him well away from Camden Street, where Christine Darby had been abducted. What we knew now, though, was that when Jim Speight had had a short conversation with him he had told him something entirely different: that his normal route home from work *did* take him past the end of Camden Street, a statement backed up by the fact that that was the way he had driven the arresting officers (in his own car) back to Walsall!

But that was only our first encounter with him on the Christine Darby investigation. He had also been interviewed on the big Walsall house-to-house operation (on 29th February, 1968) and his house-to-house questionnaire had not been checked against his car questionnaire. Why not? Simply because the house-to-house questionnaire was filed in Walsall, and the other in Cannock, ten miles away! Thus the price of "political" compromise . . . of having two centres of operation in which the theory of Walsall's subordination to Cannock had got lost. To use the military analogy, we had divided our forces and, so far at least, had lost the battle.

Had our system not been split for inter-force "political" considerations, all the papers would have been in one place and it is inconceiveable that the two would not then have been brought together. Had they been, this particular character would undoubtedly have risen instantly to the category of suspect. He would probably have been brought in for interview by Ian Forbes and Harry Bailey, for the interviewing officers (Detective Constable Ivan Walker and Police Constable Ronald Nicholls) had been so sure they were onto a good suspect that they had endorsed the questionnaire *"Very good likeness to the Identikit; not satisfied with this man due to the unsatisfactory alibi of wife alone"*.

It was bad enough that a questionnaire endorsed in this way should have been marked "NFA" by the Walsall Incident Room officer and filed away among the effectively "dead" enquiries, but Walker and Nicholls actually spoke to him to underline their suspicions and their belief that the matter should be taken up by some senior officer, but to no avail. In effect they were told that the man's wife would undoubtedly alibi him whoever went to see them and that if they themselves could take it no further, neither would anyone else be able to . . . *exactly the kind of behaviour of which I had been told nine months before and which had led to the removal of the man in charge there.*

The suspect's alibis might, of course, have been genuine, but we next came to something even more disturbing. We had spent a vast amount of time over the past four years tracing and interviewing hundreds, if not thousands, of men with previous convictions for indecency with children. What about those who had not been convicted? What about those against whom complaints had been made and investigated but who had not been prosecuted for lack of evidence? The law says people in that situation are innocent because they have not been tried and convicted, but when the police are investigating child murders they would be failing in their duty if they did not regard them as leading candidates for interrogation. Now we had found such a man, but one who had entirely escaped our notice because those who knew about it had not thought to pass on their knowledge to any of the Murder Incident Rooms.

The circumstances of this case were that, in October, 1966, (the year we did not have a Cannock Chase Murder), two girls aged ten and eleven had told the Walsall police that they were playing truant from school one day (as had the murdered girl Margaret Reynolds!) and were sheltering from the rain in the doorway of a factory in Walsall when a man came and spoke to them and invited them to go to his home and meet him when he went home for lunch. They did so, and he took them into the kitchen and gave them a cup of coffee.

The factory they showed the police was the one where our suspect was employed (at that time in Walsall), and the flat to which the two girls took the police was his flat—number 20, in Regent House, a tower block overlooking Walsall Police Station.

What was alleged to have happened next rested entirely on the uncorroborated words of the two young girls. He persuaded them, they said, to undress down to their knickers and then he photographed them. Each girl in turn was then, so they said, given the camera to take a photograph of the man with his hand on her companion's private parts, over her knickers. For this, they said, they were each paid two shillings (10p).

The police interviewed him and searched his flat. He denied everything, even when the search revealed photographic equipment.

His denial, and the absence of the alleged photographs, left the police with the uncorroborated word of two young children, a weakness not helped by the fact that they had not told their parents until some considerable time afterwards. It was this that persuaded the Prosecuting Solicitor's Department to declare that there was insufficient evidence to justify a prosecution. Thus no conviction record existed from which the murder investigators might take up the matter, and no one had thought fit to tell us about it.

All of this was enough in itself to give us the best suspect we had ever had, but our week-long enquiry uncovered something else . . . something that really did hit us between the eyes. It had been the biggest failure of all, for in running our suspect's name through the Mansty Gulley system when I was going back over the earlier Bloxwich abduction file, I had found no record of him. He should have been there, but he was not. In fact, as will be remembered, we had had no sightings of men or cars in those two cases, either at the abduction or the murder scenes. *But what was in the Mansty Gulley system was a statement made by our suspect's brother, which named him as the murderer!* The brother had visited Cannock police station of his own accord to volunteer this amazing piece of information.

In describing his brother as a man of abnormal sexual appetite, cold and cruel, and, in his opinion, quite capable of committing the Cannock Chase murders, he had not, unfortunately, been able to produce one scrap of supporting evidence. But what a ground for *suspicion*, given everything else we had on him. Why had this statement not surfaced from the system? Simply because it had been recorded only under the name of the informant and not also under that of the brother he had named as the murderer! Thus it had not been available to Harry Bailey and me on our re-check and it might have been lost for ever but for the fluke that someone remembered the affair when we were making our enquiries after the latest abduction.

Our suspect had been interviewed in the light of his brother's statement, and this time he was without an alibi for either of the material dates. Had a check been made then with the Bloxwich attempted murder system (from the previous year) they would have seen that he had the kind of car they had been looking for then.

Yet another warning light had failed to flash, for he had told the officers he was employed as a travelling salesman by a Sheffield firm, and admitted that he had been in the Aston (Birmingham) area when Margaret Reynolds was abducted, and lived within three minutes' drive of the spot from where Diane Tift had disappeared!

There we had been, CID and Regional Crime Squad men of the outside enquiry teams, checking out thousands of travelling salesmen and this one had not even been recorded in the index! He had been eliminated from the enquiry, though . . . by the application of the dreaded letters "NFA" to the Action form attached to his brother's statement.

*   *   *

As Norman Williams, Con Joseph and I surveyed the material we had collected on our suspect it was impossible not to believe that we had come upon our murderer at last. There was too much, we felt, to be written off as coincidence. Yet his wife had alibied him every time the police had interviewed them. If we were right, she must have been lying all along. If not, we were about to put an innocent man through the mincing-machine, for there could be no other way to resolve the question.

What kind of people were they? Williams and Joseph had the answer: our suspect was a hard-working engineer, highly respected and valued by his employer. He had never been convicted of any offence, lived in a well-furnished home in a respectable and well-maintained tower block, was always clean and smartly dressed, of temperate habits and obviously devoted to his wife. It was his second marriage. He had divorced his first wife on the grounds of her adultery and left his two children with her, to marry a girl of twenty-one, fourteen years his junior.

There was nothing whatever in his current wife's background to suggest that she might have any leanings towards crime or deception. On the contrary, she was a quiet, rather shy girl from a very good home, and her upbringing had been impeccable. Yet if she were telling the truth about her husband's whereabouts when those little girls were being accosted, abducted or murdered, everything we had on him must be mere coincidence. But I, in common with most experienced detectives, harboured a stubborn distrust of coincidence, which could only be dispelled by an overwhelming weight of proof to the contrary. I could see only one direction in which we could go in this particular case.

I turned away from the files. "Norman," I said, "I think we've found the bastard. I think he's on his way in again."

He laughed and slapped me on the shoulder. "Well if it ain't him, Pat, he's going to have one hell of a bloody fright all the same!"

*   *   *

Harry Bailey was at home ten miles away, but within twenty minutes of my telephone call he was in that basement with us and we were taking him through what we had found. "Yes," he said at length, "there's too much here; he's got to come back in." He picked up the telephone and dialled the Chief Constable's home: "Bailey, sir. I'm speaking from the Cannock Incident Room. Mr. Molloy called me down and we've been going through some stuff he and DI Williams from Walsall have been getting together. I think we might have found our man . . . or at least we've found enough to bring him in and have a go at him."

I heard what I took to be a delighted acknowledgement of the news, and then Harry Bailey said, "I'll explain it all to you in the morning, sir, but I think you should get in touch with the Commissioner [of the Metropolitan Police] and get Ian Forbes back as soon as possible. If we're going to have this man in, I think it's right that we should hold our foot up until he can get back to us."

He put down the receiver: "The Chief's going to ring The Yard tonight, and you can bet Ian will be back here like a shot. Let's hope it turns out to be as good as it looks." He grinned more happily than I had seem him these past three years, and I swear I saw a black cloud begin to dissipate from above his head. Every one of his men knew it had been there, and I was one of the few to whom he had spoken of it, for it had been upon Harry Bailey, as head of the County CID, that some people's sense of failure had inevitably focussed. There were many who felt that this had already begun to blight his further career. Only recently, in competition for a vacancy for Assistant Chief Constable, in which in everybody's book he had been red-hot favourite, he had been passed over, and his detectives to a man felt that his only handicap had been our failure to detect the Cannock Chase Murders. Now that cloud, real or imaginary, seemed no longer to darken his brow. "Come on, lads," he said. "This calls for a pint!"

In the bar upstairs, the four of us drank a glass or two, but quietly and without sharing our news with anyone else. After all, as things stood all we had were coincidences that could never amount to *evidence* and gave us no more than the "reasonable suspicion" the law required to justify arresting the man. We were miles away from having enough to charge him with anything. In fact, as experienced detectives we knew that all we had yet done was to identify a lifeline and grab at it. It was a long rope, and even if it were going to take us anywhere, the top of the shaft was but a small light at the end of a hard climb. But we had, at least, hauled ourselves off rock bottom.

CHAPTER EIGHT

CAUGHT IN THE RUSH HOUR

It took four days to get Ian Forbes back to Cannock. When the Chief Constable of Staffordshire telephoned his request to the Commissioner of the Metropolitan Police, Forbes (promoted Detective Chief Superintendent on his return to London) was busy investigating allegations of police corruption made by a Sunday newspaper, and it took three days to disentangle him.

He was already in Harry Bailey's office at our Stafford Headquarters when I arrived that Thursday afternoon (14th November), and his face was beaming as he gripped my hand and shook it hard. "Harry's been telling me what you've got," he said. "That bastard's good enough for me. We'll have him in and see what he's made of."

"If it is him, you were right about the car," I said, taking out my papers and spreading them on the desk.

"Of course I was bloody right. I told you Victor Whitehouse knew what he was talking about."

Forbes picked up a poster bearing the artist's impression of the man in the Identikit picture. "And what about this?"

"We could be right there as well," I said, "at least from what I can gather from the boys who saw him. Mind you, they tell me that if you regard it as a photograph it's not like him, but as a collection of facial features . . ."

But we had other and more pressing problems to discuss in the four or five hours we spent in Harry Bailey's office. Problems like the most basic one of all: what in all the records we had brought together on our suspect could amount to evidence admissible in a criminal trial and what amounted to mere suspicion and would not be admissible? *The answer was that we had no evidence at all*!

Here, though, is where the policeman parts company from the lawyer in his assessment of the strength of a case. The lawyer would say, "You have enough to *arrest* him, but not enough to *charge* him, and if you are not able to charge him you will have to release him." Quite so, but the experienced policeman would say, "Fine. I'll arrest him and we'll see what happens before we start to think about charging or releasing him." He would say that because he is well versed in the phenomenon mentioned earlier in this story: that whenever those magic words "A man is in custody helping the police with their enquiries . . ." are uttered by TV or radio newscasters, ninety-nine percent of people conclude that we have the right man. They will then be prepared to talk. They will be prepared to talk about a man *in custody* for such a crime as this, whereas they would not like to feel that they were being instrumental in putting him there. From which it is always possible that, once a suspect is "inside", the thin web of suspicion on which he was arrested might yet become filled out into a net which will hold him and keep him.

At least we could not be accused of lacking optimism!

We ended that night by laying our plans for the next day, and our first consideration was the security of the operation. When we lifted our suspect we would have a great deal to do, and the last thing we wanted was to be impeded by the attentions of the news media. We therefore had to take account of the fact that Scotland Yard (at least in those days) was notorious for unauthorised leaks to crime reporters who swarmed the nearby pubs buying drinks for talkative detectives, and already there were rumblings that Ian Forbes was about to return to "reopen" the Cannock Chase Murder Investigations. So we would not operate from Cannock but from Stafford, ten miles away, and not even our families would know where we were until the first, crucial, twenty-four hours were past. What our families did not know, no amount of pressure from a horde of crime reporters could prise from them. We knew they would be trying. From breakfast time next day, for a period of some twelve hours, the front doors of Harry Bailey's home and mine were surrounded by reporters and TV crews, and our wives did not get a minute's peace, though they had no more idea than the reporters where we might be!

There would be a lot to be done once our man was in custody and we laid on teams of officers to do it. Such things as tracing and taking possession of his Austin Cambridge car, on the long shot that there might be scientific evidence forthcoming on the Christine

Darby murder; getting hold of his wife and testing the alibis that she had given him to at least one murder; tearing his flat apart in a search for something in the way of evidence; putting our key witnesses on standby for identification parades.

We drew up our lists of officers and allocated a long list of tasks, then sent out orders for them to report early at the Cannock Incident Room and await further word from us.

Everything scheduled for the next day would have to be done simultaneously and quickly, because when you have a man in custody on the kind of "wing and a prayer" on which we would be flying, time is your enemy and the law and the lawyers will soon be at your throat. There would not be a second to lose.

And then the suspect himself. How should he be tackled? We were obviously, I told Forbes, dealing with a man of exceptionally strong will, who was as cool as a cucumber under the stress of arrest and interrogation; who, through his past dealings with the police, was brim-full of confidence as to the strength of his alibis and the lack of evidence against him, and who on past form would not even tell us the time of day, but would immediately demand to see his solicitor. Furthermore, his influence over his wife was total, and it would have been fatal to our prospects if he were allowed any chance to exercise it before we had had the opportunity to have a long talk with her.

"Shock tactics," I suggested. "Total surprise and the greatest possible psychological impact."

"So," asked Forbes, "how do you think he should be picked up?"

I gave him a sheet of paper containing details of the suspect's normal daily movement pattern, which had been discreetly observed by Norman Williams's men over several days. "Seven o'clock in the morning, I'd say. There's only one way out of the garage block at his flats, and it brings him into Blue Lane. The next step was that we could have a uniformed PC stop him on the pretext of checking his driving licence. He'll be bang on time. If we pick him up there there'll be no chance of losing him, and we'll have him separated from his wife. She won't have a clue where he is and we can have a go at her in peace."

"And if he asks for his solicitor," said Forbes, "I'll tell him he can't have one for the time being." He turned to Harry Bailey: "I'll take the responsibility of delaying notification until I'm satisfied that it won't interfere with our enquiries. There's a lot to be done once he's inside and we can't afford to risk any leak, even through a solicitor, that might get in the way of our lads out there."

For a minute or two he resumed his study of the man's daily movements. Then he turned back to me. "Right," he said. "You'll do the arrest, and you'll bring him straight up the motorway to Stafford Borough Police Station. You can sling him in the cells and have him put on the [detention] sheet. Harry and I will be there and the four of us [he included Tom Parry, his Sergeant] will take it from there."

If Ian Forbes had put a thousand pounds in my hand at that moment he could not have delighted me more. If we were right, the most wanted man in Britain was about to be arrested after the biggest murder hunt in history and I was to do it. I was to do what, to my immediate knowledge, at least three hundred men would have given their right arms for.

"Right, sir," I said, without a trace of emotion. "Seven o'clock sharp. I'll give Norman Williams a ring at Walsall and lay it on with him. Then I'll be off for a kip and an early start."

"Fancy a pint first?" asked the Yard man.

"You bet!" answered the happiest man in the world.

*   *   *

At a quarter to seven on the dark, cold but dry morning of Friday the 15th of November, 1968, Detective Inspector Norman Williams, Detective Constable Con Joseph and I stood in the charge room of Walsall Police Station drinking mugs of tea. In fifteen minutes our suspect should be leaving his flat, getting into his car and driving into Blue Lane, where a PC in a "Panda" car was already waiting to stop him and ask him for his driving licence. It would be as simple as that. The car would be stopped, a word would be spoken into the microphone of the PC's personal radio and Norman, Con and I would be there almost before he got the words out of his mouth.

A uniformed sergeant handed me the Daily Sketch from a bundle of morning papers that had just been delivered. "Like a read of the paper while you're waiting, sir?" he said cheerily.

"Thanks," I said. I unfolded the newspaper, and to my horror saw, right in the centre of the front page, a bold headline declaring that Detective Chief Superintendent Ian Forbes, the officer in charge of the Cannock Chase Murder Hunt, had returned to Staffordshire, and an arrest seemed imminent.

"Jesus wept!" I shouted, flourishing the newspaper in front of Norman Williams. "Look what they've done to us. The bloody place [New Scotland Yard] leaks like a sieve. I only hope to God he doesn't take the Sketch, or we're sunk. He'll never stir if he reads this!"

Our man was obviously not a Daily Sketch reader (no other paper carried the news), for right on the dot of seven the charge office sergeant shouted, "They've got him," and we ran to my car and sped to Blue Lane. Actually, "sped" is not the right word for seven o'clock in the morning is the thick of the West Midlands rush hour. On top of this, when we tried to get into Blue Lane we saw at a glance that my Walsall Police hosts had gone right over the top in their anxiety to help me. There was not one, but three "Panda" cars, and there was utter chaos there. All to ask a man for his driving licence!

Stationary double-decker buses, lorries, cars and motor bikes were packed as thick as flies on both sides of what had turned into a three-car police road-block, and as I drove across the lawns of the Regent House tower block to get around the snarl-up I could just make out the cream-coloured top of our suspect's green-bodied Ford Corsair car and a policeman's flat cap.

Fate plays some wonderful tricks. My car was identical to his in every respect but registration number, and I jokingly remarked to Norman Williams, as we sprinted across the grass from where I had parked it, that at least our man would feel at home while we were driving him up the M.6!

My quarry was sitting in his driving-seat when we arrived. I thanked the PC and took his place by the door. I snatched the keys from the ignition switch and took a firm grip of his right shoulder.

"I'm Detective Chief Inspector Molloy from Cannock CID," I said grimly. "I am detaining you in connection with the murder of Christine Anne Darby at Cannock on the 19th of August, 1967. You are not obliged to say anything unless you wish to do so, but whatever you say will be taken down in writing and may be given in evidence."

It was intended to have an impact on him and it did. My abiding memory is of the expression on his face. He looked, as I put it later, as if the sky had fallen on him. He sat open-mouthed for a second or two, then said quietly "Oh God! Is it my wife?"

What he meant by that remark would be the subject of considerable debate, but what mattered now was to get him out of there. He seemed to be paralysed: he just looked up at me. "Get out of this bloody car," I said quietly. He still did not move. "Get out," I said again. "Do as I tell you. Get out or I'll drag you out." Still he did not move. So I took him by the shoulders and heaved him out, Norman Williams taking his other arm as we waltzed him across the road and the lawns to where my car was parked.

We went up the M.6 at around eighty miles an hour, me driving, Norman, Con and our prisoner in the back, and with not a word uttered all the way.

The Station Sergeant in the Borough Police Station at Stafford had almost as big a shock as my prisoner as we burst through the swing doors and I pushed him to the counter. The sergeant knew me. "I've arrested this man for the murder of Christine Darby," I told him. "His name is Raymond Leslie Morris. Put him on a charge sheet, sarge, and I'll put him in a cell. He'll be interviewed by Mr. Forbes and Mr. Bailey later this morning."

The prisoner's particulars were entered on the sheet and we took him into a cell, where, as was required in instructions relating to the handling of prisoners, I removed whatever property he had in his possession, as well as such things as belt and shoelaces with which he might be tempted to do himself some harm. It must have been like the crack of doom when I slammed the door on him.

I handed his personal property to the sergeant, who listed it on the charge sheet and turned it around for me to countersign. "Now, sergeant," I said, "this man must have no contact with anyone without the knowledge of Mr. Forbes and Mr. Bailey. If he rings the cell bell for attention, speak to him through the hatch, find out what he wants and let me know. We'll be in the canteen until Mr. Forbes and Mr. Bailey get here. You'll give the prisoner his breakfast, of course, and have a look at him through the peep-hole every ten minutes or so, but he must have no other contact without Mr. Forbes and Mr. Bailey being told first."

"Very good, sir," said the sergeant, and Norman Williams, Con Joseph and I went off for our breakfasts.

*   *   *

Ian Forbes's first meeting with Raymond Leslie Morris was a brief one. It lasted only seconds, and was more to get a look at his man and try to weigh him up than to question him. The time was five minutes to nine and he had been in custody for almost two hours. "My name is Forbes," said the Yard man. "Detective Chief Superintendent Ian Forbes. You may have heard of me."

"Yes."

"You will be detained here for the time being. We have certain enquiries to make."

The man just nodded, and what Forbes made of such a brief acquaintance was impossible to tell. "What do you think of him?" he asked me as we walked upstairs. "Think of him?" I echoed. "I'll tell you this sir, he's aged ten bloody years since Norman and I saw him a couple of hours ago!"

Word had already gone out to Cannock, though no one there had been told where we were. Norman Williams and Con Joseph had left us to join the men assigned to fetch in the suspect's wife and to take her to an unused police out-station where Forbes, Harry Bailey, Tom Parry and I would meet them, for this was likely to be the crux of our whole operation.

We got to Hednesford Police Station after lunch that day and the twenty-five year old wife was waiting for us. Only four years married, she was a very smart and good-looking girl, and during our preliminary chat none of us detected any kind of hardness. If anything, there was a certain naivety about her, but the initial questioning, conducted quietly and gently, did nothing to shake her story that she had been in her husband's company, well away from any murder or abduction scene, during the periods about which she had been questioned.

Before we got there, it had been decided that Ian Forbes and I would question the woman, and that if such tactics should be needed, we should play it "hard" and "soft". He, the squat, gruff and tough-looking boss of the investigation, would naturally play the "hard" man and I, the six-foot-three one who could look down menacingly on most people, would turn on my "soft" side. It was the old-fashioned, classic way of talking to criminals, a tactic not normally employed with witnesses, but since this was a particularly crucial aspect of our enquiry it seemed to call for special treatment.

But the best laid plans "gang aft agley" and what happened at Hednesford was shaped entirely by the way in which our interview with the wife developed. Far from being the hard man and frightening the life out of her, Forbes turned into the soul of kindness and gentleness. I knew at once that my role might also have to be reversed if his approach did not work.

Her husband was the Cannock Chase Murderer, Forbes told her quietly, and difficult as it would be for her to comprehend such bestial behaviour in one so close (she evidently adored him), she would one day have to come to terms with it. Could she have been mistaken? he asked her, seeking to give her a way of avoiding outright betrayal. No, she could not. Was it not possible that the passing of time had played tricks with her memory? No it was not. The police had visited them only a couple of weeks after the murder, and, like just about everybody else in Walsall at the time, they knew exactly where they had been on the day of Christine Darby's murder.

Nothing else worked either, and after keeping it up for three quarters of an hour or so, Forbes evidently decided that it was time to pass her over to me for a change of voice and manner. He got up, made some excuse and left the room.

But our intended roles had changed. *He* had been the nearest thing to a "soft man" anyone was likely to see in that room that day. Yet what room was there for the "hard" approach with which

I imagined I was now supposed to contrast his fatherly manner towards her? I was not sure what tactic I should adopt. We were dealing with a quiet, polite and obviously well-brought-up young woman and a harsh approach might be entirely out of place, whatever kind of a liar she might be. In the event, my attitude shaped itself.

Left alone with her (except for Sergeant Tom Parry) I leaned forward, and looked into her eyes. "You know," I said quietly, "you can forget your husband. My guess is that you'll never see him again. We say he's the Cannock Chase Murderer, so the way things are going his goose is cooked. He's finished, I'd say. He's a child killer, just like Ian Brady, we've no doubt about that. The only thing left for us to decide is whether or not you're another Myra Hindley."

She looked at me with a puzzled air. "You know who Myra Hindley is, don't you?" I asked, surprised that I had had to repeat the name.

She shook her head.

"You don't?" I asked incredulously. Trust me to find the only person in Great Britain who had never heard of Myra Hindley!

She shook her head again.

"The Moors Murders?"

"Oh yes, I've heard about the Moors Murders."

I then launched into such a graphic description of what Myra Hindley had done to little Leslie Anne Downey while Ian Brady was raping her and their tape-machine was recording the events in all their gory and sadistic horror, that Tom Parry changed colour and left the room. She began to weep quietly as I continued the dreadful tale . . . the first tears she had shed. She sobbed as I painted a lurid picture of poor Leslie Downey's death-throes, of the bestial things done to her, and of the child's pitiful cries for her mother.

For twenty minutes or so she sat, sobbing quietly, as I slowly drilled the picture into her, sparing not one drop of blood, not one stab of pain and not one despairing cry.

"Well?" I whispered at length, my hand on her shoulder as she wept for that poor child. "Are you a Myra Hindley?"

"No," she sobbed. "I'm not."

"Your husband didn't get home from work on time that Saturday afternoon, did he?"

I was about to repeat the question when she raised her tear-stained face, looked at me, and whispered, "No. He was late. He told me he had been detained at work with his boss. I was upset because we'd arranged to go shopping for my mother and we were late."

This was interviewing at its most delicate; the point which comes in many interviews when it feels almost like playing on a Stradivarius and one false note will shatter the precious instrument. Softly I asked her the crucial question: "So what you told the police was not true? Did you realise what you were saying to them, so close to the date of the murder?"

"What's your name?" she asked, though we had all introduced ourselves to her.

"Molloy. Detective Chief Inspector Pat Molloy."

"Mr. Molloy," she whispered, evidently beginning to collect herself, "I didn't lie. Honestly. He was there and he told the police and I just said yes when they asked me if I agreed. I didn't think it mattered. I didn't think he could . . ."

She put her face into her handkerchief again. One more whispered question: "Do you want to make another statement telling us what really happened that Saturday?".

My heart leaped when she looked up again and said "Yes." She paused. "Do you think I could have a cigarette, Mr. Molloy?"

"Yes," I said, and being a non-smoker left the room to get her one. Coming along the passage was Ian Forbes. "For God's sake don't go in yet," I pleaded. "She's going to make another statement. The alibi's busted. She wants a fag." Being the man and the detective he was, Forbes knew that this was no time for a change of voice and he pulled no rank on me, but hurried back along the passage and returned with cigarettes and matches.

I took them and made one more request before going back into the interview room: "Can somebody get me a typewriter and some statement forms?"

The typewriter was delivered, and I was typing the heading to Mrs. Morris's statement when the door opened again and Ian

Forbes came in. "How are you now, my dear?" he asked as he sat down alongside her.

Red-eyed and gripping her cigarette tightly, she said quietly, "I'm all right now, thank you Mr. Forbes."

I typed her statement. She had told the police that her husband had arrived home at about two o'clock on the afternoon of Saturday 19th August, 1967, but she now realised that "this could not have been so, but I was not telling lies." It could not have been so because, for all her uncertainty about the events of that day, she remembered clearly that her mother had asked her to get some cakes from Marks and Spencers in Walsall, which she had forgotten to get when they were out shopping together that morning. They had gone out almost as soon as he had returned home from work, and she had got the cakes, but only just in time, as the shop was about to close . . . a vital point indeed.

She remembered that as they drove through Walsall, the police were stopping cars and speaking to their drivers. This must have been between five and six o'clock, during the hue and cry following Christine Darby's abduction. On reflection, she said, she now felt that her husband had got home much later than she had first thought, and, having arranged to go to her parents' home, she remembered how close in time his arrival had been to the time of their departure for the shops.

She had honestly believed, she said, that what she told the police was true because she "trusted him implicitly." He and she had seen the TV news coverage of the abduction, including the fact that the police were appealing to people to fix in their minds their movements on that Saturday so that they would remember clearly when police officers came and asked them. Like just about everyone in Walsall that day, they discussed their movements, ". . . and this was the conclusion we came to."

It was an important, perhaps the vital, step forward, but we still had to keep it in its proper perspective, because, when all was said and done, she could not be compelled to give evidence against her husband. True, in a case of this nature (assaulting or murdering a child) she could do so voluntarily, but my impression of her that afternoon was that she was more likely not to be prepared to go through the ordeal of giving evidence for the prosecution.

Her retraction of the alibi still had the makings of a breakthrough, and we immediately despatched Norman Williams to see her parents in an effort to establish just what time she and her husband had arrived at their home, so that we might reconstruct their movements by working back from that.

In the event, Norman Williams found a pair of willing recipients to suggestions that their son-in-law was the Cannock Chase Murderer. Indeed, we had to look at their evidence with intense care, so as to be sure to separate facts from emotional imaginings. Fortunately the facts were clear enough. What they remembered (*and they had not been questioned about this before*) was that the mother-in-law was in something of a panic about the cakes, and was watching the clock anxiously as the time drew near for Marks and Spencers to close. They arrived at about five o'clock, she said, and he "*said that he had got home from work late because his boss had been on his holiday and he had stayed behind to give him particulars of what had gone on whilst he had been away.*"

This was really getting places, especially when the suspect's father-in-law told Norman Williams that the couple had arrived "sometime after the football results on the television." That is always a good pointer to what happens on a Saturday afternoon in the Midlands in the football season—the first day of that season, incidentally—and the time he was talking about was verified by an engineer at the ITV studios in Birmingham: The "Results Roundup" programme had begun at five o'clock and ended at eleven minutes and thirty-five seconds after five . . . as precisely as that!

So far so good, but there was more. At around 8 pm on the day of the murder, after having gone back home for tea, the suspect and his wife had returned to the in-laws' home and all four had gone out for the evening to a hotel in Stone, some thirty miles north of Walsall. The venue had been our suspect's choice, and their thirty-mile drive took them up the A.34 and across Cannock Chase! To see if there was any police activity there? Who could know? It is very possible, because, according to them, as he drove past the Pottal

Pool crossroads and his mother-in-law made a remark about the missing child in Walsall and the awful possibility that her body might end up on Cannock Chase, Raymond Morris replied that the police would never catch him . . . he was too clever for them! And our minds went back to the finding of the murdered girl's knickers and shoes—thrown at the roadside just as if her killer had left them to taunt us. But that was speculation, not evidence.

So our man had not arrived home at two o'clock, as he and his wife had always said, but well after four . . . *leaving him ample time to kidnap Christine Darby, take her to Cannock Chase and murder her,* and to return home just in time to dash to Marks and Spencers to collect his mother-in-law's cakes and deliver them to her at sometime after five eleven and thirty-five seconds.

It was the breakthrough we had been praying for, but, as Winston Churchill might have said, it was only the end of the beginning, not yet the beginning of the end. We might prove that he had had the opportunity for the killing, but we still had to put him in Camden Street and on Cannock Chase at the times when Christine Darby was abducted and murdered. There was plenty being done by the forty-strong team of men scattered far and wide over the Midlands which might yet produce breakthroughs in that direction, and there was still the possibility that Victor Whitehouse and other witnesses might identify him as the man they had seen on the Chase. Who could tell? Perhaps the suspect himself might have something to say. It was a possibility which it was our duty to explore.

*   *   *

The interview that evening was one of the oddest I have ever had to record. It began at five minutes past seven, when Ian Forbes asked his first question, after administering the official caution that the suspect was not obliged to answer unless he wished to do so. "You have been detained here in connection with the murder of Christine Darby," he said. "Do you wish to say anything to me about it?"

As I wrote Forbes's question in shorthand, there followed the first of the series of long silences on the part of the prisoner which were to punctuate this strange, long-drawn-out interrogation. Forbes repeated his question, with the same result, and then tried to pierce the man's silence by asking him the direct question, "Do you admit or deny being responsible?"

The suspect sat looking away from his questioner. It was a long time before he answered. "Whatever I say will make no difference," he said eventually, with a far-away expression on his now haggard face.

"What exactly do you mean by that?"

"I'm finished."

"What do you mean?"

"It doesn't make any difference now."

"I find it difficult to understand what you are trying to say."

Morris sat in silence, staring to the front, for several long minutes.

Then the Yard man leaned forward, resting his elbows on the table, his brow deepening to a puzzled frown. "Are you feeling all right? Do you understand what I'm saying to you and the situation you are in?"

His man merely nodded several times and remained silent.

The questionnaire completed at his home on the first car-check visit by the police was produced and Forbes went through it with him. He showed him his signature at the bottom and then put to him a series of questions on his movements after leaving work that Saturday, the answers to which he carefully compared with those on the form. They were consistent throughout. "Do you still say that is what you did that afternoon?" asked Forbes at length.

"Oh what's the use of all this?" he said dismissively, arousing himself for the first time from his lethargy. "What's the use?"

Forbes again expressed concern at his suspect's demeanour and offered him a cup of tea or a glass of water, which he declined. Then he went over the house-to-house questionnaire in the same way. Again the suspect's answers were consistent with those given many months earlier, but we noted with some satisfaction that they included a restatement of his route home from work (avoiding Camden Street), which was very significantly different from that he had driven the Walsall police officers on the day of his arrest for the attempted abduction, and which he had confirmed to Jim Speight on the same day as his usual route home. We would make a liar of him yet, we thought.

The formalities over, Forbes bowled his first bouncer: "You are not telling me the truth," he said. "*I have interviewed your wife and she tells me that you did not arrive home that afternoon until at least 4.30 p.m.*"

There was no need this time to wonder what was going through the man's mind, for he bent his head into his cupped hands and muttered, "Oh God! Oh God! She wouldn't. She wouldn't," shaking his head in what one could only assume was despair.

There was a knock on the door, and Norman Williams motioned to Forbes to come out of the room. We knew what that was for. We had been waiting anxiously for the result of his interviews with the in-laws and we soon knew that he had come back with statements from them.

Forbes came back in and resumed his seat, arranging the newly arrived papers in front of him in a manner calculated to set his man wondering and, we hoped, worrying. He did not immediately raise the matter of the in-laws, but went back to the house-to-house questionnaire and took up the matter of Morris's route home from work. The suspect confirmed that the route he had given on the questionnaire was the correct one, the one he always took, but Forbes shot back at him: "That isn't right, is it?"

"What do you mean? I always come that way."

Forbes leaned forward again, his eyes boring into his adversary's. "I don't think so," he said quietly. "Didn't you give that route because it takes you away from Caldmore Green?"

We were back to the silences again.

"Well, what have you to say about that?"

"That's the way I went home that afternoon."

"Just over a week ago you were seen over another matter. Didn't you say then that every time you come from work at Oldbury you travel to West Bromwich, Tamebridge, over the Broadway into Caldmore Green, turn down Corporation Street, turning right at the lights at Wednesbury Road?"

The question met with silence. No wonder, for here were the horns of his dilemma. In his anxiety to show that he had not been anywhere near Bridgeman Street on the night before Bonfire Night, he had had to give another route, *and that one took him right by the end of Camden Street, the route he had so strenuously avoided when interviewed by the police about the murder of Christine Darby*!

Now for the punch line. "Didn't you also say that on Saturdays you go to the car wash in St. Michael's Road?"

The suspect's silence denoted another smack in the face, because St. Michael's Road was just around the corner from Camden Street, and Saturday was the day on which Christine Darby had been abducted there! And he knew it, because Forbes never did get an answer to that question.

Timing it perfectly, for his man's eyes were still on the papers he had been shuffling after his last absence from the room, Forbes went out again, still without letting him know what fresh information he had received. I noted in my shorthand record that he was out for eight minutes.

He returned to throw the alibi-breaker: "I have just read a statement which was made by your wife's mother. She says that you and your wife arrived at her house in Beddows Road just before five o'clock that afternoon, and your mother-in-law says that you told her you had only just got home from work. What have you to say about that?"

This caused the longest silence of all. The man sat there, his round, somewhat protruding eyes staring into space, his whole manner suggesting that he had willed himself far away from us. After several minutes he moved, just slightly, dipping his head and creasing his brow into a thoughtful frown: "I thought you had retired, Mr. Forbes," he said, to everyone's astonishment.

"Well I haven't," snapped Forbes. "Let's keep to the point. I am still waiting for an explanation for the lies you told about that afternoon."

He received no answer, and after another spell of watching his man look silently to his front, he made as if to conclude the interview: "I am not going to ask you any more questions," he said, "but I propose to put you on an identification parade."

At last our man came to life. 'No! No! No!" he shouted. "I won't go on one. Nothing. Nothing will . . . you can't make me!"

Shorthand is perhaps the only written medium capable of recording emotion in a person's speech, as demonstrated in its incompleteness of sentences. All the same, I wrote in brackets at the end of this outburst "(agitated)".

"Why not?" asked Forbes.

He had got hold of himself again. "Mr. Forbes," he said sternly, "I think you are being a bit over-zealous in this case. You're trying to put a fitting end to an illustrious career."

I could not hold myself. "What?" I yelled, rising from my seat, putting my hands on the table and leaning across it towards him. "Pick on you out of the one-and-a-half million people we've interviewed? If we wanted to do that kind of thing, what better opportunity did we have than when that man Cartlidge picked up those two kids in Walsall a few months ago? Everybody had convicted him, even the BBC, and it cost them two hundred and fifty quid. Don't talk so daft!"

If nothing else, it brought the man down to earth again. He turned to the Yard man: "I apologise, Mr. Forbes. I shouldn't have said that. Your conduct towards me has been exemplary."

"What about this identification parade?" asked Forbes, unmoved by the commotion. "Why do you refuse?"

There was no answer. "I repeat, why do you refuse?"

The suspect was depressed again, back to his original state of near torpor. He answered quietly and despondently: "My whole life, my marriage, my job, my future. What does it matter now? I'm finished. There's nothing left for me now. It's the end."

"Once more," said Forbes, unimpressed. "Are you prepared to go on an identification parade?"

"No."

"I ask you again. Will you tell me why not?"

"I should have thought it was obvious. I've got everything to lose. If you feel as confident as you are making out, you'd better charge me and have done with it."

Despondent and despairing he might be, but our suspect knew the score. He had put his finger right on it. There was no more point in talking to him. When, as will inevitably happen sometime during an interview with a suspect against whom one has less evidence than one pretends, he spots the weakness through your need to get something from him, it is time to go. "You will be detained overnight here," Forbes told him, "and I urge you most strongly, in fairness to yourself, to reconsider going on a parade."

There was no reply. I finished my shorthand note, we rose from our seats, and the uniformed officer outside the door was called in to take the prisoner away.

*   *   *

The night ended (where else?) in the bar, where we counted up our pluses and minuses for that long day. The first question was, did we have enough to charge him with murdering Christine Darby? *The answer was that we had not.* We certainly had plenty in the way of *suspicion*, but we had not one scrap of *evidence* which would be accepted in court. Nor could we charge him with any of the other crimes, including the attempted abduction from the Bridgeman Street bonfire. Again, we had every reason to *suspect* him, but not one iota of proof.

True, we had made something of a breakthrough on the alibi for the Christine Darby murder, but even there our evidence was shaky to say the least. There was no sign yet that his wife would volunteer to give evidence against him, for whatever it might be worth even if she did.

We could prove he had had a grey-coloured Austin Cambridge car at the time. In fact our people had already taken possession of it and it was about to be examined by the forensic scientists, but our chances of getting any evidence from that were negligible after such a lapse of time.

His answers to Ian Forbes's questions had given us nothing at all on which to hang a charge, and though it was a very odd way for an innocent man to behave (he had neither admitted nor denied the killing), that was a matter of opinion and a defending barrister would see that it would get short shrift from a jury. What we *had* got from the interview was the lie about his usual route home from work. We could just about put him at the end of Camden Street at the material time, especially now that one of our teams had checked his clocking-off card at the factory, which showed he had left at 1.13 p.m. on the day of Christine Darby's abduction. Yet even that was no more than a step in the right direction.

No. It would all be down to identification. Unless we could get him identified we would have to release him. So now (somewhat grimly, I must admit) we weighed up our chances. We had at least five witnesses who might pick him out as the man seen in the forestry plantation, elsewhere on Cannock Chase and on the roads between there and Walsall. But he had consistently refused to stand on an identification parade, so what was to be done? Every course was fraught with danger, since the identification parade was the corner-stone of acceptable procedure so far as the courts were concerned and everything else was bound to result in a stormy reception from the defence. We discussed that particular problem at considerable length until . . .

"I'll show you what we'll do," said Forbes, putting down his double Chivas Regal on the bar. "We'll confront the bastard. We'll stand Victor Whitehouse in front of him and see if he recognises him as the man he saw in the forest!"

CHAPTER NINE

MISTER WHITEHOUSE, I PRESUME

I arrived home at around half past midnight after an eighteen and a half hour day, feeling that we could be within a hair's breadth of having enough to charge our suspect with murdering Christine Darby. Whether that meant we would eventually see him convicted was quite another matter, but I thought I had a right to feel pretty satisfied with our day's work whatever the future might hold.

My wife was waiting up for me with supper, as she always did when I was on a job like this, and in the usual way she sat up in bed alongside me, listening to my account of my day's work and sensing my whirring brain gradually run down, until I fell asleep.

Many of my colleagues have sworn that they have never discussed their work with their wives. They may have been speaking the truth, but I doubt it because no man under stress can keep it totally within himself and survive. I thank my lucky stars that at the end of a stressful day I had a wife who helped me unwind so completely as to clear all thought of work out of my mind and to enjoy a sound sleep before waking to face the next day with a fresh and receptive brain.

As we had anticipated, she had been besieged by press-men and TV crews for much of the day, as had Harry Bailey's wife in Stafford. By now she knew many of them and had kept them all supplied with tea throughout their unproductive vigil. Tomorrow, I told her, they would be out early, and I would have to be ready to make a flying start around the side streets in order to shake them off and get away to my still-secret (even from her!) destination.

I set my alarm clock for six o'clock and went to sleep at around two.

My first job in the morning was to collect Victor Whitehouse, our main identification witness, and take him to Stafford. I had arranged for one of my Cannock detectives to get to his house by half past six and tell him to stay in until I arrived, and then to come down and see me for further orders. This early start was necessary because it was Saturday, and Victor Whitehouse would be spending every waking hour walking across Cannock Chase. We dared not risk missing him on this day of all days.

At half past seven I was still waiting for my man, and when he arrived, breathless and full of apologies for having overslept, he told me he had not yet been to see Victor Whitehouse. I exploded with fury and he could not have forgotten that day in a hurry. But I had little time to spend on recrimination, so we got into my car and sped up to Hednesford.

"I'm sorry," said Victor's father, "you've just missed him . . . only by five minutes."

It was twenty minutes to eight. "What time do you expect him back?"

"Oh, it could be any time. He could be out all day."

My heart sank. "Where has he gone to?"

"For a walk on the Chase."

"Anywhere in particular? Anywhere I might drop on him?"

"Could be anywhere," said Whitehouse senior. "Anywhere at all. He walks everywhere, especially on a Saturday. Never know when we'll see him again."

My heart sank deeper as I saw catastrophe looming over us. Morris had been in custody for twenty-four hours, the press were baying at our doors, some lawyer or other would soon start sniffing around, and the laws governing the detention of suspects without charge would inevitably be loaded into the breach ready to shoot us down in flames if we could not get him before a court very soon. We could not put him before a court without a charge. That moment of truth known to every detective would soon be upon us; it would be "charge or release" time before we knew it. And our prime identification witness was somewhere out there, in that eighty-five square mile expanse of emptiness. I had to find him. But how? I knew Cannock Chase was there, and I knew all its boundaries, but for me to go onto it without a definite starting-point would be like trying to cross the Sahara Desert without a compass.

I had no choice but to be seen to be doing something, even if it was totally useless, so I dropped my Detective Constable at one entrance to the Chase and headed for another, randomly chosen, myself. We arranged to meet at the Pye Green television transmitter tower after an hour's search.

I drove, it seemed, miles along a dirt track in an empty world until I came to a cross-roads in a hollow. For a quarter of a mile in all directions the tracks climbed straight to the brow of a hill and disappeared over it. In the far distance plantations of fir trees ringed the horizon. I parked my car and walked along one of the tracks until it topped the hill and I could see it disappearing far into the distance. There was not a soul to be seen whichever way I looked. I returned to the cross-roads and did the same on another branch of the track, with the same result. And then a third, and then the fourth. I trudged wearily along the fourth track to the top of the brow, looked into the distance where the ribbon of earth disappeared into the forest, and thought I saw a human figure.

It was too far away to distinguish either its sex or the direction in which it was walking, and I strained my eyes under a shading hand to detect either. It walked towards me; it became a man, and, closer still, a tall man striding purposefully in my direction. I began walking to meet him, noting the detail as he neared. I did not know Victor Whitehouse. I had never met him. I was not even sure if this man looked like him, but he was the only one in sight and he might have seen someone on his travels. I still had my car over the hill if he could give me a hint of where I might go.

Now we were only yards apart, and I saw him looking at me as if ready to pass the time of day. What made me say it, I am not sure, except that I was reminded of the meeting of Stanley and Livingstone in the heart of darkest Africa. "Mr. Whitehouse, I presume?"

"Yes," he said.

I was stunned. The thought flashed through my mind: My God! With luck like this it's *got* to get better!

I could have hugged him, but I merely proferred a handshake. "I'm Detective Chief Inspector Molloy. You've probably heard we've arrested a man on suspicion of murdering Christine Darby."

He had.

"Well I've been sent to pick you up and take you to Stafford to meet Mr. Forbes. We want you to see if he's the man you saw by the car in the forestry on the day of the murder. It's a long time, I know, but we want you at least to try.''

He smiled. "Certainly. How are we to get there Mr. Molloy?"

"I have my car back there. I'll have you there in less than fifteen minutes."

*   *   *

It was at seven minutes past eleven that morning that Ian Forbes, Harry Bailey, Tom Parry and I entered the prisoner's cell to prepare him for his confrontation with Victor Whitehouse. I had my shorthand notebook out and I wrote down Forbes's first question: "You remember last night I told you I intended to place you on an identification parade and you refused? Have you thought it over during the night?"

He had, and his answer came across loud, clear and without hesitation: "In no circumstances will I go on a parade."

"Take him out," Forbes said to me.

I took him by the arm into the police station's prisoner exercise yard, an enclosed space, open to the sky but topped by bars to prevent escape. I guided him to the far wall and stood him against it. My abiding impression of that moment is of a man facing a firing squad! Haggard and red-eyed (I always said that that twenty-eight hours had aged him ten years), he waited unquestioningly for whatever might be in store for him. But he had only to wait the few seconds it took Ian Forbes to emerge from the building with Victor Whitehouse.

Whitehouse walked across the yard and stood facing the prisoner, some five or six paces away. "Have you seen that man before?" asked Forbes.

Victor Whitehouse was not a man for quick answers. He liked to think deeply about questions of any importance, and this was the most important question he was ever likely to be asked in his life. He thought long and hard, not taking his eyes off the prisoner for one second. Then he turned to look at Ian Forbes: "Yes," he said. "I'd say yes."

I took the prisoner, shaken but impassive, straight back to his cell, while Victor Whitehouse was taken away to make a written statement about the identification. In that statement he would enlarge on what he had said in the exercise yard, explaining that in saying he had seen Morris before he was referring to their encounter in Plantation 110 on Cannock Chase on the afternoon of Saturday 19th August, 1967, when he had seen him standing alongside that grey-coloured Austin A.55 Cambridge motor car.

The significance of Whitehouse's identification was that we now had sufficient to charge our man with Christine Darby's murder and to put him before the Magistrates. Still not enough to convict him, not by a long chalk, but a major step towards putting him in the prisoners' dock at the next Staffordshire Assizes. From now on, as every experienced detective could tell, there was always the chance that things really could get better. Or so we continued to hope.

*   *   *

Our prisoner learned what was to happen a couple of minutes before we left Stafford to take him to Cannock and charge him. When Forbes told him, and cautioned him again, he said "I think I would like to see a solicitor."

"We'll make arrangements straight away," said Forbes.

At 12.15 p.m. our small convoy swept along a prepared path through a vast crowd of people into the police station yard at Cannock, and the prisoner was hustled through the back door with a blanket over his head. The blanket was a necessary precaution because there was still the matter of trying to get several other witnesses to identify him, and we did not want to risk prejudicing that aspect of the case.

At exactly twenty minutes after twelve, he stood in the cell passage, faced by Harry Bailey and Ian Forbes. I walked in with the typed murder charge and stood for a second holding it out towards my two chiefs. Ian Forbes took it from my hand and stepped forward.

"Raymond Leslie Morris," he said, "I charge you that on or about the 19th of August, 1968, in the County of Stafford, you did murder Christine Ann Darby, contrary to the Common Law. He cautioned him yet again that he need not say anything unless he

Detective Constable Jim Speight hustles Raymond Morris into Cannock Magistrates' Court through an angry crowd. *Express & Star*

Ian Forbes questioned by the press outside Cannock Magistrates' Court (the author is standing in the back-ground, behind Forbes's right shoulder).
Express & Star

wished to do so and that whatever he said would be taken down in writing and might be given in evidence. A now broken-looking figure quietly answered, "Can you arrange for a solicitor?"

"Any particular one?"

He named the solicitor who had represented him at the ill-starred (for us, at least) identification parade in Walsall.

Morris's appearance before a specially convened magistrates' court in the building behind the police station precipitated a scene of crowd hysteria such as had never been seen there before. "They only needed the tree and the rope," I would say afterwards, "and we would have seen a better lynching that day than they ever had in Dodge City!"

It was as I have said: the fact that the police had arrested him and charged him with murdering Christine Darby was enough to satisfy the whole population of the West Midlands that our hunt had come to an end. Convincing a jury would be another matter entirely, but, legal presumptions of innocence or no, this court appearance lit the fuse for the biggest celebration in the West Midlands since VE Night!

In the Green Rock pub in Walsall late that night, for instance, there occurred one of the best illustrations I have ever known of the faith the people had in their police force. It was near to closing time, the pub was packed to the doors and there was only one topic on everyone's lips: "They've got the Cannock Chase Murderer! Haven't you heard it on the newsflash?"

What follows is not apocryphal; there is (or was) a telephone message record at Walsall Police Station to prove it. A little man, the worse for drink, was musing to himself rather than for the ears of others that perhaps the euphoria was a little premature. "How can they be so sure," he said into his half-filled pint glass, "that they've got the right man after all this time?"

Two much bigger men immediately put down their pints, grabbed him and threw him through a plate-glass window! I used to joke that we afterwards tried to trace them to get them on the trial jury, but it was a touching demonstration of faith in their police force all the same.

*   *   *

We celebrated ourselves, of course, as we felt entitled to after arresting the most wanted man in Britain. We sent messages to our outside enquiry teams telling them to interrupt their work at some convenient point and join us for a drink. There would be a tremendous amount of work to get through in the next few weeks, but for now we felt entitled to let our hair down, and few, I am sure, would have begrudged us our feeling of elation.

There was no shortage of people ready to join us, judging by the way they packed into our bar as soon as the brief court proceedings were over and the prisoner had been taken off to Winson Green Prison in Birmingham. It was a massive celebration, which began by my going up to the bar to buy a treble Chivas Regal for Ian Forbes and a very large gin and tonic for Harry Bailey. "Drink this," I said to Forbes. "And let me be the first to shake you by the hand. I can tell you now that I'd begun to doubt the sense of putting everything into that picture and that car, and I wasn't the only one by a long chalk. But you stuck to it, man, and you've been proved right. I want to be the first to congratulate you. Let's hope we can see it through to a finish. Cheers!"

My congratulations to Harry Bailey as I handed him his treble gin were for the lifting of the burden he had shouldered for three whole years, as Scotland Yard Murder Squad men had come and gone. As head of the County CID, his had been the continuous torment of seeing his police force stigmatised by failure, and I had personal knowledge of how he and his wife had felt under that burden of responsibility. "You must be feeling good now," I said, with masterly understatement. "Pat," he said, "nobody can know what this means to me."

Nothing more needed to be said; I raised my glass to the pair of them, took a large swallow from my pint of Guinness, smiled with my own inward satisfaction, and turned to join the wider celebration.

At some time or other that afternoon I bought drinks for two other men whose contribution to this day deserved special recognition . . . Detective Sergeant John Farrall and Detective Constable Jim Speight, who had carried the flag for us at Walsall and sparked off the revival of the almost moribund investigations.

Detective Sergeant John Farrall and Detective Constable Jim Speight, partners on the Staffs County Crime Squad.
Birmingham Post & Mail

They could so easily have marked their "Action" NFA in the light of the failure to identify Morris and his somewhat rapid release from custody, as had so many others in no less crucial circumstances, and we could so easily have lost him. Their instincts had served us well. If we managed to get Morris convicted of one or more of the Cannock Chase Murders there would be a certain amount of glory flying about, but it can often pass by those of lower rank and less prominent position, so I wanted to say my own thank you then, as we savoured our moment of at least partial success.

It would be about four o'clock that afternoon, when I was jammed in the crowd drinking yet another pint of Liffey Water, that I saw a uniformed PC struggling towards me from the door. It was PC Ray Watton, who I knew had taken Morris handcuffed to prison. "Excuse me sir," said Watton, handing me a small brown envelope. "The prison officers in reception found this round Morris's ankle when they searched him."

I took from the envelope a man's wrist watch with a metal expanding bracelet. "Around his ankle?"

"His ankle, sir. Can't think what he was doing with it round his ankle. Does it mean anything to you?"

"Not a thing," I said, realising that I had blundered in searching my prisoner the previous morning in the Stafford Police Station cell. Searching is a strictly regulated matter and I had told men off more than once for leaving bits of property in the possession of prisoners in their cells. The wrist-watch was the item most often missed, but that was no excuse for a man in my position and of my experience. I turned to Ian Forbes and Harry Bailey, and held out the wrist-watch. "Look at this. They found it around Morris's ankle when he arrived in prison reception. What do you make of it?"

"Beats me," said Forbes. "Perhaps he's nicked it."

"Yes," I said. "Perhaps he has." I thanked Ray Watton, told him to make a note in his pocket-book about the affair, put the watch in my pocket and thought no more about it until the following day.

My wife had joined me in the bar during the afternoon, and had later left me to see to the children. I next saw her at around eight o'clock when I walked across to my home to tell her that the Chief Constable had invited us all (her included) up to headquarters, where he wished to buy us a celebratory drink. "Is Anne in bed?" I asked.

"She is. She's awake, I think, and I know she wants to see you."

My daughter (the youngest of our three children) was not much older than Christine Darby when she had been so cruelly taken and killed, and she had lived, as had all the children in the Midlands, in the climate of fear created by that and the earlier crimes. She was awake as I went into her room, knelt by her bed and kissed her. She looked up at me with her wide, hazel eyes, and gripped my hands in hers. "Well," I said. "You haven't seen me for a long time, have you?"

"No, Dad."

"There's no need for you to be afraid any more of going out to the shop or walking along to school on your own, is there?"

"No, Dad".

"Do you know why?"

"Yes," she said, smiling. "Because you've caught him, Dad, haven't you?"

"Yes," I said, fighting back tears that might have owed as much to the Guinness as to the emotion of the moment. On the other hand, even the most hardened policeman is entitled to feel emotional now and then, even though he must keep it strictly out of his work. I had a quotation from Dr. Samuel Johnson framed on my office wall, and I commended it to my men as illustrating the need for them not to allow their emotions to cloud their judgements: "If a madman were to walk into this room with a stick in his hand, no doubt we should pity the state of his mind. But our primary consideration would be for our own safety. We should knock him down first and pity him afterwards!"

That is precisely the outlook with which I had approached the arrest of a man I believed to be a child murderer. Not one jot of emotion had entered my head throughout our preparations for the day of his arrest and throughout the day itself. Every judgement, every action, was as unclouded as all my experience had taught me it should be. Had it been otherwise, I could have made mistakes that might have put at risk the whole purpose of the exercise . . . the finding of the truth about the murder of Christine Darby and the punishing of the person who was guilty of it.

Anger, elation, sadness and all the rest were emotions I was entitled to entertain as much as any man, but I was a policeman first and foremost. Only after his first appearance in court could I allow myself the luxury of elation; only now could I wipe away the tear that was not only for my daughter, but also for those poor little mites who had met their end on Cannock Chase.

I kissed her goodnight and headed back to the celebrations.

*   *   *

Harry Bailey, Ian Forbes, Tom Parry and I met next morning in an upstairs room in Stafford Police Station, to enter into our notebooks my transcription of my shorthand notes of the interviews with Raymond Morris. We were nursing massive hangovers, and found it impossible to concentrate, especially with our ears being assailed by the (at other times) beautiful peals of bells from nearby St. Margaret's Church. "I wish somebody would shut off those ******* bells," muttered Forbes, head down, into the desk.

"What bells?" asked Harry Bailey as brightly as his own condition allowed.

"It's no bloody use," said Forbes. "It'll have to wait until tomorrow. Pat's got the original notes, so that's catered for. Writing them into our books is only a formality. It'll do tomorrow." Wearily, he pushed himself up from his chair, stumped across the office and reached his battered grey trilby from the hat stand. "Call our driver," he said. "We'll go and have a chat with Christine's mum. She'll want to see us."

We drove down the M.6 to Walsall and through the streets of terraced houses to Camden Street, where our Jaguar stopped outside number 80. Ian Forbes knocked on the door and it opened. Standing there was seventy-two year old Henrietta Darby, the dead girl's grandmother. She recognised the Yard man instantly, threw her arms around him and sobbed uncontrollably. Her daughter, Christine's mother, joined in the emotional reunion and hugged him too. Was I doomed to spend this whole bloody week-end shedding tears? I turned away and dabbed at my eyes with a carefully concealed handkerchief.

"Thank God, Mr. Forbes," said the grandmother. "Is it him? Are you sure it's him?"

"It's him, me dear," said Forbes gently, an arm around each woman's shoulder as they sobbed with the relief of his assurance. They wanted to give us a cup of tea, but tea was the last thing men in our condition wanted at a time like that. We declined, and when the moment was decent, made our parting.

"Where to, sir?" asked our driver, PC Martin Woollaston.

"I don't know about you lot," said Forbes, "but I need a ******* drink. Stafford. Yes, Stafford. To the 'Why Not', Martin."

We were there just after opening time . . . at around twelve fifteen . . . and we tucked into the hair of the dogs that had bitten us. Half an hour later we were in the throes of a revival of our spirits, when in walked Detective Sergeant John Farrall, the senior of the two I had sent down to Walsall to hold a watching brief when Morris was arrested.

"Hello, John," I said. "What are you having?"

"Nothing just now, sir. I wonder if you can pop along the road with me and have a look at something interesting we've found."

I immediately took my leave of the others, and went with him to the small police station (normally out of use) which he and Jim Speight had taken over for sorting out all the bits and pieces they had taken from Morris's flat in Walsall. They and the forensic scientists had taken the flat apart: floor boards, panels, built-in furniture, everything that might have provided a hiding place had been ripped out, so much so that in the end the place looked as if it had been bombed.

From a pile of photographic equipment and materials, John Farrall picked up a Kodak photographic paper box. "We found this in the room he uses as his studio. It was sealed, and if you look here you'll see that it says it is only to be opened in a darkened room. That would keep his wife out of it, I suppose. Look what we found inside it." He removed a number of photographic negatives and nine half-plate-sized black and white prints.

John Farrall and Jim Speight had struck gold! The photographs were of a little girl of (we guessed) eight or nine years of age in various stages of dress and undress, with one which showed a man's penis by the child's vagina in close-up. Though no attempt had been made to hide the girl's face, the man indecently assaulting her appeared only in the close-up of his private parts (he was wearing trousers) and (in another of the photographs) of his hands, which, again in close-up, could be seen pulling aside the child's labia to expose her vaginal orifice.

Two of the photographs at least had obviously been taken by a camera fitted with a time switch, of which there was more than one among Morris's equipment.

I needed no telling who the man in the photographs was, for when I reached inside my pocket and withdrew the wrist-watch found around Morris's ankle at Winson Green Prison, the answer stared us in the face. That watch was on the left wrist of the hands interfering with the little girl's private parts!

Farrall and Speight were astounded. "Christ, sir!" exclaimed Farrall. "Where the hell did you get that?"

"Easy," I laughed. "It was around Morris's ankle when they searched him at Winson Green yesterday."

Whatever else had been going through the man's mind during those long hours in his Stafford cell, he had certainly remembered these pictures and the incriminating watch around his wrist. Had I done my job properly and removed it from his wrist, this stroke of good fortune could never have come our way. Life has a funny way of working out sometimes. Hasn't it?

*   *   *

When Monday morning came, we were called to Force Headquarters to attend a press conference called by the Chief Constable. A large number of reporters filled the room, while camera lighting blinded and cooked us as we sat at a table . . . the Chief Constable, his assistants, and the four of us. That we were still suffering the effects of a hectic week-end was evident from the press photograph which is still one of my prized possessions, though our four sets of closed eyes and our appearance of being asleep were ascribed at the time to the effect of the TV lighting.

It was a euphoric press conference . . . rather too euphoric, I felt . . . and I shuddered slightly at the implications in some of the questions and answers that we had already convicted Raymond Leslie Morris, not only of killing Christine Darby (which was the only charge he so far faced), but of being responsible for all the others. I seem to remember much talk about "The Cannock Chase Killer". That Morris might well have done the lot was obviously at the forefront of our minds, but whatever anyone might have been thinking we could never afford to abandon the "open mind" stance which is so essential in detective work.

A similar press conference held after the arrest of the so-called "Yorkshire Ripper" brought down a chorus of protest on the head of the Chief Constable of West Yorkshire. Perhaps the spokesmen

The post-arrest press conference at Police HQ
(L to R: Harry Bailey, Chief Constable Rees, Ian Forbes, Tom Parry,
ACC Stanley Bailey, ACC Barry Pain and the author)
Birmingham Post & Mail

at ours did not quite overstep the mark, though they seemed to me to get mighty close to it. Perhaps we were just lucky.

Pleased to see it over, we got into our cars and headed back to Cannock, calling at Hednesford Police Station to take a look at Morris's grey Austin A.55 car, which the boys had brought in for scientific examination. It was a strange feeling to stand in front of the car that every policeman in the British Isles had been looking for for fifteen months. Thirty-five thousand of them were recorded in our index, along with detailed questionnaires from every owner, and here, at last, was the only one that mattered. If only it could have spoken to us.

At Cannock, we got down to our work with a will, our first job being to get those interviews into our official pocket-books.

We also had to assess our situation, not only in relation to the murder with which Morris had been charged (and it must be borne in mind that we could still not count his wife among our witnesses for the prosecution), but also in relation to other matters, such as the attempted abduction from the Bridgeman Street bonfire. We dearly wanted to be able to charge Morris with that.

429 LOP was the number remembered—erroneously—by Wendy Lane as the green and cream-coloured Ford Corsair was driven away by the would-be abductor. The Walsall police had done a permutation of the figures 4, 2 and 9, placing the letters LOP both before and after them, producing twelve variations, one of which was 492 LOP (Morris's car). But that permutation would not have stood a chance in court, which is why the West Midlands Police report on the affair had stated that ". . . *there would appear to be insufficient evidence to obtain a conviction against Morris for any offence disclosed by his conduct in Bridgeman Street."* Quite so. A defending barrister would have driven a horse and cart through that permutation. Were there not 999 registration numbers ending with the letters LOP? Could not Wendy Lane have got one or more of the figures wrong? Worse still (and this would *really* have killed it), could she not have got a letter or two wrong as well?

It would have to be the numbers. "Go through the whole one thousand, nine hundred and ninety-eight," I had told Detective Sergeant Cyril Hurmson and his partner, Detective Constable Eric James, "and see what it throws up." They did, and what they delivered to me within just a few days gave us the charge we were looking for. To begin with, the Ford Motor Company had told them that the registration series *beginning* with the letters LOP had been exhausted before the first Corsair was produced. That eliminated one half of our problem. Then the officers went to the reverse order and found that, of the 999 cars so registered, only twenty-six were Ford Corsairs. Of those, only one was of a two-tone green and cream colour. *And that belonged to Raymond Leslie Morris!*

But good police work goes even further than that: every one of the owners of the other twenty-five Corsairs was interviewed and made a statement proving his whereabouts on the night before Bonfire Night in 1968. Not one of them was within fifty miles of Walsall, leaving in splendid isolation in Cyril Hurmson's "LOP Enquiry" the man we could now charge with attempted child abduction, even without his being identified by the victim or the witness.

Another obvious target for our enquiries was the little girl in the photographs found in Morris's flat. She turned out to be his wife's niece, who lived in Wales and had spent a few days at the flat, first in the summer of 1967, a month before Christine Darby's death, and again in the summer of 1968, in a holiday that included the anniversary of the murder. The girl was not seven or eight, as we had thought, but only five years of age. Here again things got better.

On her return home from the first visit, the child had complained to her mother of soreness around her private parts. Some signs of tenderness were found and, later, there was bleeding from a small tear. There were also some unaccountable marks on her abdomen, but eventually everything returned to normal and no more was thought about it. A year later, though, when Raymond Morris and his wife (the child's aunt) came to collect her for another trip to Walsall, the child began screaming and crying in the most distressful way, but her mother thought it no more than an upset at leaving home. When she returned, this time too she complained of soreness about the private parts, but the redness and tenderness soon cleared up and, again, her mother thought no more about it.

Everything fell into place when the shocked mother saw her child in Raymond Morris's nine indecent photographs. The dress she was wearing in the photographs was one she had had for her fourth birthday, and she had worn it on both visits, but a petticoat underneath had been bought in Walsall during the second visit. The photographs could therefore be dated to within a couple of days in August, 1968.

The child was, of course, too young either to make a statement or give evidence, so we would have to prove the case by other means, since we could expect no help from her assailant. There were three possible points of proof: first that the photographs had been taken in the flat (no trouble at all, given the childish pencil marks scrawled on the wall by the bed, and the identification of the bed quilt), second that the man whose penis could be seen against the child's vagina was Morris (no trouble either, since we had his trousers), and third, that the man whose hands were to be seen interfering with the child's private parts was Morris too. Here we were faced

The bedroom, with its childish scribbles on the wall, where Morris indecently assaulted and photographed his wife's five year old niece.

Staffs Police

with something of a dilemma. At a conference in the office of the Director of Public Prosecutions in London, about a week later, we discussed the question with the DPP's man dealing with our case.

"What we could do with," he said, "is a comparison photograph, showing side by side the indecent photograph and one with Morris's hands, with those same small scars on the knuckles, in the same position and wearing his watch."

"No trouble at all," I said. "I can fix that when he next comes back before the magistrates."

"But what if he refuses?"

"Then I'd do it by force."

"But you've no right to. It would amount to an assault."

"So let him prosecute me. We'd have our evidence!"

We all laughed, and passed on to the next item under discussion. The DPP's man, it seemed, was prepared to leave the matter to me.

In the event, I got our comparison photographs, but to my eternal regret Morris was completely passive and I was denied the opportunity to "assault" him.

By mid-December we were in a position where Ian Forbes could put three further charges to Morris . . . two of indecently assaulting his wife's five-year-old niece (one for each visit to his home), and the other of attempting to abduct the ten-year-old in Walsall on the night before Bonfire Night. To both charges, Morris, heeding the inevitable advice of his solicitor that he need say nothing, answered, "No."

*   *   *

Any murder file represents a tremendous amount of paper-work for the arresting officer and his staff, but putting this one together was a huge task. Ian Forbes and I (at the typewriter again) did the report to the DPP and thereafter I worked closely with the Director's man in putting together the thick bundles of witness statements, documentary exhibits and photographs, and tying up the loose ends he pointed out to me in the telephone calls he made

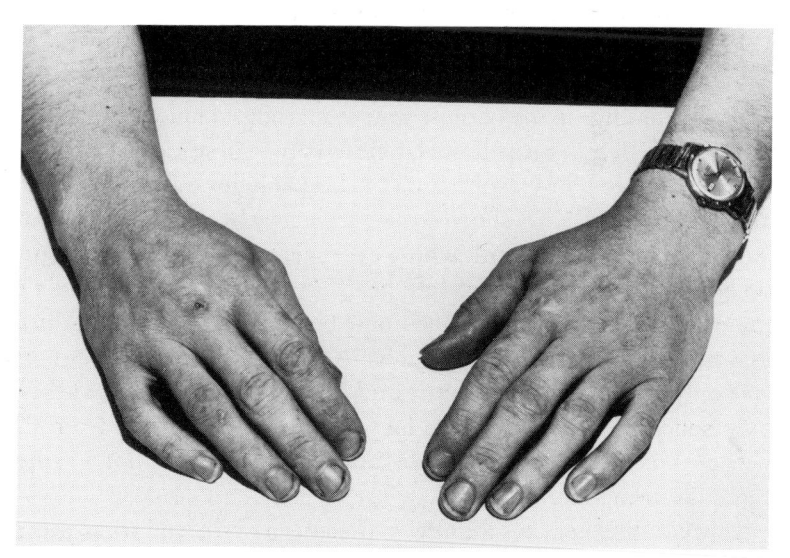

Morris's hands, with the incriminating wrist watch.   *Staffs. Police*

several times a day. Even so, we found ourselves in a position by the 7th of January, 1969, (only seven weeks after the arrest) to take Morris before the Cannock Magistrates and ask them to commit him for trial.

Under a procedure introduced by Act of Parliament only a year before, the old style Committal Proceedings (a laborious process involving many days of hearing evidence and reducing it to writing) had been superseded by what was known as the "Paper Committal", in which the proceedings could be reduced to a matter of minutes by the service and acceptance of prosecution witnesses' written statements. There could, however, still be a mixture of the two where the defence wished to examine witnesses (as, for example, where they wished to submit that there was no case to answer), or the prosecution wished to test one or more of their witnesses before putting them before the higher Court.

In this case, the attendance in person of five prosecution witnesses was at the request of the prosecution, so that they could be tested. And the chief of them was the defendant's wife, Carol Morris, who, for some reason we were not to know until several months later, had now totally abandoned her husband and was insistent upon giving evidence against him.

Mr. John Leck of the DPP's staff addressed the magistrates on behalf of the prosecution, taking them through every step of the case by reference to the witness statements placed before them, and calling the "live" witnesses as their evidence became relevant.

All eyes were on Carol Morris, who gave her evidence quietly and calmly, yet plainly showed the hurt it gave her. She did not once look towards her husband, whose eyes seemed to be trying to burn their way into the side of her head. As expected, she told the magistrates that he had arrived home between four and four-thirty and said his boss had kept him at work after finishing time. But this was only the magistrates' court and Morris was represented there by a solicitor. She still had to face his Queen's Counsel from the witness box in a Court of Assize, and she would find that a rather more daunting experience.

It was at this hearing that the prosecution first aired what was to become one of the major arguments of its case, namely that the highly damaging photographs of Morris's niece should be exhibited at the murder trial. In other words, the four charges should not be tried separately by separate juries. If they were, then only the jury trying the indecent assault charges would see the photographs.

The prosecution wanted one trial of all the charges before one jury, since, it was claimed, all the facts were so interlinked that it would be a nonsense to separate them. One did not have to be very learned in the law to guess that the defence would fight this submission tooth and nail on the grounds that the photographs would be unduly prejudicial to the defendant and would almost certainly lead to a wrongful conviction for murder. In other words, the murder case should be tried entirely on its own merits and not be influenced by those highly prejudicial photographs. If anything worried us about this case, it was this. To have a good chance of convicting Morris, we just had to have those four charges tried together.

So Mr. Leck made the same point before the magistrates as would be hammered by Crown Counsel before the Assize Judge: it was a question of *identity*. In looking for the man who murdered Christine Darby the police were looking for a man who had certain abnormal tendencies, as well as certain facial and physical features. Since abnormal tendencies are as much a part of a man's description as the nose on his face or the colour of his eyes, they, too, ought to be admissible as evidence tending to prove the identity of the murderer.

What were those abnormal tendencies? They were, first, to take away in his car, when he was alone, little girls whom he did not know by telling them a false story that would lure them in; second, having taken away the little girl, he would sexually interfere with her with his hands in the area of her private parts; thirdly, in doing this to little girls he had a tendency to lay them on their backs with their lower parts bared, their knees upraised and apart and their private parts fully exposed. Since all these points of identification were so interlinked, it was patently logical that all four charges should be tried together.

The magistrates must have thanked their lucky stars that they did not have to deal with that conundrum, which promised to make this case a *cause célèbre* in anybody's terms by taking the argument about the admissibility of the photographs at the murder trial to the highest appeal courts in the land! It was their simple duty to decide whether or not the prosecution had made out a *prima facie* case for trial at the Assizes, and this, they said, had been done.

Raymond Leslie Morris was committed to the next Staffordshire Assizes to be tried on four charges: of murder, of attempting by force to take away a child with intent to deprive her father of possession, and of indecently assaulting his wife's niece on each of her two visits to Walsall.

CHAPTER TEN

ALL IN THE GAME

There was an awe-inspiring majesty about a Court of Assize which its successor, the Crown Court, has not quite managed to preserve. For eight hundred years, Judges had travelled England and Wales on their Circuits, carrying and proclaiming in every County Town their Sovereign's Commission of Oyer, Terminer and General Gaol Delivery, with all the attendant ceremonial that such a majestic progress demanded. Met at the County boundary (nowadays the railway station) by the Sovereign's representative, the Lord Lieutenant, the Judge would be escorted to his lodgings and thence to the Shire Hall in a procession of trumpeters, javelin men, Yeomanry Cavalry, policemen and civic dignitaries. His arrival at the Shire Hall would be heralded by a trumpet fanfare and his entrance into his court from the door behind his judge's chair would be greeted by the respectful bows of bewigged barristers and court officials. He was the personification of Her Majesty's Justice, and he received no less homage and respect than would the Sovereign herself.

It was no less awe-inspiring to walk into that court, to step into the witness box, to be the focus of every eye, and to come under the scrutiny and questioning of the most learned legal minds that could be brought to bear on the matter in hand . . . the verbal battle between those who accused a man of a crime and those charged with his defence. For seven hundred years in such majestic surroundings, the arbiters in that battle (so far as the facts of the case were concerned) have been the "twelve good men [and now women] and true" who make up the jury, while "My Lord, the Queen's Justice", has presided over it all as the interpreter of the law, the jury's mentor, and the dispenser of justice to those found guilty.

To a policeman, the witness box of a Court of Assize was his supreme testing-ground (as is the Crown Court to-day), the place where his professional ability and integrity are put to their sternest test and where he can be made or broken. Strangely enough, most policemen never go near the place in their whole careers, and many of those who do go basically by choice, having chosen, or been chosen, to be detectives. In one way it can be seen as a form of masochism, but so can motor car racing or aerobatics, each of which carries its own thrill and the practitioners of which would themselves confess to loving its element of danger.

Ask a detective why he has spurned promotion to remain in his present department and rank, as I eventually did, and among his reasons will undoubtedly be the fact that it would have removed him from the arena of a Crown Court witness box, crossing swords with defending counsel and winning the duel. Masochism it may be, but it is an experience which only those who have been there can understand.

It is in the nature of a criminal trial that, when all else fails, the defence will turn its wrath on the police officer and try to destroy his evidence in the eyes of the Judge and jury. If, *in extremis*, this means trying to destroy his character as well, then so be it. What matters to the lawyer is securing his client's acquittal, and many inexperienced observers have wondered at times who it was that was on trial. To an experienced police officer, though, it is "all in the game", and he develops a skin thick enough to make it relatively painless. Others—particularly young officers—can find it a frightening and distressing experience, as they are called liars, bullies and violent thugs, while the real liar, bully and violent thug stands in the prisoner's dock, immaculate in new suit, shirt and tie, butter melting in his mouth, his long list of criminal convictions hidden from the jury unless and until they pronounce him guilty. "Mud sticks", the young officer will feel, however untrue the allegations thrown at him in cross-examination, and I have seen many of them come out of the witness box like wrung-out dish cloths, certain that their careers are in ruins, not yet wise in the ways of the game others of us laughingly call justice.

As to the equality of the contest, one only needs to know for the purpose of this story that the defence goes into court with every word of the prosecution evidence in its possession. Nothing can be introduced into that trial on behalf of the prosecution without first being put into writing and served on the defence in good time before the witness is called to give evidence. As for the case to be put for the

All in the Game 211

defence, the prosecution can only guess. There is no reciprocal arrangement. The case for the defence will become apparent only when the accused man is called into the witness box to give evidence on his own behalf. The prosecution then has only the length of time left to the end of the trial to find evidence to rebut any surprise element of the defence, whereas the defence will have had months to put together its case against every element of the evidence served on it by the prosecution.

So here we were, on a bitterly cold, snow-swept February day (the 10th), with all the hustle and bustle of an assembling Court of Assize going on around us and the trial about to open, guessing like mad as to what might be waiting for us. All we knew was that Raymond Leslie Morris was going to plead not guilty to the murder and the attempted abduction, and that, if the defence had its way, the jury empanelled to try him on those charges would not be allowed to know that he was prepared to admit, and plead guilty to, the indecent assaults shown in those damning photographs. That,

The queue forms in the snow outside the Shire Hall in Stafford for the opening of the trial. *Express & Star*

too, would be all in the game, for we knew that his defence counsel intended challenging in the strongest possible way the prosecution's submission that everything should go into one trial . . . the photographs, the evidence for the attempted abduction and the evidence for the murder of Christine Darby. We could, therefore, write off at least one half day of the trial for a start, and whatever might happen in the days that followed, that opening skirmish would be the hardest fought of the lot.

If Morris intended pleading not guilty to the murder, how would he fight it? Almost certainly he would rely on his alibi, and his wife and in-laws would undoubtedly come under severe cross-examination for their second thoughts on the matter.

He would claim to have been somewhere else at the time. If he had been somewhere else, Victor Whitehouse's identification of him must be mistaken. Furthermore, Whitehouse was the only one of a number of possible identification witnesses who had been given the opportunity of seeing Morris and trying to identify him. What would happen to the others when they stood in the witness box and tried to identify him in the prisoner's dock was patently obvious: accusations against them would range from the mistaken to (as occasion might demand) the nothing short of criminal.

There would also be questions of Ian Forbes and myself (we were the only ones to be called in reference to the interrogations) as to why no identification parades had been held. Identification was crucial to our case and we could confidently expect to be put through the mill if only on that account.

What of the rest of our evidence? Every experienced police officer preparing to go into the witness box in a contested case will give some time immediately before-hand to working out every possible line of attack, for he will be a principal target. Our interviews with Morris would come under very close scrutiny and it was highly likely that I would be challenged at the outset on the accuracy of my notes. My shorthand speed was an adequate 100 words per minute, a speed I had checked on the night before the trial in an hour's dictation exercise with my wife. Anyone who wished to ask his Lordship if I could be tested in court as to my shorthand speed was now welcome to do so.

Morris's somewhat strange demeanour and his equally strange answers to the questions put to him at Stafford would also come under scrutiny. After all, he had neither admitted nor denied the murder at any stage of our questioning. What he had said could only be described as vague and ambiguous, and if ambiguous it was open to interpretation. If there were inaccuracies in the record of the interviews that would give the defence even more room to manoeuvre, so I could reasonably anticipate a pretty strong attack on either my capability as a shorthand-writer or my truthfulness as a witness on oath. To one well-practised in the witness box in nearly nineteen years of police service, the latter would come as no surprise whatever.

I always told my men that by intelligent anticipation one could forecast ninety-nine percent of cross-examination, and if only one percent of what was to come was unexpected and unprepared for, one's experience and witness-box skills could handle it. Woe betide him who does not prepare in that way. I have seen some pretty sorry sights emerge from the ordeal and some careers ruined as a result, so whatever might befall us during this trial, none of us would be found unprepared. It had been my job to see that every other police officer giving evidence in the case had prepared himself.

We had prepared as well as we could; we had anticipated what we hoped would turn out to be ninety-nine percent of what would be thrown at us in there, and we could only wait and see what unforeseen slings and arrows would assail us when the time came.

There is one other matter which needs to be understood if one is to share a police officer's perception of a criminal trial he has instigated: he will not be allowed in court from the moment the jury is called to be sworn, until he himself is called in to give evidence.

It is a cause of frustration one never quite gets used to, no matter how long one serves in the force nor how often one attends court, that he who has put so much into finding the witnesses, securing their evidence, arresting the suspect, preparing the papers for the prosecution and serving it all on the defence, will never hear those witnesses give evidence if the plea is Not Guilty. How their spoken evidence compares with their written statements, how convincing or unconvincing they are in giving it, how they stand up to the novel ordeal of hostile cross-examination, will never be seen by the one who has nursed the case from its conception to its birth in court. He will, of course, pick up what he can from newspaper and TV reports and from what he is told by others who *were* in court, but when it comes to the turn of the police officers in the case to give evidence, he will certainly not have the latter facility, for he and any of those present in court who communicate to him what was said or asked of his partner, would, quite properly, be in serious contempt of court, if not actually accused of conspiring to pervert the course of justice.

Thus, when the time came for Forbes and me to give our evidence, neither of us would be allowed to leave the court-room after stepping from the witness box, in case he should speak to the other about the evidence he had given. If, by some quirk of the court timetable, one of us should give evidence before lunch and the other afterwards, we would have to ensure that we did not use the same restaurant, for if we were merely observed together we could be sure of being called before the Judge and ordered to account to him for the fact.

I (or Forbes, if it were the other way around) would go into the witness box knowing nothing whatever of what had been put to my colleague in cross-examination by the defence. It is perfectly logical, of course, for if defending counsel could open up a division between us, he would be well on his way to discrediting our evidence altogether.

*   *   *

The anticipated legal battle over the question of one trial or separate trials began as soon as Morris had made his pleas of Not Guilty, and, though none of this part of the proceedings was allowed to be heard by the jury or reported in the news-media, at least we who would eventually be barred from court were permitted to sit in and listen.

In many ways it was a somewhat arcane debate, involving legal precedents and questions as to when the value of some piece of evidence or other was over-ridden by its prejudicial nature, and the Judge listened to the ninety-minute submission by the defence QC with little comment, as he did to that of the QC representing the Crown. Each submission having been made, the arguments followed, with the Judge putting in his own points for one side and the other.

The prosecution's case was exactly the same as that put to the magistrates: that unusual tendencies were as much a part of a man's description as any of his physical features, and that since identification was a crucial issue in the case, every possible point of identification should be considered. The indecent photographs, the method of enticing little girls into his car, the way in which both Christine Darby and the child in the photographs had been indecently handled, and the identical nature of Morris's alibi to each of the allegations of abduction and attempted abduction were pointed to as "unusual tendencies", or "propensities" as they were called.

It was all summed up neatly in Crown counsel's statement that the accused "had a perverted lust which is found only in a small percentage of the population." Some have limps, some have brightly coloured red hair, some stutter. What counsel for the prosecution was saying was that Morris's perverted lust was just as much a part of his identifiable make-up as any of those physical peculiarities. The more features identified in the man one is seeking, the more one reduces the proportion of the population likely to possess them all. In Morris, so the prosecution hoped to prove, one could find all the main characteristics possessed by the Cannock Chase Killer, and so small was the number of men in the population of whom that could be said, that the finger of guilt must, in the end, be pointed at him.

Naturally the defence totally rejected this argument, but defending counsel laid even more stress on the gravely prejudicial effect which the indecent photographs would have on the jury. Show them these pictures, he said, and they are likely to convict him of the murder whatever weakness they might otherwise have found in the prosecution's case.

That they were gravely prejudicial, the Judge entirely agreed. He had, he said, to take every possible care over the interests of the accused in this regard. But he had also to take into account the interests of justice, and in balancing the two he came down in favour of the latter. One jury would try all three indictments (the indecent assault alleged to have been committed on the child's first visit to Walsall was "left on the file" on the orders of the Judge), and would consider all the evidence, including the indecent photographs. They would, of course, have the benefit of the Judge's guidance on the danger of allowing themselves to be prejudiced by them.

An almost audible sigh of relief went up from the side of the small court-room where we were gathered. We had scored a significant hit with the prosecution's first salvo. There was still a very long way to go, but at least the murder jury would see everything we felt they should, though what they would make of it all was no more predictable than is the outcome of any trial by jury, no matter how strong the case for the prosecution. But at least we had struck a telling blow and felt happier about our prospects for the coming battle.

The Clerk of the Court then stood, picked a small card from a cloth bag and called out a name. The Jury was being called. It was time for us to leave the room.

*　　　*　　　*

The afternoon of that first day was taken up with Crown counsel's opening speech, in which he gave the jury a very detailed account of the evidence that would be called before them, either verbally from the witness box or by the reading of witnesses' statements, according to what might or might not be challenged by the defence. In the course of his speech, he handed the jury all the photographs that would be referred to during the trial, including the incriminating photographs found in the accused man's flat.

There was time for only one witness that day . . . Detective Chief Inspector Bob Stewart, the man whose team had plotted the massive car check on our vast map of Cannock Chase. For the purposes of this case, though, he was simply proving times and distances by reference to another large map, on which were plotted in coloured ribbon the various routes it was possible to take from Morris's place of work to the two abduction scenes (Camden Street and Bridgeman Street), to and from Cannock Chase, and to his home. The argument about the timings and routes he could have taken from his work-place to his home would be an intense one, for if the jury accepted that Morris had lied to the police about them it would represent one more nail in the coffin of his case. They would assume very considerable significance when the jury was considering the question of whether or not he had had the opportunity to commit the crimes.

Young Nicholas Baldry, the boy who had seen Christine Darby taken away and who had raised the alarm, was called on the second day of the trial. Nine years old, bright and alert, he gave his evidence clearly and succinctly. It was, of course, fifteen months since (at the age of seven) he had first told his story, and, since these were the days before the courts began to allow witnesses to refresh their memories from statements made long before, it was to be expected that he would have forgotten something. In fact he had forgotten almost everything but the bare fact that Christine had got into a car and that it had gone not towards Caldmore Green (which the driver had enquired about) but Corporation Street. He remembered neither the abductor's pronunciation of Caldmore as "Carmer" nor anything of note about his car. It was only natural, then, that defence counsel should seize on the fact that he had been shown an Austin A.55 Cambridge and had said that the only resemblance between that and the one he had seen in Camden Street was its light grey colour.

"It was a different shape?" asked the QC.

"Yes, sir."

"It wasn't the same size either?"

"No, sir."

The expected challenges to our identification witnesses also materialised early in the trial. As always in such cases, much depends on the quality of the witnesses: some are brief and straightforward about what they do remember and what they do not; others will give an impression of anxiety to help and will embellish their recollections with details which anyone with experience of the frailty of human memory will know are wide open to challenge.

Such was the case with the lady who claimed to have seen a man driving a car, with a little girl in the front passenger seat, from the direction of Walsall towards Cannock, on the A.34, at around the time that Christine Darby's abductor would have been there. She was torn to pieces in cross-examination. She was presented with a copy of a local newspaper bearing Christine's photograph and was accused of knowing the facts first and remembering her sighting of the car afterwards. If she was as certain of what she had seen as she had claimed to be, why had she not come forward immediately the picture was published? Why had it taken her twenty-three days to tell the police about it?

The more she tried to explain, the more deeply she enmeshed herself in the barrister's net and the more she piled up contradictory statements which were thrown back in her face. To the question on the apparent delay in coming forward to the police, she said she was "positive I rang the police on Monday or Tuesday. That would be before it [Christine's picture] was published."

This time our "System" did work . . . for the defence. A hurried search through the files produced the actual telephone message, *and it was dated seventeen days after Christine Darby's abduction!* "It was utterly wrong of you to lend your oath that you had telephoned the police with the information before seeing this picture on August 23rd, wasn't it?" asked the defending QC.

"I said I couldn't be certain," she replied lamely.

The Judge leaned forward towards the witness box: "You have told the jury on oath that before you saw this photo you had phoned the police. Their records show it was about ten days later."

"I must be mistaken, then."

She was finished.

The poor woman had had trouble even earlier in her evidence, when she had also been the first recipient of the boomerang we had all been expecting to fly into that courtroom at sometime during the trial. Our Identikit picture and the artist's impression which had adorned posters sent all over the world were produced at the request of the defence. Was there any resemblance at all between the man in the picture and the man in the prisoners' dock, the QC asked her.

"His cheeks are more sunken," she replied, "and so are his eyes. He was more round-faced at the time." She could say that again!

That picture was to be put to every identification witness we called, and defending counsel would lose no opportunity to point out that in the fifteen months between the publication of the picture and the arrest of Raymond Morris, *not one witness had suggested him as one who bore a likeness to it*!

Our first identification witness of any substance had sunk without trace, and that lady will remember her one hour and twenty-five minutes ordeal for the rest of her life. She had begun with unbounded confidence that she could positively identify both driver and child on the basis of a fleeting glimpse of a passing car; she stepped from the witness box a very shaken woman. Having volunteered, in all honesty, to help the police solve a monstrous crime, she had failed dismally by allowing her untrained memory to play tricks with her, and she had paid dearly for it.

If there was much more of this we could be finished. This was only the first taste of what our identification witnesses were going to face from this very skilful defending cross-examiner, and identification was the whole foundation of our case. Moreover, the discrediting of this witness was the cause of a phenomenon which stalked this trial in a way I had never seen before and have not experienced since. Perhaps it was the intense interest of press and public, or, more likely, the importance of a guilty verdict to the force, whose image was thought by some to have suffered from the long delay in discovering a suspect and bringing him to trial. Whatever the reason, as soon as that poor woman stepped from the witness box an air of deep gloom and pessimism swept through the court room and into the lobbies and passages. Some said it emanated from the Chief Constable, who, they suggested, had walked out of court saying we were finished. Others thought it started with the press corps. A sense of defeatism seemed suddenly to envelope all who were hoping to see Raymond Morris convicted.

Police officers who are familiar with criminal trials understand the peaks and troughs of a prosecution case and will be relatively unaffected by them. Some witnesses come through brilliantly (the *demeanour* of a witness is almost as important as the quality of his or her evidence) while others give the worst possible impression. Yet others will forget their lines and prove impervious to gentle prompting, or be forced in cross-examination to go back on vital parts of their evidence. No one who has spent a substantial part of his life preparing and taking cases through the criminal courts expects everything to go smoothly and every witness to "come up to proof" as the jargon has it. So, though we will be as prone as anyone else to moments of elation and disappointment, we know better than to allow ourselves to be infected by the pessimism of the less experienced; we know that all that really matters in the end is the judge's summing up and the verdict of the jury.

The most common cause of depression is the moment at which the defence case begins to unfold. Even police officers who have abounding confidence in their case have been known to be cast into the depths of depression by the imagined weaknesses revealed by that first exposition of the defence.

It is, then, common to find optimism and pessimism alternating during the course of a trial; yet the Cannock Chase Murder trial stands out. But if people susceptible to that kind of thing were cast into gloom by this first hiccup in the prosecution case, it was nothing to what they would experience later on!

*   *   *

The second day of the trial saw the calling of our two most crucial identification witnesses. If we were to lose these, we could pack up our papers and go home, so we knew for sure that the big guns would be turned on them when they came to be cross-examined. We knew, too, that they would be hit hardest of all with the Identikit pictures. After all it was they who had helped the police to produce them!

Victor Whitehouse was the first, and his evidence came out exactly as he had dictated it and in exactly the style one would expect of a steady, reliable man. Then came the cross-examination, and within seconds the defending QC was asking the man in the dock to stand up so that the witness and everyone else could have a good look at him. Whitehouse was then handed the Identikit and

Raymond Leslie Morris and the police Identikit picture compared.
Staffs. Police

the coloured picture. "Neither identikit picture bears very much resemblance to him, does it?" asked the QC.

Whitehouse thought they did.

And we knew they did, because we had acquired a photograph of Morris taken around 1967 and placed it alongside the pictorial impressions of the man our two main identification witnesses had seen on Cannock Chase. We could now see how well the two compared—*provided that they were not both viewed as photographs.*

Quite independently, Victor Whitehouse and Mrs. Rawlings had helped build up the Identikit picture and artist's impression to reproduce the six facial features each had remembered clearly—the hair line, the slightly-creased forehead, the eyebrows, the rather prominent cheek-bones, the somewhat bulbous nose, and the fact that the teeth showed slightly through one side of the mouth. *They were all present in Morris.* If the jury's attention could be drawn to that and away from the idea that the Identikit and the artist's picture were to be regarded as having the comprehensive accuracy of photographs, the intentions of the witnesses would be clear to them and our objective achieved. But no defence counsel worth his salt would allow that kind of thing, and Morris's QC had soon embarked on his "smoke-screen" strategy. It would be up to our man, and, we hoped, the Judge, to guide the jury through the smoke.

After being challenged on the pictorial identification, this witness was taken, as expected, through the reasons why he had failed to come forward in response to the police appeal and had had to be found by the police through a sighting of his car on Cannock Chase.

Quite right, said Whitehouse, and the reason for that was . . . exactly what he had told the police and which had satisfied them.

After that it was simply a matter of whether or not he could have been mistaken in identifying Morris. Our witness could not be shaken, even slightly. His last words were delivered quietly yet confidently: "I think if I had happened to see Mr. Morris walking down a street on the other side, any time after August, 1967, I would have been able to pick him out."

Our second crucial identificaion witness, Mrs. Mary Rawlings, was a lady of supreme yet well-reined confidence, who knew what she had seen near to the forestry plantation on Cannock Chase and could not be deflected from it. Her evidence was simple. She had seen the car coming and had moved her dog out of its way. "I usually expect a driver to thank me if I have held a dog out of his way," she said primly. "This one did not." Asked if she could identify the driver of the car in court, she said in a matter-of-fact way and with no hint of drama, "Definitely. He is the gentleman sitting in the dock."

As to the pictures she had helped to build up she simply answered, "I think they are a pretty fair likeness of Mr. Morris."

Victor Whitehouse and Mrs. Rawlings were the kind of witnesses who are the bane of the cross-examining barrister. Their evidence was simple and to the point, delivered without histrionics or embellishment, utterly incapable of being dented by the cross-examiner's tricks. If, in the end, the jury were to decide that they had been mistaken, it would be an honest mistake and they would have done their best.

As things were, though, we had passed one of our more important landmarks, and the way was open for Harry Bailey to end that day with evidence of the finding of Christine Darby's body, and for others to deal with the identification of the articles of clothing.

*   *   *

There could be no doubt about what was to be the highlight of this trial so far as the crowded press-bench was concerned. The evidence of Mrs. Carol Morris was awaited with eager anticipation, and on the day she was to be called a queue of around a hundred people still waiting outside the Shire Hall, when the last public seat had been taken, learned that their wait had been in vain.

Her evidence was preceded by that of the police officers who had gone to her home on the September car-check and, later, on the Walsall house-to-house enquiry, and had filled in questionnaires on the interviews. It was all very straightforward. Whenever Morris had given an answer he had simply turned to his wife and asked her to confirm it, which she had done quite readily.

There was one slight and interesting hitch in this phase of the evidence, when Detective Constable Brian Porter told the court that on his visit with DC Walker to the flat (on the house-to-house enquiry) Morris had expressed some annoyance at being interviewed so often. Morris, said Nicholls, had remarked that he knew they had a job to do and that since he had no children of his own he could not know what it was like to lose a lovely daughter.

In fact Morris did have children, by his previous marriage, so that remark was immediately and understandably pounced on by the defending QC: "I must suggest to you quite categorically that that was not said."

DC Nicholls simply replied, "That was said, sir."

An innocent enough remark, we thought, to draw such a sharp riposte. What else had they up their sleeve for when we got into the box?

*   *   *

Now it was time to see what the accused man's wife was made of and the court was packed almost to suffocation. It was standing room only and from what little I could see through the door panes at the back of the court (I could hear nothing, of course), everyone was leaning forward, straining their ears, to catch every quiet word of her evidence. I could see her in the witness box, a pale-faced, slight figure now, as compared with the bonny girl we had questioned three months before at Hednesford Police Station.

The story she told was in line with that in the statements she had made to us, and a big plus came early on, when she told the court what her husband had often said about his routes to and from work. *They were not the routes he had given to the police.* They had been the ones that would not take him near Camden Street (from where Christine Darby was abducted) or Caldmore Green (where we had been able to prove he had his car washed after work on most Saturdays). But that, said Carol Morris, was the route—the most direct route—he had always told her he took, both to and from work.

That, we hoped, established her husband's normal Saturday practice: leaving the factory at about one o'clock (his boss would be producing his works time-cards) and getting home at around two, via the end of Camden Street, after a call at the car-wash in Caldmore (or Carmer) Green.

The big question was why she had given the police an incorrect time for her husband's arrival home on the Saturday of Christine Darby's murder.

"Your husband gave an account of his movements?" asked Counsel for the Prosecution.

"Yes."

"This was the same or virtually the same as what he had given on the two previous occasions?"

"Yes, I was there. I was not merely keeping quiet while he said it. I agreed with what he said."

"So that on three separate occasions you were not only allowing to be said in your presence, but confirming, that he was shopping with you?"

"I said that because I didn't think he was the person responsible."

"You believed at the time that what you were telling the police officers was the truth?"

"I believed it because I couldn't believe he was the person connected."

The Judge did not quite understand. Could she put it any more clearly?

"Yes," said Mrs. Morris. "I knew that what I was saying was untrue, but I couldn't believe it."

She still was not making herself very clear, so defending counsel intervened to tell the Judge that it was his intention, when he came to cross-examine her, to suggest that whatever may have been the reason, on each of the three occasions she had believed that what she was telling the police was the truth."

Said Carol Morris: "I believed that at the time."

What her evidence seemed to amount to in relation to her corroboration of her husband's false accounts of his movements and timing on that day was that while she knew that the police were being misled, it had never once occurred to her that there might be any sinister reason for it, even though she knew he had been late home. She told the court what her husband's excuse had been for getting home late: that he had had to stay behind to tell his boss what had been happening during his absence on holiday.

Why, she was asked time after time, both in her examination by Crown counsel and in cross-examination, had she said something was so which was not so? Her answers ranged from "Because he came home and ate his meal and acted normally without any sign of emotion or anything," to "Because he was so normal," and "Because I did not think he was the person concerned."

By the end of her main evidence, Carol Morris had made two points vital to the prosecution case: first, her husband had not arrived home until four to four-thirty that Saturday afternoon (the jury would hear that that was at least three hours after he had clocked off and left work, giving him plenty of time to abduct Christine Darby from Camden Street and take her up to Cannock Chase); second, he had walked into the house on the night before bonfire night (after the attempted child abduction in Bridgeman Street, three minutes' drive away) when Coronation Street was coming to an end on the television, and the jury would hear a television engineer time the ending of the programme at 7.56 and 42 seconds precisely. If the defence could not demolish this, we would at least have established that Morris had had the opportunity to commit both crimes.

Her cross-examination inevitably turned into a very rough ride indeed. It was hard and unremitting, and the defending QC put every ounce of his considerable skill into trying to destroy her. But there comes a time in any cross-examination when the argument reduces to perhaps one small point, in this case why the police had been misled in the first place and what had caused her to change her mind fifteen months later. After that the questioning becomes repetitious and it is time to call a halt. When this eventually happened with Mrs. Morris—after five gruelling hours in the witness box—the defending barrister sat down and counsel for the Crown stood up again to re-examine, that is to ask questions on anything new raised in cross-examination or any ambiguities brought out in it.

"You have told my learned friend about what you told the police . . . and said that you agreed with what your husband had said because you could not believe he was responsible, and then you said you believed you were telling the police the truth?"

"Yes," said Mrs. Morris. "Because I did not think he was connected with it."

"At that time did you know what time he really had got home?"

"Yes, he really got back at 4.30 p.m."

"When you left your mother's house you said you had left a steak in the oven. How long would it take for you to get back to your home?"

"About ten minutes."

"When you got home how long was it before you had your meal?"

"It was practically ready when we got home."

"Do you happen to know what time it was when you had your meal?"

"It was between six and seven o'clock. It was between eight and eight-thirty when we went out with my parents that night."

A good point on which to end her evidence, thought counsel for the Crown, to the mystification of many observers. It was a tried and tested court-room ploy, based on the premise that the last thing heard is the best remembered, and the jury were to hear from the next witness (her mother) that the steak in the oven was the reason they had had to hurry home for their evening meal, thus fixing the time in the mother's memory. This was going to be very important indeed, because prosecuting counsel had told the jury in his opening speech that the Crown did not intend to rely on the evidence of Mrs. Morris (who was not obliged to give evidence against her husband anyway) to prove the timing of the events of that Saturday. For that, said counsel, he would be relying on Mrs. Morris's parents, and the supporting evidence of a television engineer.

*   *   *

We were worried about Morris's mother-in-law. I had formed the opinion that she hated him, and hate is perhaps the most dangerous of all emotions in a witness. She had seemed to me to be relishing the possibility of his being convicted of killing Christine Darby, and she could easily spoil her performance, just as our earlier identification witness had spoiled hers, by trying too hard. But she didn't. She and her husband gave their evidence in a very matter-of-fact way and, as good witnesses should, kept it short, unembellished and very much to the point. She told of the Marks and Spencers cakes and of Morris's remarks, on arriving at her home, that he had had to stay behind at work to bring his boss up to date on what had been happening during his absence on holiday. She told how it was after five when they got to her house, and how her daughter had had to hurry home to get the steak out of the oven.

She, too, came under the hammer of a tough cross-examination. "You are completely wrong," said defending counsel of her recollection of the various times she had mentioned.

"I'm sorry, I am not," she replied coolly. "It was after five o'clock when they came to my house."

Interrupting to comment on her reference to the football results on television, the Judge remarked that "anyone who takes the least interest in life [he was a keen football supporter himself!] knows the football results don't come on the telly until five o'clock."

Everyone nodded sagely.

Her husband was if anything even better, for he gave defending counsel less material for cross-examination. He had been asleep, he said, and some hidden body-clock had told him it was time for the football results and he woke up and switched on the TV for the ITV sports results. They were coming to an end, he said, when in walked his daughter and her husband. He could not say for sure what time that would be . . . perhaps around five fifteen.

The court did not need to rely on him for the timing of this visit. Our ITV engineer could tell them that the programme ended at precisely five eleven and thirty-five seconds.

Keeping everything in its proper order and context, Morris's boss was the next witness, producing his clocking-off card and proving that he had clocked off at 1.13 p.m. that day and at 7.10 pm on the night of the attempted abduction in Bridgeman Street. There was some inconclusive questioning about whether Morris had left the factory immediately, but nothing emerged from this witness's evidence to give the prosecution any real cause for concern.

The jury now knew what time Morris had clocked off from work, and the programme timings of the ITV football results and the Coronation Street serial on television. Now they had simply to decide whether Carol Morris and her parents had been telling the truth, and if they decided they had, they would then have to ask themselves what Morris had been doing for the nearly four hours before he got home on the afternoon of Christine Darby's murder, and why it had taken him forty-five minutes to do a twenty-seven minute journey on the night of the attempted abduction.

Next came Dr. Alan Usher, the Home Office Pathologist, who gave the court the grisly details of his examination of Christine Darby's body, first in the forest and later in the mortuary. I was not in court to see it but those who were told me there were a few pale faces on the jury benches as they listened, particularly when they heard him describe the gaping and "violent" tears in her vagina and then saw them depicted in those awful photographs of the child, taken as she lay under the broken ferns and as she was examined naked on the mortuary slab. It is a cliché, but that poor child lying in the forest, really did resemble the proverbial broken doll, damaged beyond repair and thrown away without a second thought.

Dr. Usher was pressed by the defence as to whether the assailant was likely to have got blood on his clothing. It was a very difficult question to answer, since all depended on the position he had adopted in committing the assault (most likely with his fingers) and whether his clothing would necessarily come close to the wound. But it was a good straw for the defence to clutch at, for the prosecution case did not contain one iota of scientific evidence.

Since the pathologist had conceded that the assailant's clothing *could* have been bloodstained, the defence asked for Mrs. Morris to be recalled, to make the point that she had never seen any bloodstained clothing on her husband. So what? we thought, with all of fifteen months between the murder and the arrest. But it was not we who mattered; it was the jury, and who could know what miracles they might expect from the world of forensic science, and how adversely they might react if they failed to materialise?

Our tyre expert expressed his opinion on the tyre tracks found in the forest "ride": they were of the pattern (he could not identify the make) and wheel-base of a family car. More importantly for our case, only that vehicle had gone down the "ride" (to the spot opposite where the body was found), and whether it had been driven forwards or in reverse, it had come back up without being turned around. The jury had already heard Victor Whitehouse tell that the grey Austin had been parked at the top of that "ride", about fifteen yards down into the plantation.

Eventually, the evidence about the murder itself came to an end, and prosecuting counsel passed to that covering the attempted abduction of the little girl from by the Bridgeman Street bonfire. There was little to be challenged here by the defence. For one thing, the child had not identified Morris so there was nothing in her evidence to which the defence need take exception. As to the young woman who had witnessed it, it was inevitable that she would be challenged only on the car number she had taken and her description of the car itself. "I got the figures mixed up," she admitted. But they were the correct ones, she said, whichever way they should have been arranged.

"You made a mistake," suggested defending counsel.

"No," said Wendy Lane, "because you could actually see the number from the number plate at the back [they were illuminated, reflective plates]."

Just as importantly, she had later picked out Morris's make of car from twenty-one others lined up in the police station yard. Unfortunately for us, she had, as defending counsel rightly pointed out, failed to pick out Raymond Morris at the identification parade, but there was nothing anyone could do about that now, despite the fact that immediately after leaving the parade room she had told the police officers she had recognised Morris ("the man in the grey suit"), but had been afraid to identify him to his face. That came under the heading "hearsay evidence" and could not be told in court.

When it came to proving the taking of the indecent photographs of Carol Morris's little niece, the evidence was simply read from the witness statements, since the defence accepted it without question.

The time was now fast approaching when Ian Forbes and I would be called to give our evidence about the arrest and interviews, and whatever attack the defence might have up its sleeve on the way it had all be conducted would surely be unleashed on us. It was a time for re-reading pocket books, for marshalling thoughts and for toughening up those thick skins of ours.

For all the inexplicable—and worsening—bouts of depression that afflicted certain people on the prosecution side who should have known better, we did not seem to be doing too badly. That can be a good sign and it can be a bad sign. The good sign was that we might be on our way to a conviction; the bad sign was that the defence would be more likely to throw caution to the winds and chance an all-out attack on the main police evidence. So Forbes and I would also have to burnish our swords!

CHAPTER ELEVEN

THE LONELIEST PLACE

Ian Forbes and I were to be the last of the prosecution's seventy-eight witnesses. I was to go in first and he would follow, because our evidence on the interrogation of Raymond Morris (Forbes also had to give a good deal of other evidence on the circumstances of the murder and the extent and scale of the investigations) rested on my shorthand notes. Once I had introduced them in evidence, the transcript copied into his official notebook would be available for him to refresh his memory in the witness box.

Looking through the glass panel in the door behind and below the court-room, I could see that the last witness had finished his evidence and was about to leave the box. I clasped my shorthand notebook and made ready to go through the door and up to the box as soon as he stepped down from it. Suddenly the door opened and in swept the DPP's clerk: "Counsel's changed the order," he said breathlessly. "Mr. Forbes is next!"

We were both amazed. We never did figure out how counsel had come to make the change, but we had no time to think about it at that moment. In he went and there I stayed, wondering what on earth they were going to do about the fact that I was the only one who could produce original notes.

I saw Forbes take the oath and watched him give evidence as if I were watching a mime show, so sound-proof was that courtroom. He was only seconds into his evidence when he turned and said something to the Judge. In the way a police officer does when he is asked his first question, he was asking the Judge if he could refer to his official notebook for accuracy's sake. Since only notes made at the time or as soon as practicable afterwards can be referred to by a witness in the box, the Judge had asked how soon he had made his entries in his notebook. About forty-eight hours after the interview, Forbes replied, explaining that he had copied them from my transcript of the shorthand notes I had written as the interviews were taking place, and while the interviews were still fresh in his own memory. "I am sorry," the Judge had said, "but forty-eight hours is too long. I cannot allow you to use your notebook!"

To any other police officer of my acquaintance those words would have come as a thunderbolt and he or she would have been rendered speechless. Not so Ian Forbes. Being the canny detective he was, he had tried to anticipate every possible eventuality and this was one of them. He was safe: he knew his evidence off-by-heart. He also knew that to sweep through it fluently would give the fact away and possibly give an erroneous impression of glibness, so he was taking his time, gathering his thoughts and allowing the jury to take in every word he spoke.

I watched his hour and a half in that box transfixed by as brilliant a show of stage-craft as I have ever seen. The mime show I was watching would have done justice to the best of the 19th century actor/managers; I could only compare it to the style of the famed Donald Wolfit himself. Every hand to the forehead, every furrowed brow, every pause, indeed every dramatic gesture in the book was there, and those able to be in court to see and hear his performance claimed that they had never seen one like it. He even tried, so I was told later, to slip in a piece of patently inadmissible evidence as if by mistake, only to be sharply rebuked by the Judge with the words, "Mr. Forbes, you know better than that." I marvelled at his nerve. He really *did* know better!

It was, I am told, a *tour de force*, but I could not hear one word of it and I had, as the rules rightly required, to follow him into the witness box in total ignorance of any unexpected challenges that had been thrown at him. We were being subjected to the police officer's ultimate test, and woe betide our case if defending counsel were able to drive a wedge between us.

*   *   *

There are few lonelier places in this world than a witness box in a crowded court-room. In a case as sensational as this, in a court-room as tiny as are those of most Shire Halls, it is almost like a walk to the scaffold through a tight-packed throng of voyeurs waiting for the hanging. One climbs the steps, bows to the Judge, looks from him to the jury, from the jury to the row of bewigged barristers and from them to the public gallery, and one feels utterly isolated. The heart pounds, the mouth dries. It is stage-fright pure and simple, and no matter if one has been doing it for thirty-four years as I had when I stepped into the witness box for my last murder trial (fifteen years later), the feeling is always the same. It is a relief to younger officers to learn this from old stagers like me, and it is a comfort to ourselves to know that even the best of stage actors never lose it either.

"Take the book in your right hand and repeat after me," says the Clerk of the Court, as he administers the oath. Then the voice of Counsel for the Prosecution: "Will you give my Lord and the jury your full name, rank and station please, officer."

"Dominick Patrick William Molloy, my Lord, a Detective Chief Inspector in the Staffordshire County Police, stationed at Cannock."

Then it all begins: "Will you tell us, please, what you were doing at about 7 a.m. on Friday the 15th of November last?" With one eye on him and the other on the jury (one never stops looking at the jury) I tell them that I was in Walsall Police Station waiting for the word that Raymond Leslie Morris had been stopped by a uniformed policeman, so that I could go out and arrest him. When he asks me to tell the court what happened when Ian Forbes confronted him at Stafford Police Station, I, too, turn to the Judge and ask if I can refer to my notes. This time the Judge is quite happy to let me, having been assured that they had been written in shorthand as the very words were being spoken.

There was no challenge as to my shorthand speed, nor, to my surprise, was I told I must read the actual shorthand (though I was by now well practised in doing so!). When the Judge heard that I had made a typed transcript, which I had certified as accurate and signed, he asked defending counsel if he had any objection to my reading that, and I was delighted when he said he had not.

I gave my evidence exactly in line with my "proof" of evidence . . . from the arrest, through the various interviews, the handing to me of Morris's wrist-watch and the photographing of his hands with the watch replaced on his wrist. By the end of it, I had completely settled down in the box, my heart-beat was right back to normal and I was ready for anything the defence might care to throw at me.

I had already been taken by surprise by our own QC. When I reached the part of the evening interview where Morris had told Forbes he believed he was "being a bit over-zealous" and "trying to put a fitting end to an illustrious career," my notes and my proof of evidence (which had, of course, been served on the defence) said that I had risen angrily from my seat and told Morris he was talking rubbish. "What?" I had shouted. "Pick on you out of the one and a half million people we've interviewed? If we wanted to do that kind of thing, what better opportunity did we have than when that man Cartlidge picked up those two kids in Walsall a few months ago. Everybody had convicted him, even the BBC, and it cost them two hundred and fifty quid. Don't talk so daft!"

Our QC held up his hand as I began to read Morris's remarks about Forbes's over-zealousness. I paused. He told me not to read out my reply, but to go straight to Morris's apology. I could hardly believe my ears. What better answer could one give to a suggestion that one is engaged in an attempt to pervert the course of justice? But, it seemed, counsel for the defence had objected to the remark as prejudicial and irrelevant, so it was cut from my evidence by prior agreement.

The cross-examination began quietly and politely, but it was not long before defence counsel put his first accusation to me, and demonstrated that they *had* decided to throw caution to the winds and mount an all-out attack on the police evidence. No wonder he had engineered the omission of my reply to Morris's suggestion that we were trying to pin on him a crime he had not committed!

Going through my evidence line by line, the defending QC dealt first with the arrest. "Morris," he said, "did not, I suggest, say to you, 'Oh God, is it my wife?' when you arrested him."

"He did, sir. I had not mentioned anything about his wife."

"Morris said, didn't he, 'What is all this in aid of?'"

"He did not, sir."

He did not dwell on the point. He did not dwell on any of the points he made during this cross-examination, since he evidently did not feel that any useful purpose would be served by getting into a routine of repetitive accusations and denials.

"Whatever he may or may not have said," he went on, "he was sitting in his car and appeared as if numbed?"

"Yes, sir."

"You had, in fact, to get him out of the car."

"Yes sir. He did not resist. I took him out".

As he began to lead up to his next point, I thought I could see what was coming. His first question pointed the way: "The murder of this little girl was, of course, an absolutely appalling crime. There was considerable local feeling."

"Yes, sir."

"On the journey to the police station he said nothing, and when he got to Stafford I suppose he immediately asked to be put in touch with Mr. Benton [the solicitor who had acted for him at Walsall and for whom he eventually asked at Cannock]."

"He said nothing."

"He added that in view of the extreme seriousness of the matter, he wanted to see a solicitor at once."

"No, sir."

Ah, I thought, we're into the old chestnut: police perjury and denial of legal representation. Then he he suddenly changed tack: "You understand that I have to put these questions to you. Did you completely lose your temper and hit him?"

"I did not, sir."

"I want to put it expressly to you that you hit him in the stomach twice and again in his side."

"That is not true."

"And that you then held him by the lapels of his coat and said, 'Now do you want a fucking solicitor?'"

"No sir, I did not."

So this was it. Not only perjury, but assault as well.

The Judge intervened: "Did you strike that man?"

"I have never struck Morris sir." I might have added that it was not for the want of wishing to, but this was not the place for that kind of remark!

"I wanted to put those questions to you," said defence counsel, "so that you would have an opportunity of admitting or denying them." Then he turned to the interviews with his client, and we were right into an argument about the accuracy or otherwise of my shorthand record and, inevitably, my truthfulness or otherwise under oath. "I suggest that Mr. Forbes said during the short time you were with Morris on the morning of November 15th, 'We know you have done this and you are not going to see the outside of this cell for thirty years.'"

"That is not true, sir. I made a complete record of everything that was said."

"Mr. Forbes, I suggest, said, 'Son, I have just been to see your wife. She wants nothing to do with you. You are sick in the head.'"

"That is not true, sir."

"I want to ask you about certain salient points on this interview that took place. First of all, I suggest that Mr. Morris was never cautioned."

"Mr. Morris was cautioned after the first sentence spoken by Chief Superintendent Forbes."

"Secondly, that throughout the whole of the interview Morris was asking to be put in touch with his solicitor."

"He was not, sir. He did not make any reference to a solicitor throughout the whole of the interview."

"Thirdly," said the QC as if ignoring my reply, "that he was continuously saying this matter had nothing whatever to do with him."

"He was not, sir."

"Often this type of crime is done by someone who is mentally deranged and that has possibly to be kept in mind by those who are investigating a crime of this dreadful nature. When you have a suspect, this is one of the things you would think about, is it not?"

"Yes, sir. It is one of the things to look out for."

"And at that interview was not the question of Mr. Morris being sick in the head canvassed amongst you?"

"It was not mentioned."

"It was said in urging him to say whether he had done it."

"No sir, nothing at all."

Up to now he had been telling me what I had left out of the interview notes. Now he began telling me what I had put in that should not have been there, since it was not said: "I have to challenge that Morris was silent, and also that Morris said he was finished, and, when asked what he meant, that it didn't make any difference now."

"That is what was said, sir. I remember the interview very, very well, and I made a very accurate note."

Defence counsel then made what was possibly his strongest attack—on our claim that Morris had been asked on five occasions to go on an identification parade and had refused. Such a thing was never once mentioned to Morris, he said. I stood by my notes, but he was unrelenting. And I was seething with frustration, for the complete answer to that was in my jacket pocket, in my official notebook, *and by the laws of evidence I was forbidden to speak it*!

The confrontation with Victor Whitehouse in the police station exercise yard had been necessary because we needed that identification in order to charge and detain Morris for the murder. There were four or five other identification witnesses, but we did not do the same with them. In fact, on the instructions of the Director of Public Prosecutions's representative, I had made five separate contacts with Morris's solicitors, each time asking if he would stand on a parade so that the other witnesses could see him and not have to be asked if they could identify him in the Assize court. On each occasion I was told that Morris had refused. *Five times*!

Here we were, being called liars and perjurers and the complete answer was right there in my pocket book, times and dates and all. I knew it, our barrister knew it and (I could only presume), my questioner knew it. *Certainly the defence solicitors who had instructed him knew it*!

It had, of course, been a procedural blunder, for the question should have been put to Morris himself, and then I could have told the jury about it. In the way it had been done (through his firm of solicitors) it was "hearsay" evidence, and therefore inadmissible. No wonder I seethed, for I could come to no other conclusion than that they were accusing us of lying about our offers to Morris of an identification parade, knowing all the time that we had continued with our offers even after he had been remanded to prison!

But it is all in the game, so they say, and I had to stand there and take it.

We were now reaching the point at which the cross-examination was about to become repetitious, with him insisting that my whole shorthand record had been falsified and me insisting that it had not. I found myself formulating and giving him a stock answer as he put point after point to me on the alleged inaccuracy of my notes: "If it is there, sir, it was said. If it is not there, then it was not said."

Time, normally, to call a halt. But the defence QC wanted to be sure that if he found it necessary to appeal against a conviction, he would not be criticised for giving up too easily. He looked to the Judge: "Would your Lordship think I could be criticised at 'another place' [the Court of Appeal] if I did not pursue these matters?"

"I think not," said the Judge. "On the other hand, you may think you can get further with this witness on the point than you did with the last one [Forbes], and you didn't get very far with him, did you?"

The implication could not have been more clear: Forbes and I had been put to exactly the same test and, it seemed, counsel had not been able to drive a wedge between us.

My cross-examination came to an end.

The national and local newspapers loved it, and ran lurid headlines like "DID YOU THEN COMPLETELY LOSE YOUR TEMPER AND HIT HIM?', QC ASKS OFFICER"; "I DID NOT HIT MORRIS, SAYS CID CHIEF IN CHRISTINE CASE"; "DETECTIVES ACCUSED OF PUNCHING MORRIS". *Not one of them reported my re-examination by counsel for the prosecution, or the further evidence introduced by him to rebut the accusation.* 'Dog bites man . . .?'

In re-examination, prosecuting counsel first referred to the allegation of assault that had been levelled at me by his "Learned Friend", counsel for Morris, and then asked me if I was familiar with the procedures at Her Majesty's Prisons when a person was delivered on remand from a magistrates' court charged with

Murder. Of course I was. Would I, then, tell My Lord and the jury what those procedures were. I did. I told them that the very first thing that happens to a prisoner after he has been entered in the reception register is that he is stripped and given a thorough physical examination by a prison medical officer.

"So if you had assaulted the defendant in the manner claimed on his behalf, you would have done it in the full knowledge that within hours he would be stripped and minutely examined by a medical man?"

"Yes, sir."

The defence did not challenge the evidence brought later that the medical officer who had examined Morris did not find the slightest mark on him. Nor had Morris complained to him or anyone else about the alleged assault, *which, the prosecution showed, had been aired for the very first time in that court-room, three months after his arrest.*

The barristers had finished with me, but the Judge had not. He turned to me and said, "As I see it, the cross-examination put it to you, perfectly properly, firstly that your shorthand note has left out certain matters and secondly that it has wrongly included equally important matters. Do you appreciate that in a case of this sort that would be a terrible thing to do?"

"I would say, My Lord, that it would be a terrible thing in any case."

"Did you do it?"

"No, I did not My Lord."

"Thank you, officer."

"That is the case for the Crown," said our QC as I left the witness box.

* * *

Any police officer with experience of coming under fire in the witness box of a Crown Court will know that where a barrister makes a swingeing attack on his veracity and integrity he will simply be doing his duty towards his client. He will also know that if the barrister does not wholly believe in what he is doing, he will salve his conscience afterwards by seeking out the officer and making an oblique apology to him. It has never failed in my experience, and it did not at this trial. It was not said in so many words, but a passing remark and a smile when it was all over was enough to tell me that here was another such case.

*   *   *

Defence counsel rose to his feet: "Your Lordship, I call the accused, Raymond Leslie Morris."

Even as he was saying this, a prison officer was leading Morris from the prisoner's dock, and he stood guard at the foot of the witness box steps as he ascended. Morris took the Bible in his right hand and repeated the oath.

After finishing my evidence I was allowed to remain in court, so I was able to watch his performance, which was entirely predictable. His evidence followed step-by-step the points put to me in cross-examination . . . that he had not said, "Oh God, is it my wife?" when I arrested him, that I had violently assaulted him in the police cell at Stafford, that my entire record of the interviews was false in that it contained offers of identification parades which were never made and attributed to him remarks that he had never made, and that the whole exercise was an attempt to frame him.

He stuck to his original alibis and the timings in them, and said he had not adopted the short route to and from work (the one which would have taken him by Camden Street) until after some road works had made it an easier route, quite a while after the murder.

His wife, for some reason, had changed from speaking the truth when they were questioned by the police to telling lies about him.

Morris was perfectly composed, speaking quietly and politely and raising his voice only when told by the Judge that the jury might be having difficulty hearing him. Only once did his composure desert him, and that was when he was telling the court that Forbes had told him he had just seen his wife and she wanted nothing further to do with him, a remark Forbes had denied making and that was not included in my shorthand record of the interview. It wrung the only tear that Morris shed during the course of his evidence, though I was sure that he felt like shedding a few more during his cross-examination.

Raymond Morris's performance in the witness box under his own counsel's questioning was all going quietly and smoothly. Suddenly the voice of a child rang out in the silence. "That's him! That's the man! Him down there!" All eyes turned to the gallery, to see a young girl (too young, in fact, to be in that court-room), her arm outstretched, pointing at the witness box and the accused man. Morris, too, looked up, but in the commotion that followed nothing else was heard from the child, who was quickly hustled out.

No fuss was made about the incident, and one could not tell if either Judge or jury appreciated its significance. It was a moment of high drama all the same, *for the child who had pointed at Morris and said "That's him!" was the one who had been abducted in Walsall way back in December, 1964, and left for dead, raped and bleeding, in the ditch at Bentley by the man who called himself "Uncle Len"*!

Morris had not been charged with that crime and we had not a scrap of evidence (apart from his ownership of a Vauxhall Cresta car) to connect him with it. What credence could be attached to the child's outburst one cannot know, since she was still believed to be suffering from the mental effects of her ordeal. It had been quite wrong for her to be brought into court in the first place, and upon her removal from the chamber a police officer was sent to investigate her startling interruption of the proceedings. It was a thought-provoking intervention to say the least.

* * *

Morris's cross-examination by the prosecutor also began smoothly enough, with a few questions about his knowledge of Cannock Chase (he could not deny knowing the place because we had found several photographs of the area in his dark-room) and the routes and timings of his journeys to and from work. Then the prosecuting QC told him he was going to ask him to consider what had happened to Christine Darby when she was being murdered. He asked the Judge to allow Morris to see the photographs of the body lying in the forest undergrowth, and an usher handed them up.

"Whoever had killed the child must have lifted her clothing above her waist and removed her plimsolls, must he not?"

"Yes, sir," said Morris quietly.

"And the position of her body [on her back, legs apart, knees raised, private parts fully exposed] suggests that she could have been sexually assaulted?"

Morris agreed that it did.

Counsel then picked up the child's trews and knickers, and Morris agreed with him that her plimsolls (one of which was found thrown into the forest from the main road on the approach to where the body was found) would have had to be removed first.

Then Morris was handed the album of indecent photographs he had taken of his wife's niece, and asked if his wife had been in the house when they were taken.

"Yes," he almost whispered.

"In the next room?"

"In the next but one room, sir."

The whole court-room fell deathly silent. It was a moment of supreme tension. Only we who had prepared this prosecution knew what was coming next.

"Tell how it was you came to take these pictures," said the QC, turning his head as he did so to throw a glance at the jury.

Morris thought for a moment. "I was taking portraits of her, sir, and she accidentally exposed herself and I took it."

The Judge shot a question at him: "Are you telling the jury that that girl's posture in that picture is accidental?"

"No, sir."

"What *do* you mean?"

"While I was taking the pictures I am not sure whether she was leaning on the bed or if she was lying, but she fell backwards and I saw her like that and I rearranged the position."

This was amazing. Of all things to lie about, Morris was lying about the indecent photographs, to which he had already pleaded guilty. Perhaps he knew where the questioning was leading, but whatever his motive he had unexpectedly opened himself up to the onslaught of a delighted cross-examiner.

"Look at this photograph [one of his wife's niece fully clothed, sitting on the bed]," said counsel. "She looks a happy little girl there."

"She is smiling, yes."

Turning to another picture, counsel said, "Either you or the girl had raised her dress and underslip above her waist. Who did that?"

"I don't know."

"Why," asked the barrister disingenuously, "when taking portraits of a girl aged five, was it necessary for her or you to raise her dress up in that position?"

Morris was not sure.

His attention was directed to other photographs in which the child had her knickers on again, and counsel asked him when they were taken.

"On the same day," said Morris, "but after the others."

"Who asked her to put her knickers on?"

"I did, sir."

"Does she normally go about with no knickers?"

"No, sir." Then, with a look of alarm on his face, he hastily added: "I say 'No', but I have no prior knowledge of this."

* * *

At this point our civilian photographer, John Vaughan, leaned over my shoulder and whispered to me: "He's bloody lying, sir. That girl was photographed first when she was fully dressed and then as she progressively undressed."

I whispered back: "But he's saying he took them in a different order and that she got dressed after being undressed. We arranged the pictures in the album in the order they are because that was the order we found them in the box."

"Well, he's bloody lying!" said Vaughan, "and I can prove it."

"How?"

He told me and I motioned to him to step back while I hurriedly wrote a note and passed it forward. The DPP's man passed it to our junior prosecuting counsel, who showed it to his leader, who looked at it and nodded.

* * *

Evidently leaving the point about the sequence in which the pictures had been taken until the court adjourned for the day, our

QC came back to the picture of Morris's wife's niece bearing the uncanny resemblance to the position of Christine Darby in death. Why had he taken this picture?

"I did not notice it was like that," said Morris lamely. "She may have leaned back."

Then the QC plunged in the dagger. "Do you notice certain things similar to the dead body? The dress is drawn up."

"Yes, sir."

"Did you draw the dress up to the waist?"

"Yes."

Again the Judge came in, sensing the way the questioning was going: "Did you want the girl in that position for the photograph?"

"I would say yes, sir."

He agreed, too, that he placed the child into indecent positions for other photographs in the set.

Counsel pointed to the one where the man's penis was placed next to the child's vagina and elicited from Morris the fact that, between setting the timer and placing himself in that position, he would have had only seven seconds. "What was the purpose of doing these things?"

"I still don't know."

The questions came thick and fast and Morris began to reel under them, finding himself obliged to say that he couldn't stop himself, that he had been aroused and that he was lying in suggesting that some of the child's indecent poses had come about by accident.

The dagger went deeper when counsel got Morris to agree that the photographs of his wife's niece would have been taken on August 17th, 1968. Quietly he put the question to which all this had been leading: "That was almost the anniversary of the death of Christine Darby, within two days, wasn't it?"

"Of course it was sir."

"Were you re-enacting the interference you had had with Christine Darby a year before?"

"I didn't know Christine Darby, sir."

"What you did to that girl in the photograph was in some

respects the same thing that must have happened with Christine Darby?"

"I don't quite follow you sir."

Everyone else did!

With a show of patience, counsel went through the points of similarity once again. "You said you felt disgusted with yourself after you took the pictures, yet you went to the extent of photographing yourself doing so. Can you explain that?"

Morris could not.

"Is not the only explanation that you had a lust for little children?" asked counsel, summing up the whole of the prosecution's case for the the admission of the indecent photographs as evidence towards the murder. Morris denied it, of course, but that line of questioning was hammered home relentlessly . . . until the Judge intervened once again.

When he had come out of the bedroom after photographing the child, had he told his wife what he had done, asked His Lordship.

"No," said Morris.

"Did you enjoy it?"

"I don't know what to say now, sir. It was just something I had done. I had never taken any pictures like that before and I did not think, sir."

"Did the little girl enjoy it?"

"I wouldn't know, sir."

"Oh yes you would," snapped the Judge. "Tell the jury!"

"I just don't know," said Morris with a look of despair.

The questioning turned to the finding of his wrist-watch around his ankle when he arrived at Birmingham Prison. Why?

He had "just kept it on." It was something personal to hang one to, he said.

Oh no it wasn't, said the QC. Oh yes it was, insisted Morris.

And his enigmatic remark to me when I put my hand on his shoulder and told him I was arresting him for murder? "Oh God, is it my wife?"

He had not said it. I was lying.

"Were you anxious after the police first saw you that your wife would withdraw her support about your movements on August 19th?"

Morris had to admit that it would look bad for him if his wife did change her mind about his alibi, but he had still not said, "Oh God, is it my wife?"

The rest of Morris's four and three quarter hours' stint in the witness box that day was taken up with details of his movements on the Saturday of the murder, and when the day ended (it was Friday), prosecuting counsel told the Judge he would continue his cross-examination when the court resumed after the week-end.

It was now time to prepare John Vaughan's evidence about the sequence of the photographing session in readiness for the resumption of cross-examination on Monday.

*   *   *

It took only ten minutes when the cross-examination of Morris was resumed to expose his lies about the sequence of the indecent photographs. He wriggled desperately, and he came up with a couple of ideas on how the prints could have come out in a different order, but in the end he was stuck with the fact that the numbers on the negatives showed the order in which they must have been taken. He tried claiming that they could come out different if one was loading loose film instead of cassette, or if it had been put in upside down, but even his legal team was forced to accept John Vaughan's evidence. That child had begun the photographic session fully clothed and had ended up half naked.

Make a liar of a man, they say, and you are halfway to convicting him. Not that one would have guessed it in this case, for the afternoon of the previous Friday had seen yet another wave of gloom sweep through the prosecution . . . at least through some of those not actually involved in the case. My wife was in the public gallery with Mrs. Bailey and Mrs. Forbes, and they thought the gloom was almost tangible. It was a strange phenomenon indeed, and this time it seemed to have arisen from the allegations being thrown at Ian Forbes and me by the defence, which, so everyone told us, had worried even the Chief Constable.

"Only them as has been there knows," goes one north-country saying, and Forbes and I had seen it all before and had taken it in our stride, though it was unpleasant to see the effect it was having on some of whom we would have expected different. Still, it could not go on much longer and then we would see who was right, though the press, who seemed to share the gloom, were already marking down the odds on a conviction.

Counsel for the prosecution harried Morris for another two hours that morning, pressing him again on his exclamation at the moment of his arrest: "Oh God, is it my wife?", which he continued to deny. He was pressed on his allegation that I had assaulted him. Had he had any bruises? No, only a red mark. "I don't bruise easily," he explained.

His cross-examiner insisted that the reason he had refused to go on an identification parade at Stafford after agreeing to go on one at Walsall was not that he was not given the opportunity, but that this time he knew he would be seen by a man who had looked at him full face, at close quarters, in broad daylight, and he was afraid to take the chance. Morris continued to deny that any such offer had been made to him.

And then it was all over. "I have no re-examination, My Lord," said his QC as Prosecuting Counsel sat down. The prison officer returned Morris to the prisoners' dock.

There followed a sad appearance on the accused man's behalf by his mother and father, who said they had seen his car outside his in-laws' house next door during that Saturday afternoon. By the time counsel for the prosecution had finished with them, the time seemed to have been fixed at about five o'clock, though they had no means of verifying it. Furthermore, under cross-examination they admitted that they had only volunteered this evidence forty-eight hours before entering the witness box. In all kindness, there was no need for further questioning.

It was the end of the case for the defence.

CHAPTER TWELVE

NEMESIS

It was the seventh day of the trial, and it was all over bar the closing speeches for prosecution and defence, the Judge's summing up, and the jury's verdict.

The closing speeches were predictable . . . counsel for the prosecution highlighting what he felt was advantageous to him and Morris's defender refuting the police evidence and his wife's change of mind about his alibi. What everyone was waiting for was the Judge's summing up. How had he seen the merits of the arguments? Which way was he going to lean? For lean they do, having made their own assessments of the value of the evidence and the quality of those who have given it. Not to the extent of influencing the jury in its judgement of the facts, because that would undoubtedly result in the quashing of a conviction on appeal, but to the extent of reducing lengthy questioning to pithy points . . . to the esssentials . . . to the crucial questions the jurors should be asking themselves. "It is a matter for you, members of the jury," a judge will say, "but you may well ask yourselves this question . . ." or, "You may think, members of the jury, that all you need to ask yourselves about that disagreement between the prosecution and the defence is . . ."

Telling the jury that they had to be "Sure" before they could convict Morris of anything, the Judge began with an exposition of the law relating to attempted child abduction and murder. In relation to the particular cases before them, he said, no one could doubt that someone had abducted and murdered Christine Darby and someone had attempted to abduct the other little girl in just the circumstances outlined by the prosecution, of which he reminded them.

Warning them of the danger of "lumping all the charges together," he pointed out that they had to consider each separately and to deliver a separate verdict on each of them. "It would be quite wrong," he said, "to say that if he did one he must have done the others."

This led to the damning evidence of the photographs. In the ordinary way, he told them, a man's character was not disclosed to a jury, but the law allowed certain exceptions, and one of those exceptions was of very considerable importance. It was "Identity", one of the central issues of the case before them. The law permitted evidence to be given on matters other than the crime with which a person was charged if it pointed to a similarity between those other matters and the case the jury was considering. The law allowed a jury to ask themselves not only "Is he the man?" and "Have the prosecution got the right man?", but also whether features of other proven matters involving the man on trial were repeated in the case before them.

That, the Judge told them, was why they had seen "those filthy photographs." Warning them that they must judge the photographs strictly in the context of identity and not allow themselves to be swayed by a natural outrage, he said they were only relevant on the question of identity. They, and any other "similar facts" introduced by the prosecution, could show if there was a hallmark linking the man across more than one incident. *But it was only relevant on identity.*

It was no more than evidence for them to consider, and they were quite at liberty to take the view that the supposed similarities were not strong enough or not striking enough to provide any assistance in solving the real problem. The jury, however, was equally at liberty to say "There is the hallmark. That is the man."

In simple, straightforward language, the Judge took the jury through the steps they would probably follow in judging whether some or all of the similarities in the case applied to the accused. In each of the two crimes, he said, a little girl was involved, and so was a car, and a bogus story. There might be a similarity, but it did not mean that Morris was responsible. It might be Mr. X or Mr. Y who had got the same technique. But if, when they were deliberating, they came to the conclusion that in one of the charges the man was Morris, then the similarity might be carried on to other charges. It was only, he stressed, if they took an adverse view against Morris on one of the charges that they would be entitled to consider something of the technique of getting the girl into the car, and so on, and so on.

In taking their first step in this process, of course, they might be helped by the fact that of the 1,998 cars bearing the registration letters LOP which had been checked by the police after the attempted abduction, only one had turned out to be a green Ford Corsair with a cream roof. And that belonged to Raymond Leslie Morris!

Now he came to the attacks on the evidence given by Forbes and me, and here he made one of his most telling points, the one that had been contained in my outburst to Morris when he was accusing Forbes of being "over-zealous" and which I had not been allowed to tell the jury. Serious allegations had been made against the police, said the Judge, and it was important because it meant that either the police or Morris were lying.

"If at the end of the day you are sure these charges against the police are unfounded, it must follow that Morris was telling lies— and you are searching for the truth. I do not say which way your decision will go, but you are searching for the truth. Morris has alleged that Detective Chief Inspector Molloy had made a false shorthand record of the questioning. You may think it odd that Molloy is prepared to produce a false shorthand note omitting any reference to the request for a solicitor and including remarks never made about an identification parade, *but that he should refrain for some reason from including a confession.* If they were out to frame Morris, do you think they would have stopped at the shorthand notes Molloy produced?"

A devastating point. If the jury did not come down on our side now, at least we could not complain that the question had not been put before them!

As to the various identifications made in the case, "there was ample scope for mistake," so he advised the jury to ask themselves if on each occasion there was something which would imprint the memory of a face on the witness's memory. Victor Whitehouse, for example, had said he remembered because the car was parked in such an unusual place. They would have to consider that. Whitehouse had also hesitated for ten or twelve seconds before saying Morris was the man he had seen there. Was that because he was not sure, or because he was being very careful? They would have to consider that too.

While the lady who had claimed to have seen Morris driving a car with a little girl in it on the road to Cannock Chase seemed at times to get short shrift from the Judge, he told the jury that they were still entitled to accept her evidence of identification. It was a matter for them.

He thought the jury might look at the evidence of Mrs. Rawlings in a different light. The events of that day were imprinted on her mind because the man in the car had not even acknowledged the fact that she had pulled her dog out of his way. As to the Identikit she and Victor Whitehouse had helped to compile, they had said that it was Morris they wanted to describe, and Morris they did describe. "Likeness in people's minds," he said, "depends on the view they take."

Good enough for me, I thought, hoping that the jury would also remember prosecuting counsel's explanation of how one should view an Identikit . . . not as a photograph but as a collection of remembered facial features.

The time of Christine Darby's death could not be assessed with any degree of certainty, said the Judge. Dr. Usher had said she could have died on either Saturday or Sunday. Seven or eight o'clock on Saturday evening was one time suggested by counsel for the defence, and Dr. Usher could not argue against it. "If that were right," he said, "the prosecution case goes out of the window."

Slowly and painstakingly, the Judge went through both sides of the case, witness by witness, but when he came to Carol Morris he had much more to say. "What made her change her story on November 15th? It was not the filthy photographs, because the police had not yet found them. Was it the fact that Morris had previously been questioned in connection with the attempted abduction? On any view, Mrs. Carol Morris had told lies. I say that without hesitation. Either she lied originally in confirming his alibi or she is lying now."

The jury should approach her evidence with "very considerable reservation," he said, though they were entitled to feel that she had only been telling "white lies" when questioned by the police earlier in the investigation.

What neither he, nor I, nor anyone else knew at that moment was *when* Carol Morris had changed her mind about supporting her husband. We would discover it later when, in a Sunday newspaper story, she told how, as I was typing her statement with the altered times, she slipped off her engagement and wedding rings and put them unnoticed into her handbag. She later visited her husband in prison to see if he could give her some innocent explanation for lying about his whereabouts on the day of the murder. Had he done so, she said, she would have put her rings back onto her finger and not given evidence against him. But he did not. When she saw the indecent photographs of her niece, it was all over anyway, and it was at that moment that she decided to volunteer her services as a witness for the prosecution.

The Judge ended his summing up by going through Morris's own account of his movements on the day of Christine Darby's murder, and reducing things to their essentials: "The great issue here is, does that evidence which I have just recited so shake what may have been your confidence in Mrs. Rawlings and Whitehouse that you can no longer hold to them?" A good question. He left them with one more thought. Morris had consistently denied that his usual route home from work on Saturdays at the time of Christine Darby's abduction and murder took him past the end of Camden Street. He had not, on his story, begun to use that route until some time afterwards. *Yet the manager of the car-wash in nearby Caldmore Green had remembered Morris well, and had told the court that he went there at varying times every Saturday afternoon during the period in which the murder had been committed*!

"Members of the jury," said the Judge, "it is now time for you to retire and consider your verdict."

*   *   *

The retirement of the jury in a murder trial puts police officers into a state of limbo. Everything has been done that can be done; everything has been said that can be said. All discussion of the case becomes superfluous and all argument pointless. It has all been reduced to a huddled group of twelve men and women cut off from the world in a small room guarded by a court usher.

Time passes agonisingly slowly and the heart-beat quickens with every stir around the doorway of that guarded room. Was that a knock? Yes, it was. But it is only the jury passing out a written query for the Judge. The heart-beat returns to normal until the next scare. An hour passes. Is that a good sign or a bad one? Are they dealing with the important points of the case or have they missed them and become entangled in irrelevancies? Did they get the point about the 1,998 LOP-registered cars or have they been hooked by defence counsel's guess that the murder might have been committed at eight o'clock that Saturday evening, so that, as the Judge had said, "The prosecution case goes out of the window"?

Yet there is no point in our wondering what they have made of this or that part of the evidence, because we know that they do not think like police officers or lawyers. The thought-processes of a group of twelve people who are total strangers to each other and have come together from all walks of life for perhaps a once-in-a-lifetime foray into the alien world of a court of law can hardly be conceived of as representing a coherent or ordered evaluation of anything, let alone such a huge and complex volume of information as will pass before them in an eight-day trial.

If one has, for example, ever looked through the scribbles on the notepaper scattered along the jury benches when everyone but the cleaners have gone home, one has even less idea of what has influenced them. Once, for instance, after a two-week murder trial, I found a sheet of paper containing notes and doodles which I could tell followed the sequence of the trial, and I could identify one of the juror's remarks with the beginning of the accused man's own appearance in the witness box. "Too bloody clever!" it read, in large letters surrounded by intricate scroll patterns. Not another word about his three hours of evidence. They convicted him, of course!

It shouldn't work . . . but it does.

Was *that* a knock? Yes it was. The usher opens the door and cocks an ear to an unseen whisper. He closes the door, turns to the Clerk of the Court and nods. They're coming back! The word spreads through the building like wildfire; barristers hastily arranging their wigs and reporters clutching their notebooks stream back into the court-room, while every spare inch of seat and floor space in that tiny room is taken up by an incredible press of over two hundred people. Outside the building, many hundreds more pack the square and "The jury's back!" ripples through the crowd.

It is 4.28 p.m. The jury has been out for one hour and forty minutes. The Clerk checks through their names. Have they elected a foreman he asks. They have. He stands. Have they reached a verdict? They have. Do they find the defendant, Raymond Leslie Morris, guilty or not guilty of the charge of attempted abduction? Guilty! And of the murder of Christine Darby? Guilty!

The public gallery erupts in a loud cheer and the Clerk has to call for silence. The man in the prisoners' dock shakes his head slowly in disbelief. Already the word has reached the crowd in the Shire Hall square. "Hang him! Hang him!" they yell.

Queueing for the verdict. *Express & Star*

The Judge couldn't hang him if he wanted to. "I do not intend to keep you long or make any comment about this terrible murder," he tells the haggard-looking, sunken-eyed figure. "There is only one sentence, as you know. Life imprisonment!"

Raymond Morris stands for a moment as if turned to stone. Then he turns smartly, walks across the dock and takes two steps down towards the cells. But then he stops, and, as he has done on every single day of the trial, sweeps the public gallery with his eyes. For no more than a second they lock onto his wife's, but what thoughts tumble through his tormented mind at that moment no one will ever know. Then he is gone.

As Morris disappeared down the steps to the cells, the Judge's voice cut across the noise and the bustle of people beginning to leave the court-room. "Mr. Forbes," he said, beckoning him forward. Ian Forbes, as wide as he was high, his broad muscular shoulders rounded a little, stood to attention before the bench. "Mr. Forbes," said the Judge, "I am addressing you but in addressing you I am really addressing you and the many colleagues who have helped bring this dreadful case to its conclusion. There must be many mothers in Walsall and the area whose hearts will beat more lightly as a result of this verdict. It must have been a nightmare for mothers and fathers in Walsall over the last months when they heard, maybe, of a child missing."

There was total silence in which not the slightest rustle of paper or clothing was to be heard. The Judge paused. "I know," he went on, "and perhaps many of the public know, of the really stupendous efforts which, under your direction, have been made to bring a man to justice. There will be many who are truly grateful to you and to those who have served under you. It must be a great satisfaction to you, Mr. Forbes, to know that all your efforts have been rewarded by what, on my part, I believe to be a right result. It must be also, to a much less degree, rewarding for you to know that the jury must have rejected those very unpleasant allegations which were made against you and Mr. Molloy. People of this county, and, I would have said, of the whole country, owe a debt of gratitude to you and those who have served with you for what you have done."

Ian Forbes bowed, and said, "Thank you, My Lord."

*   *   *

The crowd cheered us as we walked down the steps into the square. They were still shouting, "Hang him!," but Morris had already disappeared through the back of the court and was on his way to begin the life sentence which, at the time of writing, he is still serving.

The author, leaving the Assize Court after the end of the trial.
Express & Star

End of trial photograph at Staffs. Police HQ
(L to R: John Blaauw (head of CID in Rotterdam, Holland . . . in Staffordshire to observe the investigation and trial); Harry Bailey; the author; Chief Constable Arthur Morgan Rees; Tom Parry; Ian Forbes.   *Staffs. Police*

There was the inevitable press-conference. The Chief Constable urged continued vigilance for, as the public was also reminded by the news-media, Raymond Leslie Morris had been convicted of only one of the three Cannock Chase Murders. Were the police carrying on with the other investigations?, he was asked. He chose his words carefully, in order to avoid coming into conflict with the law of libel: "The files," he said, "are still open and under consideration."

So they were, for Morris would have to be seen again and questioned about them, once he had been through the prison classification procedure and taken to a more permanent prison abode. In fact he went to Durham, where he joined Ian Brady of Moors Murders infamy, in a top-security enclosure dedicated to holding them and two other child-killers. He was visited there, but no one was ever able to connect him with any crime other than those of which he had been convicted.

Did we carry on with our investigations into the murders of Margaret Reynolds and Diane Tift, whose bodies were no more than bundles of bones when they were found in the Mansty Gulley ditch on Cannock Chase? The answer is no. We saw no point. Rightly or wrongly we felt there was nowhere else to look. I should know, for I was to spend two years more as head of Cannock Division CID, sitting on top of that damned paper mountain which was still gathering dust when I left. And, whatever significance may be seen in the fact, from that day to this there has not been one crime in the Midlands which has necessitated its resurrection.

*   *   *

There was, of course, an immediate application on Morris's behalf for leave to appeal against the convictions, and it naturally centred on the trial Judge's decision to allow the one jury to try all the counts in the indictment and to consider the indecent photographs in relation to the murder charge.

The Court of Appeal firmly rejected the application, and in its judgement referred to principles which had "been clearly laid down for a number of years" in several previous cases which had centred on exactly the same question. One of those precedents was the trial of the notorious child-killer John Straffen, who, by a strange irony, was with Ian Brady in Durham prison when Raymond Morris joined them there!

Thus did the case *Regina versus Morris (1969)* take its place in the law books as yet another precedent on the admissibility of evidence of similar facts. The last I heard of him was five years ago, when prison medical officers were classifying him as a "Dangerous Psychopath," who would still be a danger to children if he were to be released.

*   *   *

The grey Austin A.55 Cambridge car which Morris had used to carry Christine Darby to her death on the 19th of August, 1967, had occupied an almost mystical place in the saga of Cannock Chase. Ian Forbes, "The Man from the Yard", had staked his reputation on it, and our failure to identify the one belonging to the murderer after sixteen months of searching had raised in many people's minds a large question mark over his decision to do so.

By the end of the investigation just about every such car in use in Great Britain and Ireland had been traced and their owners (including Raymond Morris!) questioned and eliminated. Its image had been seen on notice boards, the front pages of newspapers and on television screens throughout the British Isles. To everyone, inside and out of the police force, it had become the symbol, the rallying point, of the Cannock Chase murder investigation.

I have described my own feelings as I stood by Morris's car, which, in my heart, I had begun to think I should never see. It was the strange feeling (certainly strange to one whose job necessitated the rejection of such emotional distractions) that the car had itself almost acquired the personality of a murderer.

So, though more appropriate to some voodoo ceremony designed to ward off evil spirits, it still seemed bizarrely fitting that the car should meet the end it did. On 28th March, 1969, five weeks after the end of the trial, a Worcestershire car dealer put it on the forecourt of his garage and publicly burned it!

"It seemed bizarrely fitting that Raymond Leslie Morris's car should meet the end it did". *Express & Star*

Just over three years after the trial, in May, 1972, the British police service celebrated its 143 years history by holding what was called The Bramshill Cavalcade, a week of exhibitions and demonstrations culminating in a daily historical cavalcade showing everything from top-hatted Victorian policemen on penny-farthing bicycles to police helicopters. It was held at the National Police Staff College at Bramshill, in Hampshire, a beautifully-preserved Tudor mansion surrounded by tastefully built modern college accommodation among its trees and parklands.

Among the attractions at the Cavalcade was a demonstration of how the police service tackled protracted murder investigations, and the cases chosen for the illustrated lectures were the Moors Murders and the Cannock Chase Murders. The lectures were given in the same theatre, alternating at intervals during each day. Detective Chief Superintendent Arthur Benfield of the Cheshire Constabulary lectured on the Moors Murders, and Harry Bailey (now an Assistant Chief Constable, having, presumably, been rehabilitated by the successful trial of Raymond Morris) dealt with Cannock Chase.

By this time I had left Staffordshire and was a Detective Chief Superintendent and head of the Dyfed-Powys (Mid and West Wales) CID, and I was sent to Bramshill to join Harry Bailey for the lectures. I had been at Bramshill only two years earlier, on the Intermediate Command Course, so I was still remembered in the Shoulder of Mutton, the pub near the entrance to the long drive which leads from the road to the mansion. "How are you?" asked the landlord when Arthur, Harry and I went into the place on our first evening. "What brings you back here? The Cavalcade?"

"Yes," I answered. "We're giving talks on murder investigation. I'm here for the Cannock Chase Murders."

"Oh yes, I remember. Ian Brady, wasn't it. And Myra . . . what's her name?"

"No," I said. "Not the Moors Murders . . ."

POSTSCRIPT

A COSTLY LESSON

There are two sides to every story. The other side to this one is that, though the "System", stretched and tested as never before, failed that test and let us down for almost four years, it would not have done us much good even if it had worked perfectly and thrown up Raymond Leslie Morris as a prime suspect in 1964, 1965 or 1967. He would not have told us the time of day, he would have been alibied up to the hilt, and, as we have seen, his confidence was growing with every interview by the police. With the best will in the world we would never have got a prosecution off the ground, even with the identification evidence of Victor Whitehouse.

As the good book tells us, "*To everything there is a season, and a time to every purpose...*" The time for Morris could have come only when it did—in November, 1968, when he tried to abduct the little girl from Walsall on the night before Bonfire Night, and when, after his arrest, we found those incriminating photographs of his wife's niece, which were almost a recreation of Christine Darby's death throes, taken almost on the anniversary of her murder. It was those events which persuaded his wife that he was the Cannock Chase Murderer, broke his alibi, and, with all the other evidence tucked away in our "System", convicted him. His time had come.

We were lucky. But how close we came to catastrophe. That child accosted by Morris by the Walsall bonfire came within a hair's breadth of being taken away in his car. Had Wendy Lane not appeared when she did, I have no doubt that he would have taken her, and that she, too, would have finished up dead on Cannock Chase. It was a thought that, to say the least, sat uneasily among my own feelings of elation.

*   *   *

By June, 1971, just over two years after Raymond Leslie Morris had begun his life sentence, I had been promoted to Superintendent (in uniform) at Burton-on-Trent. The Deputy Chief Constable telephoned me from Headquarters to say that the Home Office had asked for a report detailing the mechanics of the Cannock Chase Incident Room. It was to help a team working on a project for computerising incident room systems. Assistant Chief Constable Harry Bailey was on leave and, it seemed, I was the only one available who knew the systems well enough to give the information required. Would I go back to Cannock and prepare the report?

I was delighted to do so, because I could not get out of my mind how nearly our failure had come to causing the death of another child, and how, in all the euphoria which followed his life sentence, we seemed to have forgotten the number of things that had gone wrong. None of us seemed to remember—or if we did we were not talking about it—that Morris had appeared in our systems *five times* without once graduating into the "suspect" category. Nor had the news-media so much as remarked on the fact as it became apparent during the trial. When it was all over, the only thing that seemed to matter to us, to the news-media and to the public at large was the fact that Raymond Leslie Morris had been convicted.

Feelings of relief and elation had outshone everything else. Had the failure of our system led to another child murder, it would have been an entirely different story.

If the lessons we had learned were not to be acknowledged, then they might well have to be learned all over again at some other time and in some other part of the country. So I took the opportunity to do something about it. I ended my report by pointing out some uncomfortable truths: first, the weaknesses introduced by the existence of two Incident Rooms, ten miles apart and of equal standing (in practice if not in theory), and, second, the fact that whatever the quality of a person's alibi, it would "clear" him to the satisfaction of the System, whatever reservations might have been expressed by the officers who had interviewed him.

The first weakness had arisen from a failure in command and control, for though in theory Walsall was subordinate to Cannock, in practice it operated with a degree of independence which made failure a very real possibility from the outset.

The second would have existed anyway as a built-in flaw in the system, whether in one Incident Room or two. Since alibis or other eliminating factors were not distinguished in terms of quality or validity, there was only one place for them: they all finished up in the same massive Nominal Index with the simple and unequivocal epitaph "NFA", No Further Action. If, therefore, the investigation had eventually reached a complete dead end, with every line of enquiry exhausted, it would have been next to impossible to go back through those cleared less than satisfactorily and take a second look, because they had been lumped together with well over a million others of no conceiveable further interest.

Not that one should wait until an investigation is exhausted before taking a second look. In the perfect system, such re-checking would be a matter of regular routine. As things were, Harry Bailey and I had found, only six months after the Christine Darby murder investigation had begun, that a re-check of this kind was already quite beyond our power. It would have required a separate and substantial operation for which we did not have the additional resources.

My suggestion for removing this weakness was a simple and logical one: that alibis or other eliminating factors should be categorised according to their quality, so that they could be quickly retrieved from their various headings and re-checked at will.

Lacking this facility, I explained, the Cannock Chase system had become "*more of a filing and reference system than the 'live' thing it should have been. It became impossible to manipulate it and it did nothing with the material fed to it but store it. With a built-in facility for throwing up common factors and unsatisfactorily-resolved enquiries, it would have named the murderer of its own accord instead of waiting until he tried another.*"

* * *

Ten years after I wrote that report, it was disclosed that exactly the same things had happened again, in the investigation of another series of murders. The so-called "Yorkshire Ripper", too, had been through the system several times (*nine times, in fact!*) without becoming a suspect, and, worse still, had committed additional murders that might have been avoided had the system been capable of identifying him.

Furthermore, the fact that the murders and the massive investigation had spread over areas covered by several police forces had (as in the Cannock Chase Murders) led to divisions of command and control arising from inter-force and inter-personal rivalries; in other words, a failure to draw all the threads together under one effective leader in one efficient centre of operations.

An earlier investigation—the so-called "Black Panther" investigation into the 1974 kidnapping and murder of Lesley Whittle in the Midlands—had also suffered severely from inter-force rivalry. The force dealing with the kidnapping did not "Call in the Yard", it was not their policy, whereas the one in whose area the girl's body was found and who were now dealing with a murder, did call them in. The serious failures of co-ordination in that case led to an inconclusive debate in Parliament. But after the Yorkshire fiasco there was an even greater public outcry, and on the 19th of January, 1982, the Home Secretary made a statement to the House of Commons. He gave the House the main conclusions and recommendations of a report by Her Majesty's Chief Inspector of Constabulary, who spoke of "major errors of judgement" and "some inefficiencies in the conduct of the operation at various levels."

The Chief HMI's report also included the comments that "*Where crimes within a connected series occur, especially in different force areas, special arrangements need to be made for the command of the co-ordinated inquiry. There needs to be one officer in overall command with the authority to direct the course of the investigation in all the police areas affected*"; and "*A major lesson to be learned is that the use of categoral eliminating factors* [or what I have called in this story our 'NFA' factor] *is fraught with danger unless they are conclusive.*"

That comment related to a Yorkshire version of one of the problems we had experienced, namely the less than discriminating exercise of the right to bring a line of enquiry to an end by marking it "NFA" or its equivalent. The Chief HMI referred to the "*temptation for senior investigating officers to mis-use elimination factors in an attempt to reduce an otherwise excessive number of people any one of whom might be within the suspect category*". There were a good many detectives in the West Midlands who could have told him that . . . *all of fourteen years earlier*!

The wording was different from mine, but the message was exactly the same: Yorkshire had seen a chilling replay of what had happened in the Cannock Chase investigations, but there it had led to further, avoidable, murders.

*   *   *

I served for another fifteen years after the end of the Cannock Chase investigations, until my retirement as Detective Chief Superintendent from the Dyfed-Powys Police (in Wales) in November, 1983, and in all the murder incident room systems I operated after Cannock Chase, I built in my own solution to the "NFA" Factor—a grading system for alibis—and thus eliminated it. What a pity the "Yorkshire Ripper" investigation team did not have the benefit of our experience at Cannock. Why not? What had happened to my report?

Seven years after I submitted it, I visited the Home Office computer project team so that I could make some topical comments in my next quarterly lecture at the National Police Staff College at Bramshill on the Investigation of Major Crime, which included an examination of "The System". I asked about my report and if they had found it useful. *They had never heard of it*! They asked me to send them a copy and I did.

Four more years went by and the Home Office was then presented with the identical lessons of the "Yorkshire Ripper" investigations. But now they acted, and in the computerised version of the Murder Incident Room System which the Home Office team has recently put into the hands of British police forces (eighteen years after Cannock and five after Yorkshire), alibis and other eliminating factors are no longer lumped together. They are now categorised according to their quality and can be recalled whenever the investigating officer feels like re-checking them.

The problem of inter-force rivalry has also been tackled, in that, where a series of murders spreads over one or more force boundaries, the Home Office now exercises the power to appoint a senior officer to take overall command . . . a so-called "Supremo".

But to go back, finally, to what I have called the "NFA" Factor. The computerised Incident Room began to come into the police service only as I was leaving it in 1983 and, though I saw its development and operational trials, I never had the good fortune to employ it. I envy those who do, for it is a tool of immense value. As a super-efficient version of The System it has everything. But it has to be remembered that it is still no more than a management tool—an information storage and retrieval system, a means of identifying common factors—and it does not have the complete answer to the problem, in the shape, for example of a key marked "Whodunit", the magic button that would put up on the video screen the name of the murderer. Nor does it operate on anything but what is fed into it . . . by human beings.

It is a fact of life that, with or without computers, murder investigations will always be led, manned and brought to a conclusion by human beings. It is they who will make the crucial decisions. The computer will never replace the detective's "nose" for something that is not quite right; his instinctive feeling that there is more to something than meets the eye, the experience that interprets what the computer is telling him. Those appointed to exercise key judgements in major crime investigations (whether in the Incident Room or outside) will always, therefore, need to be of the highest calibre, for the investigator's art has not changed and will not change, whatever new technology might be brought to bear on the problem.

If those detective instincts fail, the computer will not save us. The mistakes of Cannock Chase and the Yorkshire Ripper will occur again as surely as night follows day.